HamRadioSchool.com

General License Course

*Complete Element 3 Exam Preparation
and more,
to help you really understand ham radio!*

by
Stu Turner
WØSTU

Bob Witte KØNR, Technical Editor

Second Edition: Version 2.2

General Class practice app
for quizzes & exams!

Study and practice exam questions on-the-go with your book and smart phone or tablet device!

Check your smart phone store for the
HamRadioSchool.com quizzing & exam app!

- Take short quizzes focused on just the exam questions from your current book section, for *step-by-step* learning ease!

- Take properly weighted and randomized full 35-question practice exams to test your readiness for VE examination!

- Let the app ensure you see *all the questions* and retake questions that you got wrong in previous practice exams!

- Let the app track your performance by book section so you always know where to focus your review!

- Intuitive and easy-to-use app lets you review topic knowledge and practice for your exam anywhere, anytime!

Acknowledgements: Tremendous thanks to the following for their time and assistance with this book and with *HamRadioSchool.com...* You guys rock!

Bob Witte, KØNR, for technical editing, suggestions, educational support, web site contributions, photos, gear, and for being the Elmer Supreme! Thank you Mr. Editor, I could not have done it without you. *Extra?*

James Bucknall, KDØMFO, for webmaster support, classroom support, layout advice, a fine crafted ale on occasion, and great friendship!

Paul Swanson, AAØK, for photos, educational support, and classroom support! Thanks Paul!

Steve Galchutt, WGØAT, for photos and *goatly* inspiration! Tha-a-a-a-a-a-nks, Steve!

Centennial Electronics, Colorado Springs, Colorado, for photography subject matter and for being a terrific brick-and-mortar electronics supply! Thanks for the help, Dave Givan, KØIRP.

Ham Radio Outlet, Denver, Colorado, for photography subject matter, for carrying the books, and for being **THE** ham radio retailer in Colorado.

Agilent Technologies, for oscilloscope measurement images and photographs of scopes and other electronic measurement devices.

Cole Turner, WØCOL, and Jake Turner, WØJAK, for being splendid models for illustrative photographs and for the cover art.

Joyce Witte, KØJJW, for photos, classroom support, positive encouragement, always a kind word, and very tasty treats at the club meetings!

Dan WØRO & Pam WØPRS Scott for the Flex 5000 photo!

WØTLM Tri-Lakes Monument Radio Association, for being a great radio club and providing the opportunity for me to try a hand at instructing amateur radio courses!

Waterton Amateur Radio Society, for great antenna photo subjects!

Boy Scouts of America Troop 6, Colorado, for photo subjects and wonderful summer camp radio outings! Go scouts!

Shadow, AK9DOG, for constant and unquestioning companionship during those lonely, late hours on the computer putting this thing together.

Liz, KTØLIZ, for putting up with the whole thing... *again!* Thanks honey!

v

Be sure to visit *HamRadioSchool.com* for:

- Additional multi-media learning content!

- Exam question pool review organized section-by-section!

- Practical advice, interesting articles, and fun things to do!

- *How-to* information on station set-up and ham activities!

- Sharing your comments, suggestions, and success story!

With HamRadioSchool.com's Integrated Learning System you will

Really Get It!

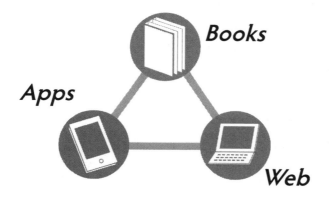

Contents

Preface

Congratulations on your decision to upgrade your FCC amateur radio license to General Class! You will really enjoy the added privileges that you will receive on the HF bands, with greatly expanded capability to make long distance contacts. The General Class ticket really opens up a whole other world of amateur radio coolness.

In this book you will learn all you need to not just pass your General Class VE exam, but to become a competent and safe ham radio operator. We really believe in preserving the quality of operations that uncountable proud amateurs have developed and maintained over the decades. We want you to really understand ham radio and keep with the tradition of *doing ham right!*

Is this book right for you? If you are interested in earning your General Class license, this book and its related web site are definitely for you, regardless of your background in science, technology, or math. This book will provide you fundamental understanding of radio along with the competence, and *confidence*, to get on all the HF bands. Inside the book and on the web site you will find easy-to-grasp explanations of the technical topics using common examples and analogies to everyday things and experiences with which you are already familiar. You will see ample pictures, graphics, and web-based multimedia that will help you intuitively comprehend everything from how radio electronics work to how to set up your first HF station.

How is this book different? Unlike some other intermediate ham radio books, this one does not pad its pages with the public domain questions from the exam question pool and try to "teach the test" by requiring you to memorize answers without understanding them. Rather, the pages provide relevant information that focuses you on the right content while providing straightforward explanations so that you really comprehend radio. When you ***really get it*** you don't have to rely on mind-numbing memorization! Oh, and we provide you those public domain questions free, online at the *HamRadioSchool.com* web site, all organized by book section and accompanied by lots of additional content to help you learn very efficiently.

Get Going! Be sure you understand how to use this book as described in ***Using This Book and Passing Your Exam*** on the next page, and then start your learning both here and online at *HamRadioSchool.com.* If you have questions or comments for us, please contact us through the web site. We'll be glad to hear from you! *Good luck, and get going!*

STU
WØSTU

Using This Book
and
Passing Your Exam

This *HamRadioSchool.com General License Course* book has been specially formatted to assist you with General license exam preparation. We recommend that you read this book's chapters in sequence first, then review material by topic, as necessary for your specific learning needs. We also recommend that you visit our web site section-by-section to take quizzes and to find additional materials that will make your learning experience an enjoyable one!

The *HamRadioSchool.com* web site provides additional learning tools organized section-by-section with the book. These enhanced learning tools may include video, audio, animations, graphics, photographs, or additional text explanations. You will also find the entire General Class exam question pool on the web site, with questions organized for ease of learning, section-by-section along with this book. The combination of this book and the web-based learning tools offers a powerful combination for really understanding ham radio.

Heavy Bold Text like this provides the answer to an exam pool question in *objective language* that mirrors the language of the question. All the exam pool questions are covered this way in this book. The tab in the outer margin adjacent to the heavy bold text provides you the question identifier. You will find the complete exam questions and response options online, conveniently organized section-by-section, at *HamRadioSchool.com*. A page index of question identifiers and topics is also included at the end of this book.

Example of Exam Question Objective Language Highlight and Exam Question:

Book text: **The 30m band is a digital mode band only; phone operation and image transmission is prohibited.**

G1A02

Question Item: **G1A02** (B)   *Section 1.1, Page 12*
On which of the following bands is phone operation prohibited?
  A. 160 meters
  B. 30 meters
  C. 17 meters
  D. 12 meters

We recommend that you read a book section, check for and review the section's online learning enhancements, and review the section's questions in exam pool format online or with our app. As you get into later book chapters, begin comprehensive practice tests online or with our app. When you are consistently passing practice exams you are ready for the real thing!

The General License (Element 3) Exam: The bottom line on passing the General exam is that you need at least 26 correct responses out of 35 total questions. That's about 74% correct answers to pass. There are 464 questions in the complete exam pool. Each question provides four multiple choice responses from which to choose. The order of the four question responses is not static -- the order will be scrambled on your exam among the "A B C D" designations.

Each exam will be comprised of questions drawn randomly from the exam pool, but with specific weighting applied by question topic, or sub-element. The exam sub-elements and question quantities drawn from each on a typical VE exam follows:

G1	FCC Rules	5 questions
G2	Operating Procedures	5 questions
G3	Radio Wave Propagation	3 questions
G4	Amateur Radio Practices	5 questions
G5	Electrical Principles	3 questions
G6	Circuit Components	2 questions
G7	Practical Circuits	3 questions
G8	Signals and Emissions	3 questions
G9	Antennas & Feedlines	4 questions
GØ	Safety	2 questions

The third character in each question identifier specifies a topical group of questions within the sub-element. Each sub-element may have several groups of questions. The last two characters in the identifier specify a question from the group.

The Exam Session: All amateur radio exams are administered by Volunteer Examiners (VE). A VE is a licensed ham who volunteers to help administer the tests and develop new licensed operators. A minimum of three VEs must administer every exam. VE sessions are conducted regularly in every state. Check with your local club or online for sessions near you.

The exam is usually administered on paper, although some computer-hosted exams are being implemented as of 2016. With the paper exams you will need a pencil (bring two, just in case one breaks), and you may use a calculator with any and all memories cleared. Take your time and RTFQ! That is, *Read The Fine Question* carefully! Your exam will be graded immediately by the administering VEs, so you'll know right away if you have passed. If you have used the *HamRadioSchool.com* learning system well, we're confident you will succeed the first time through! Good luck!

HAM RADIO SCHOOL.COM

VERE ADEPTO IS

Turn the page and start your preparation for
General Class today!

But, before we begin...

0.0 Before We Begin...

Before we begin our trek into the General Class topics and exam questions, let's review a few important themes from Technician Class material and beyond. Technical backgrounds and familiarity with the Technician Class material are likely to vary quite a lot across the population of potential readers seeking to upgrade to General Class license, so it's a good idea to make sure we all have some common foundational understanding before getting into the thick of the General Class material. That's what this little prelude chapter is all about.

If you have recently earned your Technician Class license with the *HamRadioSchool.com Technician License Course*, you've probably got a solid background for proceeding. If it has been a while since you have practiced or even thought about that material much, or if you are one of the many thousands who *memorized without comprehension* to pass your Technician VE Exam, this chapter is especially for you. You may also want to snag a copy of the *HamRadioSchool.com Technician License Course* book as a reference as you work through the General Class material. It will help you to *really get it*, and you'll be a more competent, safer, and overall happier ham by really understanding amateur radio. And don't fret if you don't have total recall of all topics briefly reviewed here. We'll cover each in more depth throughout the book.

Some of the topics on which we'll refresh ourselves in this chapter include:

- What's different about operating on HF?
- Modes
- AC signals and RF signals
- Interpreting time domain and frequency domain signal representations.
- Oscilloscopes
- Decibels
- Impedance matching and SWR
- Oscillator circuits and resonance

Fire up your neurons, here we go!

What's different about operating on HF? The bulk of on-air experience of most folks with a Technician Class license is VHF and UHF FM operations – simplex or repeater QSOs with a handheld transceiver or mobile/base FM station. With a General Class ticket the world of HF privilege really opens up to you, and the typical HF band operations are significantly different from those on VHF and UHF FM.

Single sideband (SSB) operations are most popular for voice communication on the HF bands. Being a special form of amplitude modulation, SSB is more subject to electrical noise than FM, such as that produced by lightning or other electronic devices. The quality of audio with SSB does not usually match that of local FM signals. You'll find SSB sometimes scratchy, noisy, weak, and inconsistent due to atmospheric and transmission path effects. The frequencies of the HF bands are commonly bent back to earth by the ionosphere, so HF SSB signals can travel far over the horizon, unlike the typical "radio line of sight" limits of VHF and UHF bands. Since SSB signals travel great distances they become quite weak, sometimes making the reception of distant stations challenging, but all the more rewarding!

Unlike typical VHF/UHF FM local operations, the HF band plans do not identify specific *channels* for use. There are no designated repeater paired frequencies or simplex frequency channels to skip among with pre-defined proper spacing to avoid interference. Rather, the HF bands allow contiguous tuning across the band, with any frequency available to any operator with the license privilege for it. Combined with the fact that HF signals can skip over the horizon great distances, contiguous band tuning makes the potential for interference between stations much more likely. This has two main implications for HF ops: 1) You need to be polite and willing to share the spectrum of the bands with your fellow hams, else chaos ensues, and 2) You must be very aware of your transmitted signal's bandwidth to help ensure you are not interfering with other communications on the band.

All of these factors and others require that phone operations on HF SSB proceed with somewhat differently than FM. For instance, the use of a phonetic alphabet is much more prominent to ensure positive exchanges because of the poorer signal quality. Operators will often "set up shop" on a specific frequency to which they have meticulously tuned their rig and amp and call "CQ" until found by other operators surfing across the band. Many operators will specifically seek stations in foreign countries only by calling "CQ DX." (DX = Distant stations, outside of the calling country.) And often there will be interference between stations on a busy band, with transmissions overlapping with various power levels, requiring the careful adjustment of receiver filters to isolate the desired signal.

The HF bands have sub-bands dedicated to particular modes of operating. Below the phone sub-bands you'll find digital operations with beeps and chirps and mournful droning. Further down is usually CW, with various speeds of Morse Code exchanges. You must take care to transmit only in the sub-bands designated for the General License Class operator, too! The higher license classes of Advanced and Extra have sub-bands exclusively for their use.

But you will learn about all of these factors of HF in the coming chapters and sections, and with just a little practice on the air it will all become second nature to you. No need to worry. Let's move on for now...

Modes: We have already touched on the matter of modes. Single sideband, digital, and CW are modes, each referring to a type of signal modulation. The matter of modes can get a bit complicated, and I will refer you to the *HamRadioSchool.com* web article *Loads of Modes* to help disentangle it all. Generally, there are two connotations to the term "mode:" Operating Mode and Modulation Mode.

> *Operating mode* refers to what the operator is doing to send and receive signals. Common examples are phone mode (voice ops), or digital mode (use of a computer connected to the radio).

> *Modulation mode* refers to the specific method by which information is encoded into the radio emissions. Single sideband is a modulation mode, as is FM, CW, and PSK-31 digital.

Sometimes this terminology gets combined and mixed together, and it can be confusing. Keep in mind that SSB is a phone mode (SSB = modulation type, and phone = operating technique). "FM phone" is a similar combination of modulation and ops description. Packet radio is a digital mode (Packet = modulation type, digital = operating technique). And there are others, of course. Some modes are more popular on certain bands than on others. Single sideband is very popular on the HF bands due to its narrow bandwidth efficiency. FM is more popular on the VHF/UHF bands due to the greater bandwidth available on those higher bands, as FM requires greater bandwidth for each transmission. Some digital modes perform quite well on the HF bands, while others need the greater bandwidth available on VHF and higher frequencies.

AC and RF Signals: You probably realize that the oscillating radio frequency (RF) signals that radiate from your station's antenna are the result of alternating electric currents (AC) flowing back and forth rapidly in the antenna. The oscillations of the RF signal's electric field, or *cycles*, equal the frequency of the back-and-forth AC frequency in the antenna. Frequency is measured in *cycles per second*, whether referring to AC electrical cycles in a circuit or RF electric field cycles flying through the air. The unit of one cycle per second is one *hertz*, and frequency is defined in hertz, kilohertz (thousands of hertz), megahertz (millions of hertz), etc.

We represent each of these types of cycles with a sine wave. For electrical AC in a circuit the sine wave's up-and-down flow represents the direction and magnitude of the electric voltage that is the force, or pressure, shoving the electric current back and forth in the circuit. Above the zero line the voltage is pushing one direction in the circuit, and below the zero line the voltage is pushing the opposite way. We call these two directions of flow positive and negative (+ and -), and the magnitude of the voltage is represented on the vertical dimension, or the vertical axis, in units of volts. Time is represented on the horizontal axis, or the zero line, left to right.

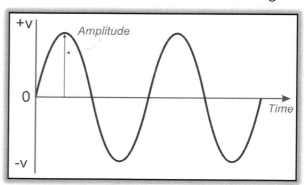

Figure 0.1: A sine wave signal time domain view.

With radio wave signals, the sine wave represents how the electric field of the radio signal is oscillating as it travels through free space. The field extends itself in two opposing directions from the axis of propagation. The zero line is again a measure of time, and also represents the axis of propagation – the direction the wave is traveling at the speed of light as the electric field changes back and forth at radio frequency.

The height of the sine wave at its peak is called the amplitude of the signal, and amplitude is a measure of the signal strength, or power.

Time Domain and Frequency Domain Views: The sine wave view of a signal described above is a *time domain view.* This is because the horizontal axis is depicting the progression of time. The time domain view defines how the signal voltage is changing over time, defining both the frequency and the amplitude of the signal. However, a typical radio transmission is comprised of a small band of many contiguous frequencies, defined as some *bandwidth.* A sine wave in the time domain view is usually depicting only one frequency out of a few thousand hertz of frequencies in a transmitted band. To depict the entire band we use a *frequency domain view.*

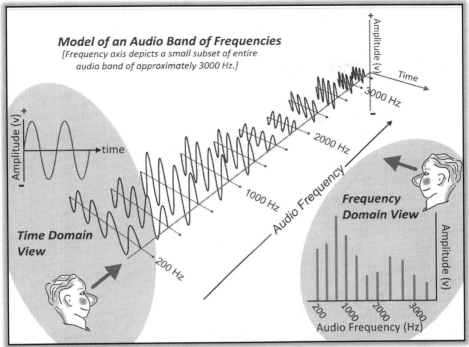

Figure 0.2: Two related views of signals provide different types of information. The horizontal axis represents either time or frequency, depending on the view.

The frequency domain view has frequency (in hertz) on the horizontal axis, and amplitude on the vertical axis. This depiction provides a definition of the band of frequencies comprising a signal, and it defines the amplitude of each frequency across the band. This is much like an audio equalizer display in which the power of the various audio frequencies is indicated over time by a set of vertical LEDs or segments that dance with the music frequencies in electronic display.

Figure 0.2 illustrates how the frequency domain view and time domain view are related: You can imagine the time domain view as taking a slice of the frequency domain view and turning it 90 degrees to its side. Alternatively, you can imagine the frequency domain view as the entire band of time domain frequency slices aggregated together and turned 90 degrees to look across all frequencies. The time and frequency domain views can depict audio frequencies, such as the signals generated by a microphone to serve as modulating signals, or they may depict radio frequencies, such as a band of transmitted RF signals. We will use both time domain and frequency domain depictions of signals and bands throughout the book.

Oscilloscopes: An oscilloscope is an electronic measurement device that allows us to measure and view signals in the time domain (and other views, depending upon the device capabilities). With an oscilloscope we may tap into an electric circuit and get a dynamic picture of the voltage variations ongoing inside the circuit. A typical oscilloscope will display time across the horizontal dimension and voltage on the vertical, just like the time domain view of waveforms. The amount of time displayed in total across the screen can be varied, and the scale of voltage can be altered to view a wide range of signal strengths. With RF signals the oscilloscope may be set to display only a few microseconds (millionths of a second) or nanoseconds (billionths of a second) in order that we can view and measure a few cycles of waveforms in great detail as they rapidly oscillate. We will refer to oscilloscope measurements in several sections of the book.

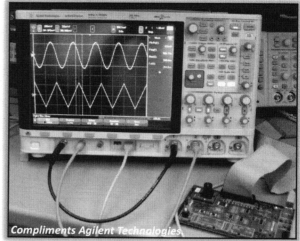

Figure 0.3: An oscilloscope displaying a time domain view of two different signals.

Decibels (dB): The decibel is used to compare two measures, much like a ratio of two numbers. In amateur radio a common comparison using decibels is power changes. For example, you might measure with a signal strength meter on a receiver that the strength of a received signal has increased by 6 dB or decreased by 3 dB. Notice that these measures indicate nothing about the absolute power value of the signal – there is no quoting of watts or any other absolute unit of power. Notice also that the measure is meaningful only in comparison to the previous power level – an increase in power or a decrease in power as related by the size of the decibel change.

The decibel is a logarithmic unit. This means that it is based on factor of 10 changes. The "bel" is a unit indicating change of a factor of 10, or 10X. For instance, a power increase from 10 watts to 100 watts could be characterized as a 1 bel increase – a factor of 10 increase. But the bel is usually too coarse of a unit, so the decibel is more typically used. The decibel is 1/10 of a bel.

You may recall from your Technician Class studies some useful rules of thumb equating decibels to relative change values. For instance, a doubling or halving of power equates to a change of 3 dB, either increased (doubling) or decreased (halving). Put another way, a 2X change equals a 3 dB change. So, an increase in power from 50 watts to 100 watts is a 3 dB increase. Another rule of thumb alludes to the bel as 10 dB. A 10X change equates to 10 dB. Our example above, going from 10 watts to 100 watts, is a 10 dB increase. We will use these rules for decibels again in our General Class studies.

Impedance Matching & SWR: Impedance (Z) in an electrical circuit is the opposition to the flow of alternating current (AC). The unit of impedance is the ohm (Ω). Every AC circuit, including RF *transmitter / feed line / antenna* circuits, will have some impedance due to the components comprising the circuit and their impact on AC. Maximum power transfer occurs when all of the components have identical impedance. For instance, to get the most power transferred to an antenna for transmission of RF energy the transmitter circuit, the feed line, and the antenna feed point should be matched in impedance.

When components of a circuit do not match in impedance, some of the power in the circuit will be reflected from the position of the mismatch. For instance, if your transmitter and feed line are each 50 Ω, but your antenna feed point is 100 Ω, you will have an impedance mismatch and some of your transmitter's power will be reflected from the antenna feed point back down the feed line toward the transmitter. The poorer the impedance match the greater the magnitude of reflected power. A ratio comparison of the forward power with the reflected power is called SWR, or standing wave ratio. We will examine SWR more closely in Chapter 5, *Antennas*.

Oscillator Circuits and Resonance: Much of radio functioning is based upon the concepts of oscillator circuits and resonance. An oscillator circuit produces the very rapid AC that is necessary for the generation of RF signals. A common oscillator circuit will include electronic components called capacitors and inductors.

A capacitor is like two parallel conductive plates separated from one another. When AC flows back and forth in a circuit with a capacitor, the capacitor rapidly charges and discharges, with positive and negative electrical charges building up alternatively on opposite sides of the capacitor with each reversal of AC. A capacitor will allow high frequency AC to flow freely, but it impedes low frequency AC or DC current. So, a capacitor will increase impedance for low frequencies but not for high frequencies. This capacitive contribution to a circuit's impedance is called *capacitive reactance* (X_c).

An inductor is a coil of wire that creates a magnetic field about itself when current flows through it in one direction, just like an electromagnet. The direction, or polarity, of the magnetic field is determined by the direction of electric current flow. When an inductor is in an AC circuit, the inductor builds a magnetic field first with one polarity, and as the current reverses the magnetic field is collapsed and rebuilt with opposite polarity. All of this building, collapsing, and building again with each AC cycle causes the inductor to impede AC also. But, exactly opposite of the capacitor, the inductor impedes high frequency AC and allows low frequency AC or DC current to pass easily. The inductor's contribution to a circuit's impedance is called *inductive reactance* (X_L).

Inductive reactance, capacitive reactance, and regular old electrical resistance combine and total to a circuit's overall impedance. We will discuss the concept of reactance in several sections.

In circuits containing both capacitors and inductors, a special state of AC flow may arise called resonance. Resonance means that energy can be transformed between different states very easily, or with very little loss of energy during transitions. In this case, energy is easily shifted from electric charge (capacitor) to magnetic field (inductor), with great efficiency. Resonance occurs in LC circuits (circuits containing an inductor, L, and a capacitor C) when the inductive reactance and capacitive reactance are equal. This equality will occur only at a specific AC frequency in the circuit, and the frequency of resonance is determined by the values of capacitance and inductance of the LC components in the circuit.

So, we can select inductors and capacitors to build LC circuits that will become resonant at a desired AC frequency. Or, we may use variable components to build LC circuits that will resonate at variable frequencies. In this way oscillators are constructed to generate RF frequencies of alternating current for radio tuning operations.

In the chapters that follow we shall see more on how capacitance, inductance, and each type of resulting reactance effects circuit behavior, and particularly how it impacts antenna circuit performance.

With this concept review under our belts, let's move on to become General Class Amateur Radio Operators! We now begin, in earnest, with a look at General Class rules and regulations. Good luck with your studies!

~ Stu WØSTU

1.0   Rules & Regs

❝ *Radio is called a medium because it is rare that anything is well done. — Fred Allen*

OK, so we are indeed *amateur* radio operators, by FCC designation. And we all learn and improve as we proceed along in our various efforts. But contrary to Fred's sentiments amateur radio can, and should, be *well done*! All amateur license classes should strive to conduct their on-air operations with a pride of competence, within the rules and regulations established by the FCC. Especially now that you endeavor to upgrade your license to General Class I hope that you will seek to make your station operation as well done as a crispy, blackened burger forsaken on a blazing grill!

In Section 1.1 we will examine all the new frequency band privileges that you'll have as a General Class operator. The HF bands really open up to you now! In Section 1.2 you'll get a peek at some "special services" that you may want to become involved with as a General Class licensee. In Section 1.3 we will expand on a few more detailed rules and regulations that are particularly relevant to the more advanced operator.

Before we dive into the rules and regulations with which you should comply to keep your operation crisp, let's see just how your General Class adventure will begin! First you need a CSCE for General Class.

CSCE: The *Certificate of Successful Completion of Examination* is awarded to you immediately when you pass your General license examination, and **it is valid to prove your exam element credit for 365 days,** one full year. You will rarely need that long of proof, as your upgraded license will usually appear on the FCC ULS within days or a couple of weeks. The *Universal License System* (ULS) is the FCC database of issued licenses and applications that has web-based interface for your convenience.

G1D09

The coolest thing about having that CSCE in your pocket is that you can walk out of the exam session and immediately transmit on General license frequencies. No waiting around for the ULS to catch up to your new status. **As a Technician Class operator having a CSCE for General Class privi-**

G1D03

leges you may operate on any General or Technician Class band segment, but you have to make it known on the air with a special call sign identifier. The proper way to identify on General Class frequencies if you have a CSCE for General but your upgrade from Technician has not appeared in the FCC database is to give your call sign followed by "slant AG." (Or "stroke AG" or "slash AG.") Just think "*Approved General,*" and remember that **you must add the identifier "AG" when you operate using General Class frequency privileges,** but not when you remain within the Technician Class privileges. When your upgraded license appears on the FCC ULS database you may stop using the AG self-assigned indicator. But while you do use it, you'll likely receive many hardy congratulations on your upgrade from fellow hams on the air, and that's kind of nice to hear!

What if you held a ham license before, but now it is expired? Do you get any credit for that in examination? Yes! **Any person who can demonstrate that they once held a FCC issued General, Advanced, or Amateur Extra class license that was never revoked by the FCC may receive credit for the elements represented by that expired license.** Thus, **anyone with an expired General Class or higher FCC amateur license must pass only the current element 2 exam** (Technician Class exam) **before they can receive a new license** at the higher class level.

With that tidbit dispensed, let's rule!

| 1.1 | Rules and Regulations
Bands and Privileges |

❝ *It's a privilege - I make the most of it.*
– David Bailey

The General Class license really adds to your operating privileges. Of course, you lose none of the Technician license band privileges that you've already earned, but you will:
- expand your 10 meter band phone privileges above 28.5 MHz
- get phone privileges on eight more HF bands
- increase your CW privileges by six HF bands
- increase your digital data privilege by nine HF bands

The step up to General Class from Technician Class license represents a substantial expansion of your privileges, and with those privileges come the expanded responsibilities of being a more knowledgeable and responsible station operator. Become very familiar with these new General Class license privileges and responsibilities so that you can make the most of them!

Band Privileges for General Class: Your General Class privileges are defined much like the Technician Class privileges, using bands, sub-bands, and mode-restricted sub-bands. Four of the HF bands on which your new General Class privileges apply will also have Extra Class and (grandfathered) Advanced Class exclusive frequency ranges. Be careful not to transmit in those exclusive sub-bands with only General Class privileges. However, in six of the 10 HF bands **a General Class license holder is granted all amateur frequency privileges: 160, 60, 30, 17, 12, and 10 meters.** There are no Advanced or Extra Class exclusive re-

Figure 1.1: Boy Scouts work the HF bands with a summer camp portable station.

gions on these six bands to worry about. On the four bands **where General Class licensees are not permitted to use the entire voice portion of the band, the portion of the voice segment that is generally available to them is the upper frequency end.**

HF Band Definitions and Operating Provisions (reference Figure 1.2):

10 Meter Band: 28.0 – 29.7 MHz. **All frequencies in this range are available to a control operator holding a General Class license.** The phone sub-band ranges 28.3 – 29.7 MHz, and the digital sub-band

G1A01

G1A11

G1A10

extends 28.0 – 28.3 MHz. **Repeaters may be utilized on 10m band above 29.6 MHz.** Note that **a 10m repeater** (FM repeater) **may retransmit the 2m signal from a station having a Technician Class control operator, but only given that the 10m repeater control operator holds at least a General Class license.**

12 Meter Band: **24.890 – 24.990 MHz.** All frequencies in this range are available to a control operator holding a General Class license. The phone sub-band ranges 24.930 – 24.990 MHz, with the digital sub-band below 24.930 MHz.

15 Meter Band: 21.0 – 21.450 MHz. **The General Class portion of the 15m phone band ranges 21.275 – 21.450 MHz.** The phone range 21.2 – 21.275 MHz is exclusive to Advanced and/or Extra Class licenses only. The General Class license digital mode sub-band is 21.025 – 21.2 MHz, with frequencies in this band below 21.025 MHz exclusively reserved for Extra Class.

17 Meter Band: 18.068 – 18.168 MHz. All frequencies in this range are available to a control operator holding a General Class license. The phone sub-band ranges 18.110 – 18.168 MHz, and the digital sub-band extends 18.068 – 18.110 MHz.

20 Meter Band: 14.0 – 14.350 MHz. **The General Class portion of the 20m phone band ranges 14.225 – 14.350 MHz.** The phone range 14.150 – 14.225 MHz is exclusive to Advanced and/or Extra Class licenses only. The General Class license digital mode sub-band is 14.025 – 14.150 MHz, with frequencies in this band below 14.025 MHz exclusively reserved for Extra Class.

30 Meter Band: 10.1 – 10.150 MHz. **Amateur operators are secondary users of this band and by FCC rules are allowed to use the band only if they do not cause harmful interference to primary users. The appropriate action if, when operating on the 30m band, a station in the primary service interferes with your contact, is to move to a clear frequency. The 30m band is a digital mode band only; phone operation and image transmission is prohibited. The maximum transmitting power an amateur station may use is 200 watts PEP output.**

40 Meter Band: 7.0 – 7.3 MHz. The General Class portion of the 40m phone band ranges 7.175 – 7.3 MHz. The phone range 7.125 – 7.175 MHz is exclusive to Advanced and Extra Class licenses only. The General

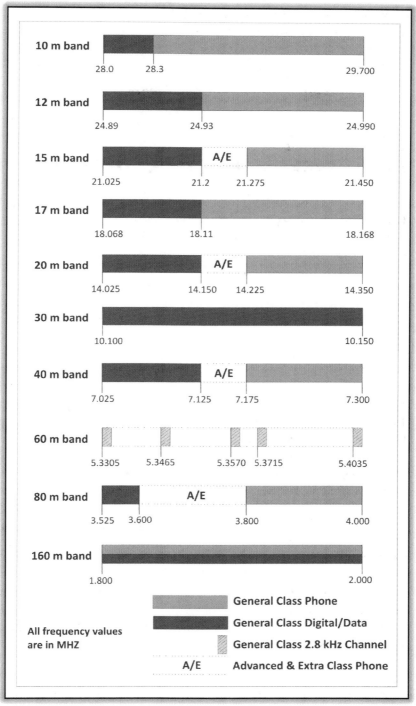

Figure 1.2: General Class HF Frequency Privileges.

Class license digital mode sub-band is 7.025 – 7.125 MHz, with frequencies in this band below 7.025 MHz exclusively reserved for Extra Class. Note that **in ITU-Region 2 (includes North America) this band extends up to 7.3 MHz for amateur operators.** In other ITU regions the range 7.2 – 7.3 MHz is used by short wave broadcasters outside the Americas and is not available to amateurs outside of ITU Region 2.

60 Meter Band: The 60m band is really different from any other band. Instead of a contiguous range of frequencies it allows **only five specific channels** – 5330.5, 5346.5, 5357.0, 5371.5, and 5403.5 kHz. Only one signal at a time is permitted on any channel. **USB on these channels is limited in bandwidth to 2.8 kHz** and power is limited to 100 watts PEP for all modes. (Note: **If you are using other than a dipole antenna, FCC rules require that you must keep a record of the gain of your antenna when operating on 60m band.**) Amateur operators are secondary users of this band and by FCC rules are allowed to use the band only if they do not cause harmful interference to primary users. **The appropriate action if, when operating on the 60m band, a station in the primary service interferes with your contact, is to move to a clear frequency.** (Note: Special rules apply for centering frequency, as detailed in FCC Report and Order of November 18, 2011.)

75 / 80 Meter Band: 3.5 – 4.0 MHz [3500 – 4000 kHz]. **The General Class portion of the 75/80m phone band ranges 3.8 – 4.0 MHz [3800 – 4000 kHz].** The phone range 3.6 – 3.8 MHz is exclusive to Advanced and/or Extra Class licenses only. **The General Class license digital mode sub-band is 3.525 – 3.6 MHz,** with frequencies in this band below 3.525 MHz exclusively reserved for Extra Class. This band may be referred to as either 75m band or 80m band, as the wavelengths extend from 75 – 85 meters across this band. Since CW ops are in the lower frequency end of the band, that segment is usually called "80 meter band" while the higher frequency phone segment is the "75m band."

160 Meter Band: 1.8 – 2.0 MHz [1800 – 2000 kHz]. All frequencies in this range are available to a control operator holding a General Class license. No sub-bands are imposed on 160m band. The entire band is available for phone or digital modes.

Transmitting Power Limits: The general FCC rules regarding transmitting power limits apply to all of the General Class bands, but two bands are more restrictive (30m and 60m). **Only the minimum power necessary to carry out the desired communications should be used on any band.**

Further, **the maximum transmitting power an amateur station may use on any HF band is limited to 1500 watts PEP output.** The 30m and 60m bands only have lower restrictions on maximum power output, as noted in the description of each: The 30m band is restricted to 200 watts PEP output, and the 60m band is restricted to 100 watts PEP output.

Examination Strategies: Wow, that's a lot of band limits, sub-band limits, and special rules to remember, huh? In practice you will likely have a copy of a band chart next to your rig and you can practically check that you're within your General Class privileges. But for the exam you'll need to use some different strategies, even including just some rote memorization (ugh!), since you cannot reference a band plan chart or notes. Let's see if we can minimize that memorizing just a bit…

Identifying Band Frequencies & Limits: Memorize that the only four bands with exclusive sub-bands for higher license classes are 15m, 20m, 40m, and 80m. Use the frequency and wavelength calculation to help determine which band a given frequency resides within. This will usually help narrow the response options to just two items. Remember from Technician material that:

Wavelength in meters = 300 ÷ Frequency in MHz.

So, for instance: **G1A09 Which of the following frequencies is in the General Class portion of the 15-meter band?**

    A. 14250 kHz [300 ÷ 14.250 = 21.05 m] Not near 15m.
    B. 18155 kHz [300 ÷ 18.155 = **16.52 m**] Near 15m, possible.
    C. **21300 kHz** [300 ÷ 21.300 = **14.08 m**] Near 15m, possible.
    D. 24900 kHz [300 ÷ 24.940 = 12.05 m] Not near 15m.

This is a little tricky since the formula requires frequency in MHz, and here it is provided in kHz. But you know to move the decimal 3 places left to convert from kHz to MHz. (See HamRadioSchool.com Technician License Course, Section 4.1.)

The calculations have narrowed to two possible responses that are very near 15 meters, responses B and C. Which is correct? *In this one case the higher frequency value 21300 kHz is correct,* and this is a unique case in the question pool. Here is an exam rule of thumb to apply in all other question cases:

Narrow the frequency options to two possibilities using the wavelength calculation, then select the lower frequency value of the two possibilities. Works every time in the current question pool excepting G1A09. Try it.

Here is one more specific example of this rule of thumb, G1A07: **Which of the following frequencies is within the General Class portion of the 20-meter band?**
A. 14005 kHz
B. 14105 kHz
C. 14305 kHz
D. 14405 kHz

Once again convert the responses to megahertz instead of kilohertz to fit with the formula and calculate wavelength. You will find that responses A and B each result in wavelengths of greater than 21 meters, while responses C and D each result is wavelengths just under 21 meters, and thus, are closer to 20 meters than A or B. (You may also recall that the General Class 20-meter band phone segment begins at 14.225 MHz and goes only higher, ruling out A and B.) **Option C, 14305 kHz** is the lower frequency of the two narrowed responses, and it is the correct one. Additionally, the 20-meter band's high end is 14.350 MHz, so response D is out of the band entirely.

Practice the calculations, learn the exam rules, and you'll be privileged to ace the questions on the General Class bands. Test yourself online with the quiz for Section 1.1, the come back to see what special services you can contribute to the ham community!

HamRadioSchool.com/general_media

Rules and Regulations

1.2   Special Services

❝ *The little waiter's eyebrows wandered about his forehead in confusion.*
— *Douglas Adams, The Restaurant at the End of the Universe*

As is often lamented, good service is sometimes hard to come by. Fortunately, the amateur radio community is one with a strong commitment to service and we all benefit from the efforts of others who choose to step up and take on the myriad chores and challenges that keep ham radio going. You can do the same, joining many of your fellow hams in serving the amateur radio family with your new and expanded General Class knowledge and skills. This section highlights just a few of the ways you can give something back, all the while keeping your eyebrows firmly attached to a singular location on your forehead.

Volunteer Examiner (VE): As a General Class license holder you can serve as a Volunteer Examiner, administering VE exams for Technician licensing. Volunteer examiners are licensed radio amateurs who give their time to administer FCC licensing examinations. You've likely already interacted with a VE team when you completed your Technician exam, and you'll see another when you test for General.

To become VE you must read the *Volunteer Examiner Manual*, complete a 40-question, open-book review, and submit a VE application to **the Volunteer Examiner Coordinator (VEC), the accrediting organization for VEs.** You can get more information about becoming a VE online at the ARRL web site, but here are a few big picture rules about VEing that every ham should know:

- **The minimum age to qualify as an accredited VE is 18 years.**

- **An FCC General Class or higher license and VEC accreditation are sufficient to be an administering VE for a Technician Class operator license examination.**

- **As an accredited VE holding a General Class license, you may**

Figure 1.3: Serving as a Volunteer Examiner helps new hams get licensed. Consider becoming a VE!

administer only Technician Class license examinations. (You may not administer General or Extra Class exams.)

- **A requirement for administering a Technician Class examination is the presence of at least three VEC accredited General Class or higher VEs.**

- **Any non-US citizen wishing to become a VE must hold an FCC granted Amateur Radio license of General Class or above.**

The bottom line on administering examinations as an accredited VE is that you may administer exams only for the license classes below your own license class. So, you must be at least a General Class VE to administer Technician Class exams. You must be an Advanced Class or an Extra Class VE to administer General Class license exams. Extra Class VEs must administer Extra Class exams. At least three accredited VEs of the proper license class must be present for any VE exam.

Consider becoming a VE and help expand the amateur radio community with new licensed operators!

Amateur Auxiliary: The ARRL **Amateur Auxiliary is comprised of amateur volunteers who are formally enlisted to monitor the**

airwaves for rules violations. Approximately 700 volunteer-appointees serve as *Official Observers* (OO). **The primary objective of the Amateur Auxiliary is to encourage amateur operator self regulation and compliance with the rules.**

G2D02

The OOs help and advise amateur operators; they are not *band cops*. They are intended to provide unbiased operational advice and assistance to amateurs, helping to correct errors, but not to find fault or to place blame. They promote good amateur operating and engineering practice.

However, the OOs are trained and certified to collect and provide evidence to the FCC in enforcement actions related to any serious rule violations. For instance, in the case of malicious, repeated interference, an OO may record on-air transmissions and use **direction finding techniques to establish the location of an offending station.** So, **skills learned during "hidden transmitter hunts" are of help to the Amateur Auxiliary.** But the OOs are not allowed to enforce the rules in any way. That is a function exclusively of the FCC.

G2D03

An OO might send you a card in the mail called an Advisory Notice. Don't panic! It is not a citation. Rather, an OO Advisory Notice is a friendly note to highlight to you possible operating practices or equipment issues that you may need to modify. You do not need to reply to any OO notice, but you should consider what caused the problem described in the notice and take action to get in line with the regulations and good amateur practice.

And don't worry about nit-picky things. The OOs are trained to avoid minor, easy-to-slip discrepancies such as untimely station identification. They're more concerned with the clear, unambiguous rule violations. Still, take pride in your on-air procedures and endeavor to keep closely to the rules and to the guidelines of good amateur practice. After all, you're going to be a General Class operator now. Set a good example! You might get a *Good Operator Report* from an OO for operating practices of the highest standards, a model for others to follow.

If you are interested in becoming an OO, and if you believe you can be a friendly guide and assistant to other amateur operators (and not a *band cop!*), you may apply online at the ARRL web site or by contacting your ARRL Section Manager.

Emergency Communications Services and Procedures: Amateur radio tends to be a low-visibility hobby (except for those massive aluminum antenna farms, of course). Unless you're really looking for it, you won't hear too much about ham radio. There will almost never be features about ham radio operations in the news or the church bulletin, and the local pub chat will usually steer clear of the topic altogether. But if there is any time when amateur radio gets a little publicity it's when operators come to aid in an emergency or disaster. This is when ham radio really shines!

A few special rules apply in emergency situations, and response organizations such as Radio Amateur Civil Emergency Service (RACES), Amateur Radio Emergency Service (ARES®), and Community Emergency Response Team (CERT), may use amateur radio to help manage communications traffic and to coordinate relief efforts.

G1B04 **When it comes to emergencies in which communications are directly related to the immediate safety of human life or protection of property,** almost anything goes regarding the amateur rules **if no other means of communication is reasonably available.** For instance, in such emergency conditions **you may ignore the broadcasting restriction and provide communications to broadcasters for dissemination to**

Photo: Bob, KØNR
Pictured: Joyce, KØJJW

Figure 1.4: Radio Amateur Civil Emergency Service (RACES) volunteers typically receive special training to serve as communications specialists for civil authorities during emergencies or disasters. You can serve too!

the public, if that is required to save life or property. Note, simply describing the scene of an accident or emergency for the convenience of broadcasters is not the same as advising an evacuating public on travel routes to take to avoid a wildfire that has suddenly exploded in a nearby forest community. Be sure your communications relate directly to the security of life or property if you dispense with amateur rules in an emergency, but remember that **an amateur station is allowed to use any means at its disposal to assist another station in distress at any time during an actual emergency.** Regardless of your license class or the radio service at your disposal, **whatever frequency has the best chance of communicating the distress message should be used when sending a distress call.**

RACES organizations consist of volunteers trained to assist civil authorities during times of emergency or disaster. RACES is provided for by FCC Part 97.407, and a RACES organization is certified by a local, county, or state civil defense agency in the area it serves, or by a related organization within civil defense such as law enforcement or fire response agencies. A RACES organization may be activated to utilize the amateur radio resources available to it to provide communications support to the civil agencies. **Only a person holding an FCC issued amateur operator license may be the control operator of an amateur station transmitting in RACES to assist relief operations during a disaster.**

During a time of war, when the President's War Emergency Powers have been invoked, the FCC may restrict normal frequency operations of amateur stations participating in RACES. That is, RACES stations may be the only communications allowed on amateur frequencies at such a time and restricted to only certain RACES frequencies. However, this has never happened since the 1952 establishment of RACES.

Consider volunteering for your local RACES organization. You will learn more about emergency communications and you can serve your community when it really counts!

Beacon Operations: A beacon transmits a repeating signal, usually a CW identifier and sometimes additional tones, **for the purpose of observing radio frequency propagation and reception, as identified in the FCC rules.** Many HF beacons operate on the 10m band and can be good indicators of sporadic E propagation and other ionospheric conditions.

Any amateur radio license holder may establish a beacon station, but some Part 97.203 regulations apply. **The power limit for beacon stations is 100 watts PEP output.** Further, you cannot establish a whole family of

G1B02 beacons on the same band from your station location. **There must be no more than one beacon signal in the same band from a single location.** Most beacons use automatic control, but the FCC regulations allow this only in certain sub-bands of the 10m, 6m, 2m, 1.25m, and 70cm bands, or on the 33cm and shorter wavelength bands (microwave bands). A beacon may transmit only one-way communications (no receiving), and it must cease transmission if an FCC District Director notifies that it is causing undue interference to other operations.

Beacon operators provide a great service to the amateur radio community, particularly to operators who like to chase DX by ionospheric skip propagation. The beacons can help you identify when conditions are right for propagation to particular regions of the earth and when those coveted sporadic E openings are available! You may find an interest in establishing your own beacon, especially if you are in an area where few beacons are currently operating.

These are just a few special services in which you can become involved in amateur radio. You may also consider forming a new amateur radio club, becoming a *Boy Scout Radio Merit Badge Counselor*, organizing or becoming a member of a CERT, helping to teach an amateur radio course, becoming an ARES volunteer, helping out a local amateur radio school club, or any of the other ample opportunities offered by amateur radio to provide service to your fellow citizens and your fellow hams. Give one or more of these opportunities a try. I think you'll find one that suits you and that becomes very rewarding!

For now, check out the question pool items for this section and test your new knowledge!

HamRadioSchool.com/general_media

Rules and Regulations

1.3

Rules and Regulations
DX and Details

❝ Men who wish to know about the world must learn about it in its particular details.

— Heraclitus

You have already learned a lot about the FCC Part 97 rules and regulations as a Technician Class license holder, and you have probably been complying with them regularly without much thought to the matter, and perhaps without digging into *particular details*. But, if you need a refresher on some of the FCC's most fundamental rules and regulations that apply to almost all stations, check out the *HamRadioSchool.com Technician License Course*, Chapter 2.

In your Technician license preparation you no doubt learned about activities that are prohibited on the amateur frequencies such as the use of codes or ciphers, creating harmful interference to other stations, transmitting music or obscene/indecent language, and broadcasting for a general audience. You learned that transmitting for pecuniary interests (payment or compensation) is disallowed, and that you must make your station available for FCC inspection upon request. You probably also learned a little about communicating with the world, although you may not have accumulated a lot of experience with those "DX" (distant) contacts to date as a Technician.

As a General Class license holder you are expected to be more knowledgeable of the Part 97 rules and regulations, and since you will be granted access to a vastly larger slice of the HF frequency pie some emphasis should be placed on the rules related to DX communications provided largely by those HF frequencies. Let's discover more about the *DX and General Class world* by highlighting some *particular details* especially pertinent to General Class operations.

DX Communications: DX communications commonly use ionospheric skip propagation to transmit and receive weak signals outside of the US. (See Chapter 3, *Propagation.*) Of course, it is necessary and efficient to have some agreement among nations on how various frequencies will be used, otherwise some country's commercial broadcast services or military transmissions may severely interfere with another's amateur radio signals, and vice versa. Such international interference is rude, if not potentially incendiary. But fear not!

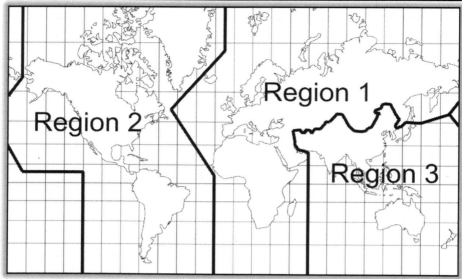

Figure 1.5: ITU Regions for Radio Spectrum Coordination.

We have international agreements regarding the use of the spectrum.

ITU: *The International Telecommunications Union* is a United Nations agency for information and communication technology issues. This agency, by international agreement, has partitioned the world into three geographic regions for managing and coordinating radio frequency use, as depicted in Figure 1.5. North America resides in ITU Region 2.

International Waters: Within the international agreements made through the ITU, the FCC governs all spectrum use and radio stations inside the US, and FCC licensed amateur stations may transmit from any vessel or craft located in international waters that is documented or registered in the United States. So, as long as your yacht is out on the high seas and not within the international boundary of another nation, you can PTT with liberty and confidence under your FCC license and within the frequency use plans for the particular region.

Foreign Contacts and Communications are limited by some nations and by agreements (or lack thereof) between nations. FCC licensed stations are permitted to make international communications that are incidental to the purposes of the amateur service and remarks of a personal character. What's that mean? Normal chit-chat about life and work, discussions about radio, call sign exchanges of course. It is prudent to minimize political conversations with some nations. **It is permissible to communicate with amateur stations in countries outside the areas administered by the FCC when the contact is with amateurs in any country except those whose administrations have notified the ITU that they object to**

G2D05

such communications. Presently, very few nations have ITU registered general restrictions on amateur radio communications, although the *Democratic People's Republic of Korea* and *Yemen* do not allow citizens to operate amateur stations at all.

Third Party International Communications: FCC Part 97.3 defines the term "third-party communication" as a message from the control operator (first party) of an amateur station to another amateur station control operator (second party) on behalf of another person (third party). Third party communication is also a non-licensed person transmitting on your radio under your licensed control operator supervision. Some countries get a little antsy about this sort of thing. Keep these in mind:

- **In order for any non-licensed person to communicate with a foreign amateur radio station from a station with an FCC granted license at which a control operator is present, the foreign amateur station must be in a country with which the United States has a third party agreement.** `G1E08`

- **Third party traffic is prohibited by every foreign country unless there is a third party agreement in effect with that country, with the exception of messages involving emergencies or disaster relief communications.** `G1E07`

- **The types of messages for a third party in another country transmitted by an amateur station should only be messages relating to amateur radio or remarks of a personal character, or messages related to emergencies or disaster relief.** `G1E05`

Station Identification: What if you are practicing speaking your freshly learned Mandarin, French, or Spanish with a new DX contact friend? How do you identify your station? **Even if you are using a language other than English in making contact using phone emissions, you must identify your station using English.** Je suis désolé, c'est la règle! `G1E09`

Operating from Foreign Countries: Many hams enjoy the challenge and thrill of "DXpeditions," traveling to foreign nations and perhaps to quite rarely contacted geographical areas to operate a station. Be aware that you may operate an amateur station in a foreign nation only when authorized by that nation. Check the law carefully before traveling!

Reciprocal Agreements: The US has reciprocal operating agreements with many nations that allow FCC licensed stations to operate on foreign territory. Two notable international reciprocal agreements in which the US participates

Buddipole's Chris, W6HFP, sets up a Mini-Buddipole on the east coast of 8P6/Barbados. Photo by Steve, WGØAT; Courtesy of Buddipole. www.buddipole.com

Figure 1.6: A DXpedition to a foreign nation can be both rewarding and challenging, and offer some once-in-a-lifetime operating scenarios!

are the *European Conference of Postal and Telecommunications Administration* (CEPT) and the *International Amateur Radio Permit* (IARP). CEPT includes most European nations and several others, but carefully research the reciprocity provisions by FCC license class and frequency privileges. The IARP is issued by the *Inter-American Telecommunications Commission* (CITEL) that includes many North American and South American nations. Again, check the reciprocity provisions of the IARP, as the operating privileges are not perfectly aligned to those of an FCC licensed station in the US.

Handling Interference: Interference happens. Stations bump into one another or occasionally stomp all over each other. Changing atmospheric conditions, less-than-careful operators, and improperly operating equipment are a few of the reasons for accidental interference between stations. In most cases interference can be handled by one station simply moving to a clear frequency, but a few situations are a bit more unambiguous and require specific action to be taken.

Repeater Coordination: Repeaters are usually fixed stations with fixed frequencies, and they are coordinated to minimize interference with one another. They don't usually move around changing frequencies like mobile stations.

Each region of the US has a designated *Frequency Coordinator*. It is the job of the coordinator to recommend frequencies for proposed repeaters so that interference between repeaters and with simplex operations is minimized. If you wish to install a repeater station, first check with your area's Frequency Coordinator and be certain your machine will not impose interference.

Uncoordinated Repeaters are sometimes placed into operation in spite of the efforts of frequency coordination bodies and their appointed Frequency Coordinators. **In the event of interference between a coordinated repeater and an uncoordinated repeater, the licensee of the non-coordinated repeater has primary responsibility to resolve the interference.** Don't go to the trouble and expense of establishing a repeater only to find you have to take it off the air due to interference! Adhere to good operating practice and be sure to coordinate properly.

G1E06

Uncoordinated repeater tower

Additional Interference Provisions: Some other less common situations may require you to cease transmissions if you are creating interference. Here are three situations that most operators will not encounter in typical operations, but of which you should be knowledgeable:

FCC Monitoring Stations – The FCC operates monitoring stations to ensure compliance with regulations across the various radio services, including the amateur service. **If you are operating within one mile of an FCC Monitoring Station you may be required to take specific steps to avoid harmful interference.** According to the *Code of Federal Regulations, Title 47*, FCC Protected Field Offices are located in or near the following US cities:

G1E04

Kenai, AK	*Waipahu, HI*	*Canandaigua, NY*
Douglass, AZ	*Belfast, ME*	*Santa Isabel, Puerto Rico*
Livermore, CA	*Laurel, MD*	*Kingsville, TX*
Vero Beach, FL	*Allegan, MI*	*Ferndale, WA*
Powder Springs, GA	*Grand Island, NE*	

Secondary Privileges – As noted in the *Bands and Privileges* section of this chapter, **some bands are available to the Amateur Service** only on a secondary basis, and interference with the primary service users requires that you move to a clear frequency or cease transmissions.

Spread Spectrum – Spread Spectrum (SS) is a transmitting method that spreads the power density of transmissions over a very broad band of frequencies. This is accomplished through *frequency hopping* or other methods where the transmitting station and the receiving station utilize a very broad band of frequencies. With frequency hopping stations skip rapidly from one frequency to another, transmitting only briefly on any given frequency. In amateur radio specific standards of frequency hopping and other spread spectrum implementations are imposed in order that transmissions may not be made covert through this operating mode's nature. **Stations transmitting spread spectrum emissions may be required to cease operations or take other steps to avoid harmful interference with other users or facilities.**

Antenna Height: I know you want to erect a giant antenna farm to get on all the new General Class bands that will be available to you, but the height of those antennas has some liming rules.

The maximum height above ground that an antenna structure may be erected without requiring notification to the Federal Aviation Administration (FAA) and registration with the FCC is 200 feet. If your antenna is less than 200 feet high you do not need to register your antenna… unless…

If your antenna is at or near a public use airport, you must notify the FAA in some cases. Specific rules that relate the distance from the airport (or heliport) to antenna height by slope computation apply. If your antenna exceeds the height as determined by the slope calculation, you are required to notify the FAA. See the *Code of Federal Regulations, Title 14, Part 77.9* for the specifics of filing requirements if your station is within 20,000 feet (3.79 miles) of a public use or military airport.

Exceptions to Rules: You're probably very familiar with most of the commonplace rules and regulations governing the Amateur Service, but let's review a few exceptions to the rules that you need to keep in mind also.

Codes and Ciphers: You recall from your Technician studies that secret codes or ciphers are not allowed on the amateur bands. **This restriction does not apply to abbreviations or procedural signals**

(prosigns) as long as they do not obscure the meaning of a message. For any of the standard Q signals this is no problem. Those Q signals are known, open shortcut codes commonly used by amateur operators. However, if you invent your own covert abbreviations with your pals and use them on the air to hide the meaning of your transmissions, you are in violation. Keep your transmission open and above board! But you should know that there is an exception to this rule. **An amateur station is permitted to transmit secret codes to control a space station,** such as an amateur radio satellite. This makes perfect sense, as the operator of an expensive satellite has every reason to protect it from accidental or purposeful control hijacking!

G1B06

Music Transmissions: You also learned in your Technician studies that transmitting music on the amateur frequencies is a rule violation. You should also recall the singular exception to this rule as well. **Music may be transmitted by an amateur station only when it is an incidental part of manned spacecraft retransmission.** Music is sometimes be incidentally transmitted from NASA Mission Control or from the ISS during amateur radio contacts. Sometimes the music may be retransmitted in periodic amateur radio news features that many repeater operators support. So, music from space on the amateur bands is OK. Music from your banjo on the amateur bands is a rules violation!

G1B05

Courtesy NASA/JPL-Caltech

Figure 1.7: Amateur Radio on the ISS – Music Transmissions OK!

Pecuniary Interests: Every technician knows that you can't receive money or other compensation for amateur transmissions and that you can't use the amateur bands for your business communications. Both of those are prohibited operations. However, **an amateur station may transmit communications in which the licensee or control operator has a pecuniary (monetary) interest when other stations are being notified of the sale of apparatus normally used in an amateur station and when such activity is not done on a regular basis.** So, it is fine to advertise on the air that you wish to sell your HT or that old 2m antenna in your garage, and even haggle over prices! Just don't market non-ham equipment or merchandise, like that vintage pickup truck up on blocks in the yard!

Revoked License: It is a very rare situation, but it can happen. If a person has ever had an amateur license revoked by the FCC, that person is not allowed to transmit on the amateur frequencies even as a third party operator. **A license revocation disqualifies a third party from participating in stating a message over an amateur station.**

You have now expanded your knowledge of the particular details of DX and other General Class amateur radio operations! You have also completed the first chapter material in your drive to General Class. Congratulations! Next we will examine some of the cool operating methods you can implement as a General Class licensee, but first be sure to check your recall online with the question pool items from this section.

HamRadioSchool.com/general_media

2.0　Operating Your Radio

❝ There's a fine line between fishing and just standing on the shore like an idiot.

– Steven Wright

If you want to hook lots of contacts as a General Class operator, how you operate can determine which side of Mr. Wright's line you fall upon in the ham radio fishing derby. This chapter will help you understand how to really *RF fish*.

In Section 2.1 we will define the concept of *Good Amateur Practice* and examine some specific examples of what it is, and of what it is not. In Section 2.2 you'll study some common operating tips and techniques for the HF bands that will open up to you as a General licensee. We'll particularly focus on single sideband operating techniques. The topic of Section 2.3 is *Continuous Wave* (CW). Even if you do not immediately become proficient sending Morse Code, you should be familiar with CW mode and its unique operating characteristics, and just maybe you'll catch the bug and try your hand at it! Finally, we will dig into digital modes in Section 2.4, with particular coverage of the digital modes commonly used on the HF bands.

Ready to toss your line into the General Class waters?

2.1　Good Amateur Practice
Operating Your Radio

❝ Good Amateur Practice is not operating so that whoever hears you becomes sorry they ever got into Amateur Radio in the first place.❞

– Riley Hollingsworth

The FCC requires an amateur station to be operated in all respects not specifically covered by the Part 97 rules in conformance with good engineering and good amateur practice.

G1B11

What does that mean, "good amateur practice," and who gets to decide whether an amateur practice is good or not? Seems rather vague, I know. However, it is **the FCC that determines "good engineering and good amateur practice" as it applies to the operation of an amateur station.**

G1B12

Former FCC Special Counsel for the Spectrum Enforcement Division, Riley Hollingsworth, had some excellent words about good amateur practice in 2002. He said that while hard to define, it is "…operating with the realization that frequencies are shared, that there's going to be occasional interference and that's no reason to become hateful and paranoid." Other *Riley-isms* regarding the definition of good amateur practice include:

> *Giving a little ground – even if you have a right not to – in order to help preserve Amateur Radio and not cause it to get a bad name…*

> *Not acting like an idiot just because you were stepped on.*

> *Operating so that if a neighbor, niece or nephew or news reporter hears you, that person will be impressed with Amateur Radio.*
>
> Source: ARRL

So, with thanks to Mr. Hollingsworth for his wisdom and wit in framing this issue, let's cover a little ground on good amateur practice.

Log Keeping: Memory is tenuous. Very often I simply tilt my head and items of recall roll right out my ear and bounce off my shoulder, never to be found again. When it comes to radio station operation, contacts, call signs and the like, there is a virtual avalanche spewing from my auricles. To help with this exact problem, **many amateurs keep a station log,** even though the FCC does not require it. **A log may help with a reply if the FCC requests information** regarding your transmissions, station control operator, or other items that have long since exited your ear and disappeared into the couch. A log is also handy in keeping track of contacts for which you may seek a QSL card, particularly if you are chasing an award like Worked All States (WAS) or DXCC (for working 100 different countries).

At a minimum, **the information traditionally contained in a station log includes:**

- **Date and time of contact,** usually using Coordinated Universal Time (UTC, or "Zulu" or GMT time)

G2D08
G2D09

- **Band and/or frequency of the contact**
- **Call sign of the station contacted and the signal report given**
  (RST format)

You may wish to keep additional information about your contacts in your log, such as the contacted operator's name, geographic location or grid locator, and notes regarding the exchange or QSO content. This way, if you are ever called upon to provide information for an FCC in-

> ### RST Signal Report
> **R**eadability 1 to 5 (5 is best)
> **S**ignal Strength 1 to 9 (from S-meter)
> **T**one 1 to 9 (for quality of CW note)
>
> Phone reports are usually RS only.
> **"C" added to a CW report means "chirpy" or unstable signal tone.**
>
> G2C07

vestigation or if there is any question about your own station's operation, you have the records necessary to provide the requested input.

Logs may be hand written or electronic. There are numerous electronic log book programs available as free downloads online or as commercial products, or you may prefer a simple formatted spreadsheet. The advantage of an electronic log book is that it usually includes a search capability, making it easy to zero-in on previous contacts, dates, call signs, or other recorded information. Particularly with your HF and DX contacts you will want to keep a log of all the different places to which you have reached out on the air and of all the new friends made there!

Avoiding Interference: Mr. Hollingsworth's statements about good amateur practice focus on interference between stations and how to behave properly as an operator in handling it. The best behavior is to avoid the interference in the first place – head-off interference before it happens!

Contact Log

Rec #	Call Sign	Date	Band	Mode	Power	Sig Sent	Sig Rec	Time on	Time off	Country	State	City or County	Name	Freq	
1	KE7NCO	26-Oct-09	20	USB	100	5/9	5/9+	10:10	10:26	USA	NV	Sparks, NV	Scotty	14,251.00	Logged eQSL
2	W0KEN	26-Oct-09	20	USB	100	5/5 - 5/9	5/1 - 5/7	10:25	10:32	USA	WI	Hayward WI	Ken	14,251.00	Logged eQSL
3	AE4QK	27-Oct-09	40	LSB	100	5/7	7-May	13:25	13:35	USA	KY	Owensboro	Ron	7,237.00	Logged eQSL
4	K5LMI	28-Oct-09	80	LSB	100	5/9++	5/9++	10:05	10:10	USA	NM	Clayton	Herb	3,868.00	
5	W0DGG	28-Oct-09	80	LSB	100	5/9++	5/9++	10:05	18:10	USA	CO	Littleton	Dale	3,868.00	
6	KA1RBU	28-Oct-09	20	USB	100	6/9	5/9	17:35	17:43	USA	CA	Martinez	Phil	14,310.00	
7	K7IT	29-Oct-09	40	LSB	100	5/7	5/5	15:10	15:17	USA	MT	Townsend	Gary	7,195.00	Logged eQSL
8	W7EJB	29-Oct-09	40	LSB	100	5/7	5/7	15:10	15:17	USA	MT	Roundup	Cort	7,195.00	Logged eQSL
9	W6MWV/7m	29-Oct-09	40	LSB	100	5/7	5/3	15:10	15:17	USA	NV	Hwy 93	Jim	7,195.00	
10	KL7LF	30-Oct-09	20	LSB	100	5/5	5/8	16:43	16:46	USA	AK	Fairbanks	Joe	14,244.00	Logged eQSL
11	KH7DX	1-Nov-09	20	LSB	100	5/9	5/9	17:45	17:55	USA	HI	Kailua, Kona	Stuart	14,245.00	
12	W1SW	5-Nov-09	20	LSB	100	5/9	5/9	9:36	9:36	USA	CT	Newington	Pete	14,266.00	Logged eQSL
13	4U1WB	5-Nov-09	20	LSB	100	5/9	5/9+	16:22	16:22	USA	DC	Washington	Fasa	3,868.70	
14	K4MDX	5-Nov-09	40	LSB	100	5/9	5/7	17:45	17:49	USA	VA	Charlottesville	Mario	7,195.00	
15	KI4KSY	8-Nov-09	40	LSB	100	5/7	5/5	17:12	17:17	USA	FL	Pierson	Tim	14,247.60	Logged eQSL
16	YW5F	8-Nov-09	20	LSB	100	6/9	5/7	17:25	17:26	Venezuela	n/a	Caracas	?	14,237.00	
17	K8V	11-Nov-09	20	LSB	100	5/7	5/7	7:45	7:46	USA	MI	Iron Mountain	Scott	14,234.00	Special Event Veterans Day Station
18	N4TAT	11-Nov-09	20	LSB	100	5/9	5/9	8:30	9:05	USA	GA	WarnerRobbins	Don	14,313.00	Logged eQSL
19	K8MGA	11-Nov-09	20	LSB	100	5/7	5/7	10:00	10:05	USA	OH	Chillicothe	Jerry	14,249.60	Logged eQSL
20	K5KJD	11-Nov-09	20	LSB	100	5/9	5/7	13:19	13:20	USA	LA	Baton Rouge	Mike	14,263.00	Special Event on USS Kidd Navy vessel, MS river

Figure 2.1: A simple spreadsheet logbook extract. A log book should record the contact call sign, date, time, frequency, and signal report, as minimum information. Most logs will include additional notes, such as locations and names of contacts.

Except during FCC declared emergencies, no one has priority access to frequencies, and common courtesy should be a guide. So, while no operator has a lock on the use of a frequency, things tend to work on a first-come, first-serve basis with common courtesy. It would be rude to muscle in on an ongoing QSO between two operators, or to do the same to a single operator calling CQ on a given frequency unless you are responding to the CQ, of course. How can you head-off accidental interference like this?

First, **choose your transmitting frequency with good amateur practice:**

- **Insure that the frequency and mode selected are within your license class privileges.**
- **Be sure you are following the generally accepted band plans agreed to by the Amateur Radio community.**
- **And then monitor the frequency before transmitting** to avoid interfering with ongoing communications. It is usually good to listen for at least several tens of seconds, as you may be able to receive only one half of a QSO between two operators, and the one operator you can receive may be listening to his contact!

Second, **send "QRL?" on CW, followed by your call sign; or, if using phone, ask if the frequency is in use, followed by your call sign. This is a practical way to avoid harmful interference on an apparently clear frequency when calling CQ on CW or phone.** If you are answered with a CW "C," YES, or QRL, or if the phone response is "Yes, the frequency is in use," then graciously move on to another frequency and give it another shot! Sometimes the bands are crowded and finding an open frequency can be a challenge. Keep your courtesy and maintain your diligence, or possibly move to another, less crowded band.

Choosing a Frequency: Let's consider this frequency choosing step above in a bit more detail. What factors besides your license privileges are important when selecting a frequency on which to transmit?

Mode: Follow the voluntary band plan for the operating mode you intend to use. Remember, sub-bands are designated in many amateur bands for CW, digital, and phone transmission modes. Choose a frequency in the mode sub-band that complies with band plan guidelines.

DX Window: Depending upon your selected band and mode, you may need to consider whether or not you are in a *DX Window*. **A DX Window in a voluntary band plan is a portion of the band that should not be used for contacts between stations within the 48 contiguous United States,** but rather used for making DX contacts outside of this region. The ARRL recommends DX windows on some bands and modes, as defined in the *ARRL Considerate Operator's Frequency Guide* that may be found at the ARRL web site. **An operator using the expression "CQ DX" indicates the caller is looking for any station outside their own country,** so if you're within the lower 48 states you should not respond to such a call from a US station.

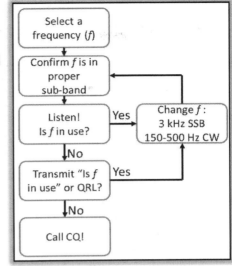

G2B08

G2A11

Figure 2.2: Flow chart of steps in selecting a frequency to call CQ.

Frequency Separation: A CW or Single Sideband (SSB) transmission uses a small band of frequencies adjacent to the carrier frequency to which your station is tuned. The bandwidth of CW is typically quite narrow, perhaps 150 Hz, while SSB is usually around 3 kHz wide. Further, the bandwidth consumed by those modes of transmission will all be piled on one side of the carrier frequency, as depicted in Figure 2.3 – all above the carrier for upper sideband (USB) mode or all below the carrier for lower sideband (LSB) mode. Be sure there is adequate separation between your chosen frequency and nearby frequencies in use for the bandwidth of the mode you are using. The customary minimums are as follows:

For CW mode, the minimum frequency separation you should allow in order to minimize interference to stations on adjacent frequencies is 150 to 500 Hz. Notice that this separation allows for the bandwidth of a CW signal.

G2B04

For SSB signals under normal conditions, the customary minimum frequency separation is approximately 3 kHz. Again, notice that this conforms to the bandwidth of the typical SSB signal.

G2B05

Example: Reference Figure 2.3. Suppose you want to call CQ on the 20m band with USB phone mode per the normal conventions for the band. You have checked that you are between 14.225 and 14.350 MHz, the General Class phone sub-band. You dial around the sub-band and note it is crowded, but there seems to be a clear frequency, 14.250 MHz. After listening a bit you hear one side of a QSO right on

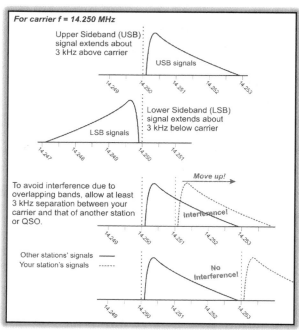

Figure 2.3: Minimum frequency separation of SSB carriers is customarily 3 kHz.

that frequency. To make sure you do not interfere with this ongoing QSO you move up at least 3 kHz to 14.253 MHz – a USB signal will extend 3 kHz above the carrier frequency shown on your transceiver display. You should also make sure your receive bandwidth is set to be *at least 3 kHz* so that you will hear any signals within your intended transmit band. If you hear no obvious signals after a few seconds be sure you are tuned on frequency and then make the call "Is the frequency in use? Is the frequency in use?" Follow with your call sign so that in the case you get a response you do not have to interrupt further with identification. If you hear no response, start your CQ calls! If you do get a response indicating the frequency is in use, politely move on.

Changing Propagation: Due to changing conditions in the ionosphere, HF propagation will ebb and flow through the day, sometimes changing suddenly. The direction and effectiveness of propagation may shift such that a station you heard at RS 5-9 a moment ago suddenly dips into the background noise, and a different station that you could not hear previously becomes prominent. In a matter of seconds you have lost your contact and you are interfering with another QSO of which you were completely unaware! It's all part of the magic, so don't let it rattle you. **If propagation changes during your contact and you notice increasing interference from other activity on the**

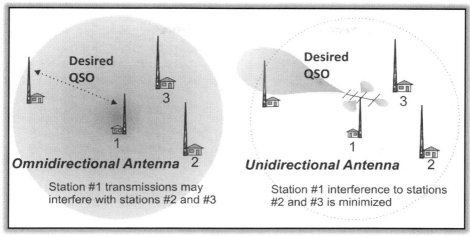

Figure 2.4: Comparison of omnidirectional and unidirectional (AKA *Directional* or *Beam*) antenna patterns.

same (or nearby) frequency, as a common courtesy move your contact to another frequency.

Directional Antennas: The type of antenna used can have a significant impact regarding interference between stations. Although we'll cover more about antennas in a later section, you probably already understand that *omnidirectional* antennas radiate equally in all horizontal directions, while a *unidirectional*, or simply a *directional*, or *beam* antenna points most of the RF energy in a particular direction. A quarter-wave vertical is an example of an omnidirectional antenna, and a Yagi is an example of a directional antenna.

A directional antenna would be the best to use for minimizing interference, since you can point the beam in the direction of your contact, thereby reducing the RF signal strength radiating in other directions. The potential of interference from your station in those other directions is minimized. With the omnidirectional antenna you have no control over the directionality of your signal, so the potential for interference is generally greater. However, erecting directional antennas for the HF bands is no small or inexpensive chore, and your first HF station will likely employ a more omnidirectional antenna like a quarter-wave vertical or a horizontal dipole. Don't fret, many thousands of hams use these antennas successfully every day without imposing undue interference!

Additional Considerations: Just a couple more good amateur practices to be knowledgable of... What if you are dialing through the bands and encounter a truly spellbinding QSO in which you would just love to take part? Or, what

G2D11

if you hear a friend or familiar contact in a QSO to whom you wish to say howdy? There is a courteous practice to use: **The recommended way to break into a conversation when using phone mode is to say your call sign during a break between transmissions by the other stations.** Simple as that. Just throw your call sign in there and await a courteous response inviting you to transmit.

G2A08

Of course, **if you are communicating with another amateur station and hear a station in distress break in, the first thing you should do is acknowledge the station in distress and determine what assistance may be needed.** Then do everything you can to provide the assistance. A station in distress will usually break in using the term *emergency, mayday,* or *priority.* But it could also be a simple "Help!"

G2B02

Now, the next time someone asks you what is meant by "good amateur practice," you are armed with superb, sage advice from Mr. Hollingsworth as well as numerous examples of it! You should be able to paint a clear, unambiguous picture of good practice, and you should be able to conduct your own station operations in conformance with it. Please do try your best, and take pride in your success. Your fellow hams are counting on you to help uphold our legacy of self-policed, on-air courtesy.

Go tackle the online quiz associated with this section, then come back for a little insight into common HF operating conventions.

HamRadioSchool.com/general_media

2.2   Operating Techniques

" *In extreme situations, the entire universe becomes our foe; at such critical times, unity of
mind and technique is essential – do not let your
heart waver!*   *– Morihei Ueshiba*

There you are: It's the busiest point of the contest! You're working a giant SSB pile up, your VOX headset tweaked to perfection, your azimuthal projection map keenly guiding your commands to your directional's rotator, a thousand yearning contacts screaming call signs in your ear, and now you can distinguish none of them! You quickly decide to go split mode and wonder if you can sneak away under cover of the adjustment for that long-needed comfort break with the plumbing. You don't want to lose the pile up or the frequency – you'll have to shift to the split fast! Are your mind and technique unified? Can you do it? *Or will your heart waver?*

Marshall arts Ōsensei Ueshiba would have made a fine ham operator, and while his advice may be just a smidgen over the top for most ham ops, the point is well taken. Technique matters.

With a General Class ticket your operations will likely focus much more on modes commonly used on the HF bands, including single sideband (SSB) phone, and on some of the associated operating techniques that will enhance your ability to make HF contacts. In this section we will explore commonly accepted HF conventions and describe some of the more advanced operating techniques that come in handy on the HF bands. Ready, *kōhai*?

Single Sideband: We will cover more detail on single sideband (SSB) mode a bit later in the *How Radio Works* chapter, but let's review some of the basic characteristics and then discuss SSB use on the amateur bands. (You may want to review the HamRadioSchool.com Technician License Course section 6.3, *Bandwidth and Sidebands*, for a refresher on the nature of SSB.)

Single Sideband phone (voice) mode is a special form of amplitude modulation, or AM. Its primary advantage for voice transmissions over AM or FM is its narrower bandwidth. As depicted in Figure 2.5 a modulated true AM signal has two bands of signals either side of the carrier frequency to which the

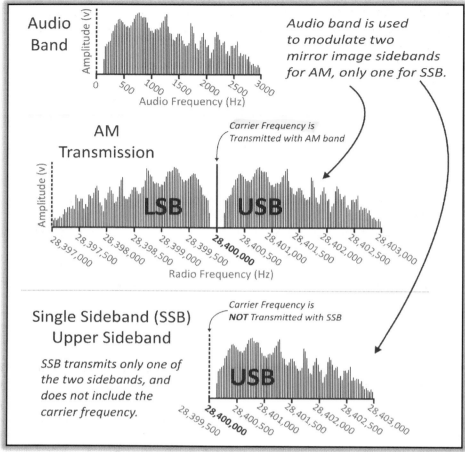

Figure 2.5: Comparison of AM and SSB.

transmitter is tuned – one band above the carrier frequency (*upper sideband*, or USB) and one band below the carrier frequency (*lower sideband*, or LSB). The USB and LSB are redundant mirror images of one another, each representing the phone modulation in approximately 3 kHz of signal bandwidth. Thus, the entire AM signal consumes about 6 kHz of bandwidth in total, and it offers a robust and good fidelity signal.

However, since the USB and LSB each contain a complete phone modulated signal, only one of these sidebands is necessary to affect voice communication. Single sideband mode is exactly that – the use of only a single sideband of approximately 3 kHz for phone transmissions. Either the USB or the LSB may be used in a SSB transmission at the discretion of the control operator. The carrier frequency signal, also transmitted in a true AM signal, is omitted from SSB transmissions as well. Using less than half the bandwidth of AM and much less bandwidth than typical FM signals, SSB is a very efficient voice mode, and **SSB**

is the most commonly used phone mode on the HF amateur bands.
As you may surmise, some fidelity of signal is sacrificed for this efficiency as compared to AM.

SSB Conventions: While either of the sidebands may be selected for use by a SSB operator, random selection of USB or LSB within a band would cause some hassles. For instance, a pair of operators using opposite sidebands will not be able to understand one another's demodulated audio. In such a case signals intended for high audio frequency reproduction will be demodulated as low frequency audio and vice versa. The result is usually a garbled *"wah wah, grrr flump wah wah"* kind of audio reproduction that almost sounds like speech but is indecipherable. Such random selection would also complicate transceiver operations on a given band and muddle the matter of avoiding interference described in the previous section on *Good Amateur Practice*!

So, standard operating conventions for USB and LSB use have been established and accepted by the amateur community. It is good amateur practice to follow these conventions:

Upper Sideband (USB): The sideband most commonly used for voice communications on frequencies of 14 MHz (20m band) or higher (17m, 15m, 12m, 10m), including VHF and UHF bands.

Lower Sideband (LSB): The sideband most commonly used for voice communications on frequencies of 7 MHz (40m band) or lower (75/80m, 160m). [Note exception: The five 60m channels are restricted to USB only.]

Variable Frequency Oscillator (VFO): The VFO is the name used for the *big knob* on the radio, the one that is used to make incremental or continuous adjustments to the tuned frequency. Recall from the *Before We Begin* chapter, pre-designated or assigned channels are not typically utilized with HF operations as with VHF/UHF

Figure 2.6: The BIG KNOB, A.K.A. the VFO.

repeaters or simplex band plans. Rather, the VFO tunes the carrier frequency for both transmitter and receiver across the continuous range of frequencies available in a HF band. Typically a transceiver's VFO will allow a minimum frequency change step size of 100 Hz or smaller.

G2A05

G2A01 G2A03 G2A04 G2A02 G2A09

G4A03 G4A12

Split Mode: Many modern HF transceivers offer **dual VFOs that permit the monitoring of two different frequencies.** In HF operations, **operating in "split" mode is a common technique in which the transceiver is set to different transmit and receive frequencies,** thereby utilizing the dual VFO feature. A very common reason for doing this is to help reduce interference from many calling stations during a pile up.

Pile Up: A situation in which many stations are attempting to contact a single operator, such as a very rare or desirable DX station, is called a pile up. If numerous stations are calling a single DX station, many of those calling stations cannot hear the DX station respond due to the stronger and multiple signals of more local operators striving to make themselves heard over several seconds following the DX station's "QRZ?" (who is calling me?) transmission. So, even if the DX station replied to your call sign, you may not hear it, resulting in delay, confusion, and finally a repeated cacophony of station calls. Rinse and repeat until frustrated.

One way to resolve this problem is for the DX station to operate in split mode, transmitting on one frequency and listening on another. The calling stations should be in the opposite, complementary frequency arrangement, listening on the DX transmit frequency but transmitting on the DX listen frequency. That way, the DX station's calls are clear to everyone, making for more efficient and effective contacts.

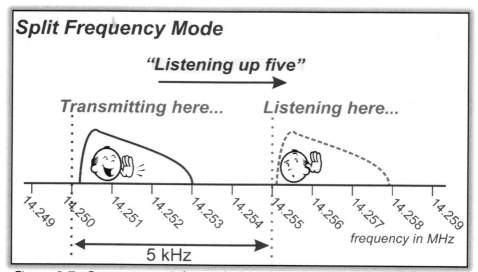

Figure 2.7: Operating in Split Mode sets the transceiver to different transmit and receive frequencies. This technique is often used during busy "pile ups."

However, the station *running the pile up* (the single highly desired station) needs to be sure to announce his transmit and receive configuration for this to work. Usually the station will announce something like "listening up five," meaning that the station will receive your transmissions 5 kHz higher than it is transmitting. You should put your station into split mode, listening to the DX station's frequency but transmitting 5 kHz higher. If you are fortunate enough to be running a pile up (*It can happen to you!*), it is a good practice to provide listening up/down instructions frequently so that late arrivals to your pile up understand the convention being used and will not re-create the problem you sought to solve by operating in split mode at the start of your pile up! Refer to your transceiver operator's manual for specific instruction on establishing a split frequency arrangement, or split mode.

SSB VOX: Voice operated transmit, or VOX, may be used with SSB. This is not different from any other VOX operation on VHF/UHF FM – **SSB VOX operation simply allows "hands free" operation** by activating the push-to-talk function automatically when the relatively strong audio signal of the operator's voice is detected. Many HF operators prefer VOX for the convenience of hands-free operation, especially for extended time on the air such as a contest. Implementing VOX operation requires a special VOX circuit that most modern HF transceivers will support. The VOX circuit usually will provide a control to adjust the microphone sensitivity (gain) for actuating the PTT function and a delay control for adjusting the time that PTT will be held on after your voice is silent, thereby avoiding rapid and persistent on-off-on PTT actuations with brief verbal pauses. Use VOX with caution, and adjust it meticulously, as ambient sound can inadvertently key your transmitter.

G2A10

QRP: QRP operation is low power transmit operation. This is the mode for operators who care to send the very least. The Q signal QRP refers to the CW shortcut "Reduce power" or "Shall I reduce power?" QRP operations typically imply 5 watts of power or less in transmissions, and often much less than that. Due to battery power necessity, low power operation is very popular for operators who enjoy operating portable from remote locations such as mountaintops or back country camps, and many operators simply enjoy the thrill of making long distance and DX contacts on just a few watts of power. Some digital modes in common use work particularly well for QRP, such as JT65, JT9, and others, but QRP using CW, PSK31, and even phone mode is also very popular. Try it! You may get a big kick out of very little.

G2D10

Running Barefoot: Most modern transceivers include output power of about 100 watts PEP for HF operations. When using such a transceiver without any additional RF power amplification a station is said to be *running barefoot*. In good conditions 100 watts is more than enough power to talk around the world on the HF bands with SSB and a simple dipole wire antenna. In poor propagation conditions a power amplifier may be used to boost power well above "barefoot" level to complete contacts, and we will examine amplifiers in greater detail in Chapter 6.

Azimuthal Projection Map: A handy tool, especially for the DX chaser, is an azimuthal projection map. **The azimuthal projection map** is a world map projection that **shows true bearings and distances from a particular location,** such as your station location. With such a map you can readily determine where in the world your signals are pointing when using a directional antenna, ensuring that you are pointing in the shortest path to your targeted geographical area. This determination might seem trivial at first consideration, but it is not!

G2D04

The desired pointing direction of your RF signals to any given receiving station is depicted as a straight line from your station to the other. However, combining straight lines with a spherical planet is sometimes a tricky feat of mental gymnastics. The azimuthal projection keeps the mental gymnastics to a kindergarten-level playground exercise.

For example, suppose you are operating from the central US, perhaps near Kansas City. If you point your awesome 20m Yagi directional antenna due west, where will your signals go? You may be surprised to know that you will be pointing directly into Australia in the southern hemisphere! Japan and South Korea will be nearly 45 degrees north of your directional projection. To point to central Europe you'd turn your antenna northeast to roughly 030 degrees.

Long Path Contacts: Armed with azimuthal projection knowledge and excellent propagation conditions you can also try **long-path contacts with another station, in which your antenna is pointed 180 degrees from its short-path heading.** So, in our example above, to take the long-path to Europe you'd point your directional antenna 030 + 180 degrees, or to a southwest heading of 210 degrees. Such contacts are usually more difficult, and success may depend on atmospheric conditions. Either way, long path or short, it's all for fun and for the reward of achieving it!

G2D06

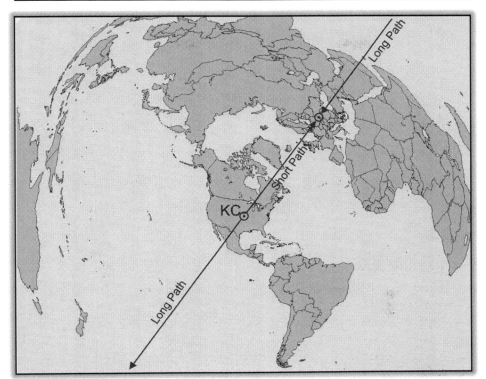

Figure 2.8: Example azimuthal projection map centered on Kansas City, MO, indicating both short path and long path propagation to a European contact.

Is your heart wavering yet? Maybe just thumping a little faster, anticipating getting on the air and trying out some of this newly acquired technique? You will learn much more about HF operational techniques and conventions when you're on the bands. Don't be afraid to ask your fellow hams questions, and listen to other QSOs to glean additional insight. Before long no one will be able to tell the operational difference between you with your sparkling new General ticket and an ancient, grey beard Ham Ōsensei!

Next we'll get find out how to achieve zero beat and hone our prosigns with an examination of CW operations. But first, be sure to review the questions for this section!

HamRadioSchool.com/general_media

Jake WØJAK and Cole WØCOL take turns sending and receiving CW with a touch key tone generator and using visual mnemonics as an initial method of quickly memorizing Morse Code. The tone practice is critical to proficiency, as it reinforces learning the sound of code character patterns. The ultimate learning goal is to "hear" each pattern as a letter.

> ❝ *Wave after wave*
> *Will flow with the tide*
> *And bury the world as it does*
> — *Neil Peart (Rush), Natural Science*

The joy of CW! Although proficiency with Morse Code is no longer required for any of the FCC Amateur Service licenses, continuous wave (CW) mode operations are far from buried in ham radio! Indeed, continuous wave continues!

Many operators prefer CW to any other mode, as it offers a pleasure and pride of skill development like nothing else in the hobby, and its power efficiency remains unmatched by any other mode. The prevalence of CW on the HF bands is greater today than ever, and you should try your fist at it! After all, popular theory is that the moniker of our hobby, "ham" radio, derived from the pejorative comparison of professionally competent wireless telegraphers whose code was beautifully consistent and readable with those "ham fisted" amateurs whose code exhibited numerous auditory warts. So, let's continue with some fine points about continuous wave.

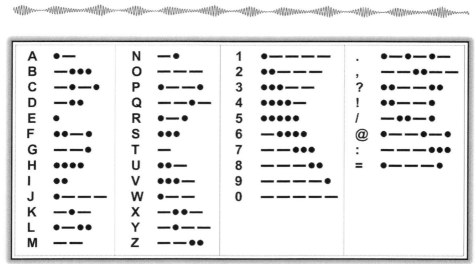

A	•—	N	—•	1	•————	.	•—•—•—
B	—•••	O	———	2	••———	,	——••——
C	—•—•	P	•——•	3	•••——	?	••——••
D	—••	Q	——•—	4	••••—	!	••——•—
E	•	R	•—•	5	•••••	/	—••—•
F	••—•	S	•••	6	—••••	@	•——•—•
G	——•	T	—	7	——•••	:	———•••
H	••••	U	••—	8	———••	=	—•••—
I	••	V	•••—	9	————•		
J	•———	W	•——	0	—————		
K	—•—	X	—••—				
L	•—••	Y	—•——				
M	——	Z	——••				

Figure 2.9 International Morse Code Characters.

CW Band Use: Recall from the *Bands and Privileges* section that most HF bands have digital and data sub-bands in the lower portion of the bands where phone transmissions are prohibited. This is where most of the CW action will be found, down where it doesn't have to contend with the broader band emissions and associated interference of the phone modes. However, a little-noticed line in the key of the ARRL US Amateur Band Plan chart states, "CW operation is permitted throughout all amateur bands." So, you may occasionally hear CW code in the phone and image portions of the bands, and that's OK, but good amateur practice avoids using CW in the phone bands. Most operators prefer CW using the lowest frequencies for which they have privileges.

Keys and Keyers: You are probably familiar with the look and action of a conventional *straight key* for CW, as depicted in Figure 2.10– press the key down and a contact is made that activates the CW transmitter. Morse Code tones of *dits* and *dahs* are created by the duration of the key press by the operator. It requires quite some skill development to send consistently timed characters, words, and intervening spaces. Also depicted in Figure 2.10 is a paddle key and a touch key, each of which may be connected to an *electronic keyer*. **The purpose of an electronic keyer is to automatically generate strings of dots and dashes for CW operation.** A keyer is a digital circuit or

G4A10

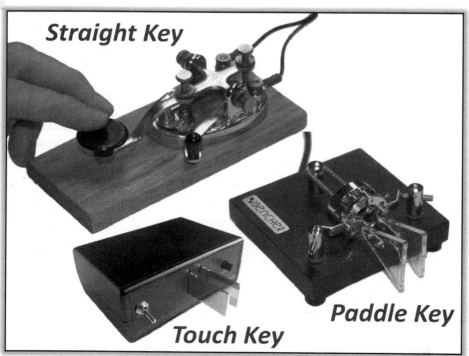

Figure 2.10: Example Keys and Paddles.

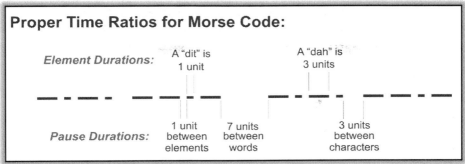

Proper Time Ratios for Morse Code:

Element Durations: A "dit" is 1 unit   A "dah" is 3 units

Pause Durations: 1 unit between elements   7 units between words   3 units between characters

Figure 2.11: No matter your send speed, strive for a consistent 3:1 ratio of elements, in which the 'dahs' are three times the duration of the 'dits.'

microprocessor that detects activations of a paddle and generates the associated Morse Code element. For instance, pushing or touching one paddle will cause the keyer to generate a consistent duration *dit*, while the other paddle's activation will generate a consistently timed *dah*. While this helps make an operator's code more consistent, most operators find that electronic keyers promote faster sending speed as well, but the timing of character and word spacing remains with the operator's technique and skill. Some well-practiced operators are able to achieve speeds upwards of 50 words per minute (WPM). That's screaming!

Break-In: Suppose that you are sending a lengthy message with CW, at beginner's slow speed of perhaps 5 words per minute (WPM). If interference occurs during your send, or if the receiving station needs to interrupt you for an urgently required break, or if a station in distress desperately needs to break-in with an emergency message, how will you know of these problems if you're steadily transmitting? The answer is break-in telegraphy, or QSK. **Full break-in telegraphy means that transmitting stations can receive between code characters and elements.** In other words, when you are transmitting code characters your transmitter is rapidly switching on for the sending of each dit and dah element and just as quickly switching back to receive in between those elements – millisecond durations – while your relatively slow brain is coordinating your fingers. So, there is no solid, uninterrupted block of transmit time with full break-in operation, and it is possible to hear other stations transmitting or requesting to break-in even while you're frantically trying to pour out your CW heart to them.

Semi-break-in telegraphy is similar, only there is a somewhat longer delay after each dit or dah transmit time during which the transmitter continues, or 'hangs on.' The time for another operator to break-in is reduced, but still available, and you will hear the other's keying effort between your own transmissions. You may be able to adjust your transmitter's delay time to affect varying degrees of break-in capability. That is, you can adjust the duration that your transmitter will remain in transmit mode following the completion of a code element. Additionally, **transmitter keying circuits sometimes include a time delay to allow time for the transmit-receive changeover operations to complete properly before RF output is allowed.** This is a protection mechanism for the circuits, but most modern transceivers will have incredibly short time delays, usually on the order of a few milliseconds, and even the speediest operators will not usually notice interrupted code elements due to this feature.

CW Operating Conventions: Here are a couple of basic operating tips and tricks of the CW trade that may help you get started on the air once you have mastered basic code production and decoding.

The best speed to use answering a CQ in Morse Code is the speed at which the CW was sent. As a beginner it may not be feasible for you to answer a rapidly coded CW transmission at equivalent speed, but there are many beginners and beginner's nets on the air that will allow you to exchange code at comfortable speeds before jumping into the fray of faster code. Further, most speedy CW operators will slow down if you reply to them slowly, and you should never send faster than you can receive for the same reason – the more practiced operators will match your speed.

Zero Beat: In CW operations "zero beat" means matching your transmit frequency to the frequency of a received signal. That is, you want the received signal tone to sound the same as your transmitted tone, aligning your CW transmitted band center precisely with the other operator's band center. (You will hear your *sidetone* for comparison when you transmit CW.) Achieving zero beat makes the received signal tone sound the same as your sidetone, helping to distinguish your contact from any interfering signals on a busy band. Zero beat also helps minimize the bandwidth that your QSO consumes, leaving more spectrum for others to

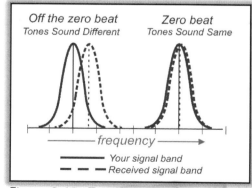

Figure 2.12: Zero Beat is achieved when the center of your transmitted band matches the frequency of the received signal's band, and the two tones sound identical.

enjoy. Most transceivers will provide a capability for checking the tone of your transmitted signal, so dig into that operator's manual and become more familiar with your rig. Usually this will involve the generation of a sidetone without transmitting it, while simultaneously listening to the received CW signal to be matched. The VFO is adjusted until the received signal tone and the comparison sidetone sound identical and have no *beat frequency* warbling sound. The tones should remain identical when you *reverse your sideband*, as well.

Reverse Sideband: On a busy band you will experience CW interference. Even though CW signals may be as narrow as 150 Hz, your receive filters will usually allow a significantly wider band of signals to be detected and demodulated. So, you're going to hear the guy next door on the band sometimes and, depending on where that other signal is located relative to your own frequency, its tone may be higher or lower than the one you are decoding and perhaps significantly annoying. A technique that most receivers will allow is reversing the sideband and, thereby, reversing the orientation of audio tone demodulation. Doing this, perhaps with a "CW-R" control on your transceiver, can turn that annoyingly high-pitched tone into a mellow low-pitched tone that is easier to ignore, thus allowing you to concentrate on your decoding. The reverse effect is feasible as well. So, if like me you have lost much of that high frequency perception the interference may seem to disappear altogether with sideband reversal! Thus, **an advantage of selecting the opposite or "reverse" sideband when receiving CW signals is the possibility of reducing or eliminating interference from other signals.**

G4A02

Prosigns and Q Signals: Procedural signals, or *prosigns*, and *Q signals* are abbreviations for commonly used terms and were developed by telegraphers to reduce the burden of spelling out things all the time. Prosigns are two letters (three in the case of "SOS") that are transmitted together without pause, as if a single letter, and that have specific meanings in code exchanges. Q signals are three letter shortcuts beginning with the letter Q that are used extensively in CW and that have crept into phone mode usage as well. On the following page is a short list of prosigns and Q signals followed by an example CW exchange that uses many of them. A more exhaustive list of prosigns, Q signals, and other popular CW abbreviations may be found online at *HamRadioSchool.com*.

Pro sign	Meaning	Q Signal	Meaning
AR	**Indicates end of a formal message**	**QSL**	**I acknowledge receipt. Do you acknowledge receipt?**
K	"Over" or "Go ahead"	**QRN**	**Static;** natural noise. **I am troubled by static.**
KN	**Similar to K, except listening for a specific station or stations.**	**QRV**	**I am ready to receive messages. Are you ready to receive messages?**
CL	At the end of a transmission to mean "Closing station"	**QRS**	**Send slower. Shall I send slower?**
DE	"From" or "This is"	**QRL**	**Are you busy? Is the frequency in use?**
SK	Similar to AR, but used only at the end of last transmission of QSO	QRP	Reduce power. Shall I reduce power?

Example brief CW QSO:

Station 1: QRL
Station 1: CQ CQ CQ DE WØSTU WØSTU WØSTU K
Station 2: WØSTU DE KØNR KØNR KØNR K
Station 1: KØNR DE WØSTU UR 599 IN MONUMENT CO NAME IS STU STU AR KØNR DE WØSTU KN
Station 2: WØSTU DE KØNR UR 579 IN RICHMOND IN NAME IS BOB BOB AR WØSTU DE KØNR KN
Station 1: KØNR DE WØSTU QSL QSL TNX QSO MUCH QRN 73 SK KØNR DE WØSTU
Station 2: WØSTU DE KØNR QSL TNX 73 SK WØSTU DE KØNR CL

Now you're ready to go study code and practice it, getting up to speed! While CW is not for everyone, it adds a completely new dimension to your amateur radio fun, and I hope you will endeavor to pick up code. But first, let's get this General Class ticket under your belt. Check out the question pool quiz on CW, and then we'll get digital!

HamRadioSchool.com/general_media

Operating Your Radio
2.4 | **Digital Modes**

❝ I am not the only person who uses his computer mainly for the purpose of diddling with his computer.
— Dave Barry

❝ The Universal Purpose of Amateur Radio is to have fun messing around with radios.
— Bob Witte, KØNR

A singular conclusion is reached by combining these two incontestable tenets of technological brilliance: *Delight in technological diddling increases as the multiple of radio-computer linkages.* This conclusion is the fundamental theorem of the ham digital modes. Let's see just how this diddling proceeds.

The Basics: As you probably learned in your Technician studies, digital modes utilize discrete signals or bits to encode characters and transmit them by radio frequency signals. Each character, whether a letter of the alphabet, a number, or other symbol is represented by a pattern of bits. In binary digital codes this is usually represented as a sequence of the digits 1 and 0, such as *10010110*.

A digital mode must have a defined protocol. A protocol is a set of established rules for encoding, sending, and decoding the digital patterns. The protocol will usually define a set of allowable characters, the structure of the transmitted patterns, and other characteristics of the data exchanges between stations.

Of course, a digital mode must also have some RF modulation technique such as FM or SSB. The digital codes are often translated into sequential sets of shifting audio frequencies that may be RF modulated for transmission over the air and then demodulated back into audio tones by a receiver for decoding back into the intended character sets. In these instances a computer will be interfaced to the transceiver to affect both the translation of characters into audio signals for the transmitter and the decoding of characters from audio signals via the receiver. In other cases the RF frequency is directly shifted via computer control, avoiding the audio modulation step. Let's examine first where digital signals are found in the HF bands, consider some of the digital protocols that are used for digital communications, and then dig into several of the various digital modes commonly used in ham radio.

HF Band Frequency Use: Recall from the *Bands and Privileges* section that digital mode sub-bands reside in the lower portion of most of the HF amateur bands. The very lowest portion of these sub-bands tends to be used for CW operations, while portions of the sub-band above the typical CW regions are commonly used for data transmissions.

The HF digital sub-band segments commonly used for data transmissions are:

10m band	28.070 – 28.189 MHz
12m band	24.920 – 24.930 MHz
15m band	21.070 – 21.110 MHz
17m band	18.100 – 18.110 MHz
20m band	**14.070 – 14.100 MHz**
30m band	10.130 – 10.150 MHz
40m band	7.080 – 7.125 MHz
80m band	**3.570 – 3.60 MHz [3570 – 3600 kHz]**
160m band	1.800 – 1.810 MHz [1800- 1810 kHz]

We will explore some of the digital modes commonly used on the HF bands including RTTY, PACTOR, PSK 31, and JT65 / JT9. Be aware that many others exist and that new digital modes seem to spring up frequently. But next lets consider some of the common digital protocols used by digital modes.

Packet Delivery: A packet is a formatted package of data that includes additional information necessary for accurate transmission and reception. Some digital modes such as packet radio (using *ASCII code*) and *Automatic Packet Reporting System* (APRS) are used to deliver messages to specifically addressed receiving stations. Email by packet radio and text messages by APRS are two examples, and the PACTOR mode utilizes packet delivery. A digital message or file may be delivered in multiple packets of data.

ASCII: American Standard Code for Information Interchange represents characters with a seven-bit code. It defines 128 characters, 33 of which are control characters for text spacing, appearance, and other functions. Many variations of ASCII have been developed using greater bits and greater variety of characters.

Each transmitted digital packet must have routing or destination information. Further, such packet structures require the receiving station to synchronize with the protocol structure and in some cases to facilitate retransmission of packets received with detected errors. **This type of routing and handling information is contained in the header part of a data packet,** and that is followed by the data or body of the message. A trailer segment of infor-

Header	Data	Trailer
1001100011100011101	1111000110101110100001111011001011	11100110000111101101111
- Routing Data - Error Correction - Control Data	Message Data or "Payload"	- Message Status - Error Detection

——————— Packet Send Sequence ——————→

G8C03

Figure 2.15: A generic packet communications format of information. Many protocol variations of this general format are used by different systems.

mation usually concludes a packet's data sequence. If the digital mode is an ***Automatic Repeat Query*** **(ARQ) data mode and the receiving station detects a packet containing errors, the receiving station will request the packet be retransmitted.**

G8C07

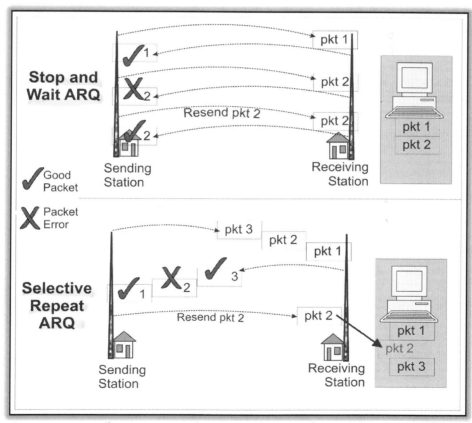

Figure 2.16: Different protocols may implement Automatic Repeat Queries (ARQ) in different ways, but each requires the receiving station to transmit a repeat request and/or an acknowledgement of valid packets received.

Various protocols are used for ARQ, including simple stop and wait ARQ in which an acknowledgement of valid packet receipt must be received by the sender within a limited time and additional packets are not transmitted until acknowledgement is received. *Selective repeat* ARQ protocols provide more continuous sending of packets and packet resends when errors are acknowledged by the receiver, but the receiver must re-sequence packets into proper order based upon packet header control data.

G8C10

A different packet error correction method, *forward error correction*, allows the receiver to correct errors in packets by transmitting redundant information with the data. The redundant information is often efficiently encoded into the packets using mathematical algorithms that allow error detection and self-correction without the need for an ARQ or other retransmit request. However, the quantity of transmitted data is necessarily increased by this method, so it represents a trade-off with the ARQ method of error correction.

G8C04

Baudot Code: Pronounced "*baw-doh*," Baudot Code was a precursor to modern ASCII code and it is used by the RTTY mode that we will examine subsequently. With **Baudot Code** each character is represented by **a 5-bit code sequence with additional bits used for start and stop data.** With five binary digits Baudot code may represent $2^5 = 32$ different characters. However, two Baudot characters (called *FIGS* and *LTRS*) are used to implement something like the shift function of a keyboard by which a second set of characters is referenced. All characters that follow the FIGS character will be interpreted as the alternate set characters that include items like numerals, punctuations, and other special characters. The code interpretation is reset to the normal text character set by transmitting the LTRS characters. Thus, the total number of characters including FIGS and LTRS is 64.

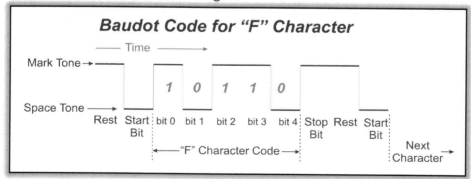

Figure 2.14: RTTY uses 5-bit Baudot Code for each character, with each bit value represented by either the "mark" or "space" frequency/tone. Start-stop bits maintain timing and sequence synchronization between sending and receiving systems.

With a little protocol knowledge in our heads, let's now poke into the nature of several specific digital modes used in amateur radio.

RTTY Mode: Radioteletype, or "ritty," is an older technology that was originally used to transmit text that was immediately printed upon reception by a mechanical printing device. Computers have replaced the teletype machines now in order to encode and decode RTTY data for computer screen display. A computer interface may directly manipulate frequencies, or a *sound card interface* (SCI) may be used to easily link computer and transceiver, with software to provide tone sequences for transmission and to decode received tones. RTTY mode employs Baudot Code.

RTTY is a *frequency shift keying* (FSK) method. **The FSK signal is generated by changing the transmitter oscillator's frequency directly with a digital control signal. The two separate FSK frequencies are identified as *Mark*** (binary 1) **and *Space*** (binary 0). The frequency shifting may also be implemented by *audio frequency shift keying* (AFSK) using two audio tones of different frequencies that modulate mark and space RF shifts.

G8A01 G8C11

In both frequency shift methods, the frequency shifts back and forth between the mark and space to encode a Baudot sequence of five 1s and 0s that represent each character. **The most common frequency shift for RTTY emissions in the amateur HF bands is 170 Hz,** with the standard AFSK tones being 2125 Hz (mark) and 2295 Hz (space). These tones are transmitted by SSB mode on the HF bands, and **normally the lower sideband (LSB) is used when sending AFSK RTTY signals with a SSB transmitter.**

G2E06 G2E01

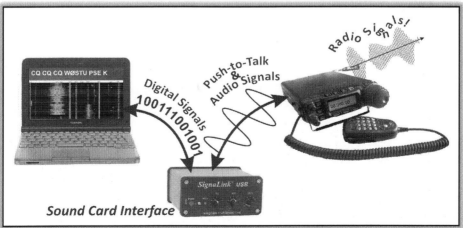

Figure 2.13: Many digital modes use a Sound Card Interface (SCI) between transceiver and computer, using tones to modulate digital signals.

Digital symbol rates are measured in baud. Derived from the use of Baudot Code, baud is a measure of the number of symbols that a digital mode transmits each second. With a simple code like Baudot each symbol transmitted represents one bit of data (a single 1 or 0 digit). So, with Baudot the baud is equivalent to *bits per second* (bps). With more complex digital communication codes this simple relationship equating baud and bps does not hold true, as multiple bits may be simultaneously transmitted with other codes in other digital modes, and structural, synchronization, or formatting bits for a data exchange protocol further complicate the baud calculation.

Principles of information science tell us that as the rate of information or data transmission increases the bandwidth used by the transmission must also increase to preserve the accuracy and reliability of the information. For instance, the rate of information exchange with CW is rather low, one character at a time tapped out by human hand relatively slowly, and the bandwidth required is narrow (~150 Hz). But with SSB phone mode you may transmit an entire word or two in the same time required to send just a dit or dah in CW, so the information transfer rate is much greater. Commensurately, SSB consumes much greater bandwidth (~3 kHz). With RTTY (or other digital modes) **the same relationship holds between transmitted symbol rate and bandwidth: Higher symbol rates require wider bandwidth.**

In order to maintain reliable RTTY information transfer with efficient bandwidth values, each of the amateur bands has a maximum permitted RTTY symbol rate in baud. Generally, the maximum permitted symbol rate decreases with lower band frequency. (Notice that total available bandwidth narrows generally with lower frequency of the amateur bands.) **The maximum symbol rates permitted for RTTY or data transmission on the amateur bands is as follows:**

1.25m and 70cm bands	**56 kilobaud**
2m band	**19.6 kilobaud**
10m band	**1200 baud**
Below 28 MHz (10m)	**300 baud** (includes 20m band)

Common Errors: Some caution is necessary to ensure that a RTTY or other FSK system is properly set up. **Some things that could be wrong if you cannot decode a RTTY or FSK signal even though it is tuned in properly include: The mark and space frequencies may be reversed, the wrong baud rate may be selected, or you may be listening on the wrong sideband.** Check your station settings carefully.

Let's take a look at a great digital mode for noisy HF bands, PACTOR.

PACTOR Mode: *Packet Teletype Over Radio* blends packet radio efficiency with the robust FSK modulation of RTTY. It sends packetized teletype over radio that allows error correction methods to be used. PACTOR offers very good performance on the noisy HF bands, and improvements have been made with PACTOR 2, 3, and 4 variations. **The approximate bandwidth of a PACTOR 3 signal at maximum data rate is 2300 Hz,** slightly narrower than a typical SSB signal. (An AFSK-based mode very similar to PACTOR is known as WINMOR, providing slightly reduced performance as compared to PACTOR, but using a sound card interface in lieu of a more expensive PACTOR modem. WINMOR maximum bandwidth is approximately 1600 Hz.)

The PACTOR protocols utilize two-way transmissions that are limited to just two stations, so joining an existing contact between the two stations is not possible. PACTOR implements ARQ in which an *Acknowledgement* (ACK) transmission of error-free receipt is returned to the sending station after each block of data. Conversely, **a *Not Acknowledged* (NAK) response is sent by the receiver to request the packet be retransmitted.** PACTOR can achieve high data rates and is useful for transmitting large blocks of data on HF bands, including use with the Winlink amateur radio email system.

A PACTOR modem or controller may be placed in a monitoring mode without two-way connection to determine if the channel is in use by other PACTOR stations and thereby avoid accidental interference. **Other signals interfering with a PACTOR or WINMOR transmission may result in failure to establish a connection between stations, long pauses in message transmissions, and frequent connection retries or timeouts. (The PACTOR or WINMOR connection is dropped from a failure to exchange information due to excessive transmission attempts.)**

Winlink Email: As noted above, PACTOR and WINMOR represent two of the more popular methods of accessing the Winlink amateur radio email system. **The Winlink system frequently transfers messages between the Internet and amateur radio stations** via internet gateway stations. Winlink requires users to register to be recognized by the system, but once you are part of the system you can access your messages from any worldwide Winlink station. Winlink is also accessible with VHF and UHF signals using a terminal node controller and connecting to a local Winlink Radio Mail Server (RMS) station. **To connect to a** Winlink **digital messaging system gateway station simply transmit a connect message on the station's published frequency.**

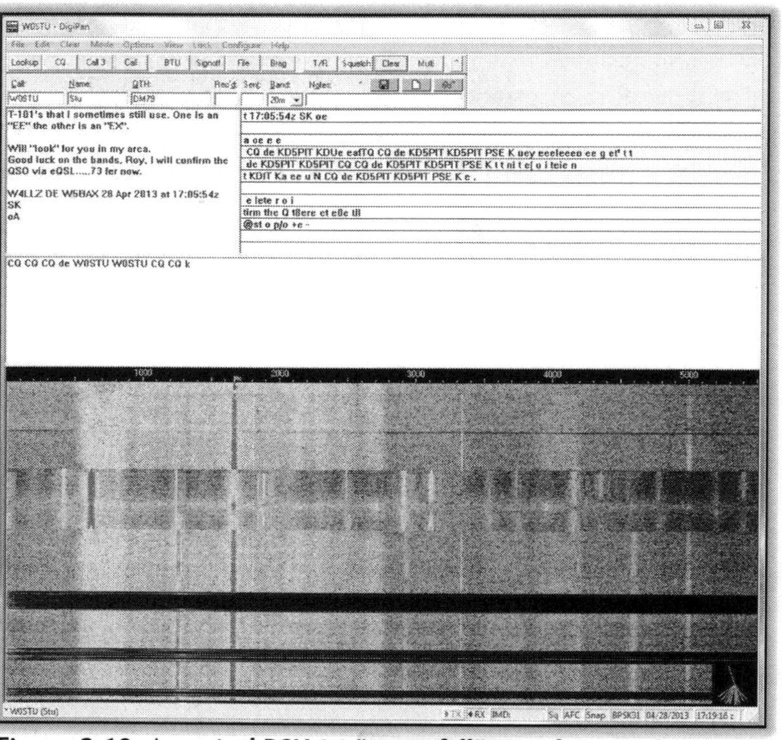

Figure 2.18: A typical PSK 31 "waterfall" interface. Each signal is displayed as a vertical pattern in the audio receive band that may be selected by mouse pointer for decoding and QSO.

PSK31 Mode: *Phase Shift Keying 31* is a popular keyboard-to-keyboard text chatting mode that utilizes only a single transmission tone and uses very narrow bandwidth. It encodes characters as binary sequences by reversing the tone's waveform phase in timed intervals. An interval exhibiting a shift in waveform phase represents a 0, and the absence of a phase shift represents a 1 for the interval. Characters are encoded using **Varicode, in which the number of bits sent in a single PSK31 character varies.** In a manner similar to Morse Code, the PSK31 Varicode uses shorter symbols for the most commonly used characters, thereby enhancing the efficiency of communication. **Upper case letters use longer Varicode signals and thus slow down transmission.** During any given station transmission a continuous tone is transmitted, with strings of 0 bits sent when no data is included in the transmission. This is necessary to keep the receiving station's decoding protocol synchronized with the transmission's phase shifting interval sequence.

The 31 in PSK31 represents the approximate transmitted symbol rate (baud rate), 31 baud. Although this symbol rate is slow relative to many other digital modes, it is quite adequate for most keyboard-to-keyboard communications. PSK31 provides very good performance on HF bands even in noisy conditions, and the narrow bandwidth of the mode provides a lot of punch with just a little power. It is a terrific QRP mode, with propagation performance similar to CW.

PSK31 tone sound is a unique, ghostly sounding whine, and easily distinguishable on the bands. **On the 20 meter band most PSK31 operations are found below the RTTY segment, near 14.070 MHz.** Similarly on 40m, you'll commonly find PSK31 near 7.070 MHz. Other bands have recommended calling frequencies and typical segments of the digital sub-bands where PSK31 is found, and just dialing through the sub-band will usually suffice for finding the group of ethereal PSK31 sounds.

A PSK31 waterfall display is depicted in Figure 2.18. **A signal's frequency is** depicted as a narrow linear flowing stream across the **horizontal of the display. Signal strength is depicted by intensity, and time flows in the vertical. One or more vertical lines adjacent to a PSK31 signal indicates overmodulation,** a condition that may be corrected by adjusting the gain of the transmitting station's sound card.

WSJT Modes: The WSJT family of digital operating modes developed originally by Joe Taylor, K1JT are for very weak signal communications. **The JT9 and JT65 modes are designed to operate at extremely low signal strength on the HF bands,** and these modes perform amazingly well even with very low signal-to-noise ratios. The JT65 mode is also used for VHF and UHF earth-moon-earth (EME) bounce signals, and the protocol uses precisely timed intervals for signal transmit and receive cycle synchronization between stations. **Both JT65 and JT9 use AFSK on the upper sideband (USB) as a standard** and employ multiple tones/frequencies. The JT65 signals use 65 unique tones to modulate signals, while the JT9 signal uses a similar protocol with just nine tones and occupying less than 16 Hz bandwidth. If you want the ultimate in QRP operations, JT65 and JT9 are for you!

Transmitter Duty Cycle Caution: The *duty cycle* is the ratio of on-air transmission time to total operating time of a transmitted signal. That is, the portion of time is your transmitter is actually on and transmitting during a QSO. Each mode has a duty cycle, and with digital operations **some modes can have high duty cycles, possibly exceeding the transmitter's average power rating. So, be sure you know the duty cycle of the data mode you are using when transmitting,** as well as your transmitter's limits. A digital mode's duty cycle can usually be found in the creator's documentation or in online user group forums.

Digital Rules and Regs: Let's wrap up the digital diddling with a few special provisions from the FCC Part 97 rules and regulations, and some practical comments about digital QSOs.

Automatically Controlled Digital Stations: The FCC Part 97 regulations have some special rules regarding digital stations that operate under automatic control. **Automatically controlled digital station is the FCC term referring to unattended digital stations, including those that transfer messages to and from the Internet,** such as messaging gateways.

G1E11

Only certain bands and sub-bands may be used for automatically controlled digital stations communicating with other automatically controlled digital stations. **Auto controlled stations transmitting RTTY or data emissions may communicate with other auto controlled stations only in the 1.25-meter or shorter wavelength bands, and only in specified segments of the 80-meter through 2-meter bands. Any automatically controlled digital station operating outside of the automatic control band segments may communicate only with a station initiating the contact that is under local or remote control.** So, for example, an automatically controlled Winlink gateway station with a contact frequency outside of the auto-control band segments may only be contacted by a station under the control of a human by local or remote means, and it may not serve as a relay link for digital messages from another auto-controlled digital station. Check FCC Parts 97.221 and 97.305 rules if you plan to operate an automatically controlled digital station.

G1E13

G1E03

Third Party Digital Communications: Because of the ease by which email, texts, and other digital messages may be forwarded to others, and because of the linkages between amateur radio stations and the Internet, it is prudent to make special note of regulations about third party communications. **Under no circumstances are messages sent via digital modes exempt from Part 97 third party rules that apply to other modes of communication!** Remember, third party messages may be transmitted to other countries only if that other country has a third party agreement with the US. The control operator must be present at the control point when third party traffic is transmitted, supervising and monitoring the third party's participation. Except for RTTY and data emissions, automatically controlled stations may not transmit third party traffic. (See FCC Part 97.115.)

G1E12

Digital QSOs: Beyond the typical emails or text messages that are really not different from Internet messages when delivered by radio, some digital modes have unique QSO characteristics. For instance, with the PSK31 mode many operators are fond of using pre-programmed stores of texts, called *macros*. With the click of a button a PSK31 macro will transmit your stored text data, such as a description of your transceiver, antennas, computer and software, or just about anything else. CQ calls and standard sign-off strings are other common macro transmissions. However, in between the macros and CQs and KNs there is often room for genuine *rag chewing* with a new friend, albeit in text form.

I recommend downplaying the use of macros and just chat with your contacts. This keeps the mode more personable and encourages real conversational exchange that many hams find as the most enjoyable aspect of the hobby. Of course, you can simply make contact, exchange your robotic macros, and move on to the next signal if that's all you really want. But be prepared to see the CW-like shortcut language combined with more ample use of normal text language than in CW. It requires a little practice, but you'll pick up the community techniques in no time.

With the very low signal power JT65 and JT9 modes, messages may require quite some time to be exchanged, usually several minutes for a short QSO. As such, they are characteristically brief and to the point, often using many of amateur radio's shortcuts and abbreviations. With these modes patience is required, as is brevity.

More information on specific digital modes may be found online with user forums and wikis, or at the ARRL digital modes web page. Additional basic information on digital modes is available in Chapter 10 of the *HamRadioSchool. com Technician License Course* book.

Linking computers and radios to communicate via the digital modes can be a lot of fun and they add yet another intriguing facet to the ham radio hobby – greater techno-diddling opportunities! You can use digital modes to transmit electronic files, still images, text, telemetry, email, digital control commands, digital voice, and more! It's easy to get started with Winmore, PSK 31, or RTTY with free software and a sound card interface. Don't miss out on the fun. Diddle digitally!

But first, review the summary table of question pool topics for this section on the next page, and then go examine the online quiz questions on digital modes.

HamRadioSchool.com/general_media

Summary of
Question Pool Topics
Section 2.4: Digital Modes

Digital Sub-bands

20m band: 14.070-14.100
80m band: 3.570-3.60

RTTY – Radio Teletype Digital Mode
- FSK method (direct freq. shift of tx oscillator)
- AFSK method (two tones, 2125 Hz & 2295 Hz)
- Baudot Code – 5 bit code + start/stop bits
- Two frequencies, "Mark & Space"
  ○ Mark & Space 170 Hz separation
- Higher symbol rates require wider bandwidth
  ■ Max RTTY symbol rates on bands
    ■ 1.25m & 70cm: 56 kBaud
    ■ 2m: 19.6 kBaud
    ■ 10m: 1200 Baud
    ■ Below 10M: 300 baud
- Common problems with decoding
  ○ Mark & Space reversed
  ○ Wrong Baud rate
  ○ Wrong sideband (LSB used for AFSK RTTY)

Packet Radio: Header contains routing and handling information.

Automatic Repeat Request (ARQ): Receiving station detects errors & requests packet retransmission.

NAK: Not Acknowledged response set by receiver to request retransmission.

Forward Error Correction (FEC): Redundant info sent with packet for receiver correction of errors.

PACTOR & WINMOR Digital Modes
- FSK method
- PACTOR 3 has ~2300 Hz bandwidth
  ○ (WINMOR is AFSK similar method)
- Limited to two-station links only, no break-in join
- 'Monitoring mode' of PACTOR modem to check if frequency in use
- Interference to PACTOR or WINMOR may cause:
  ○ Failure to connect
  ○ Frequent connection retries, timeouts
  ○ Long pauses in transmissions
- Excessive trx attempts = dropped connection
- Used with Winlink email system and other digital messaging systems linked to Internet
  ○ Transmit 'connect message' to connect with digital messaging systems.

Auto-Controlled Digital Station Rules:
- Specific sub-bands for comm between two auto-controlled stations
  ○ 1.25m and shorter wavelengths.
  ○ Specific segments of 80m – 2m bands.
- Outside auto-control bands comm must be only with local controlled or remote controlled stations.
- No exemption from standard 3rd party rules.

PSK31 – Phase Shift Keying 31 Digital Mode
- Uses Varicode, number of bits varies
- Upper case letters use longer Varicode, results in slower transmissions
- 31 is approximate symbol rate
- On 20m band, ops near 14.070 MHz.
- Waterfall display
  ○ Horizontal Position: Frequency
  ○ Intensity of line: Signal strength
  ○ Adjacent vertical lines: Overmodulation

JT69/JT9 Digital Modes
- USB as standard sideband used
- Designed for extremely low signal strengths on HF bands

3.0   Propagation

> **❝ *You must live in the present,
> launch yourself on every wave.***
> **– Henry David Thoreau**

That's just what hams do. On every wave we propagate ourselves on an invisible journey to parts unknown and often to peoples unknown. That's half the fun of it! But we can know quite a lot about the paths of that invisible journey, even if we can't see our waves propagating. With a little insight about the nature of radio waves, the atmosphere, and even the sun, we can make some reasoned estimates of where we launch ourselves on every wave.

This chapter is all about RF propagation. We will start in Section 3.1 with a journey to the surface of the sun – sunspots, solar eruptions, and lots of thermonuclear violence! In Section 3.2 we'll soar through the atmosphere to study the ionosphere, magnetosphere, and some of their effects with frequencies. We will wrap up Chapter 3 with consideration of the practical impact on our radio operations resulting from all of that solar violence and related atmospheric reactions.

Ready yourself for launch into our local neighborhood's solar inferno!

3.1   Propagation
Solar Activity

> **❝ *A day without thermonuclear fusion is
> like a day without sunshine.*   – Anonymous**

Let's start our exploration of HF propagation with a journey to the surface of the sun! An incredible place born of thermonuclear fusion where complex solar dynamics rule and superheated tendrils of plasma erupt larger than thousands of earths and surge along invisible magnetic loops in spectacular displays of the star's power!

And where relatively dark sunspots dot the star's face like an adolescent's acne.

Sunspots: Those solar blemishes are really important to ham radio operators. Sunspots are correlated with solar energy output. That is, the more active and energetic the sun, the more sunspots there will be. Sunspots are regions of high magnetic activity on the sun's surface that produce relatively cool interiors, hence the somewhat darker "spot" appearance. But the perimeter of a sunspot will radiate much more intensely than other parts of the solar surface, and the net result is an increase in solar energy output with sunspots. In particular, sunspot edges absolutely glow with ultraviolet (UV) radiation, and UV is critical to the creation and maintenance of the ionosphere around our earth!

Of course, the ionosphere is the giant mirror in the sky that bends HF and lower VHF frequencies back toward earth to provide that amazing *over-the-horizon* propagation we call skip. Sunspot activity is strongly correlated with the signal-bending effectiveness of the ionosphere, and **high sunspot numbers result in enhancement of long-distance communications in the upper HF and lower VHF range** due to the greater density of ions in the atmosphere created by the UV rays.

G3A09

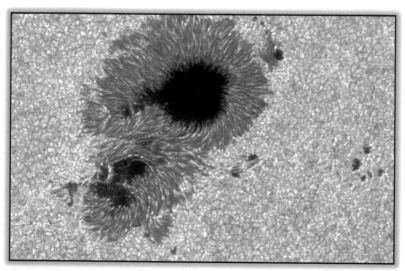

Figure 3.1: Sunspots increase solar ultraviolet radiation that helps create the earth's ionosphere. Courtesy NASA/JPL-Caltech

The sunspot number is a measure of the solar activity based on counting sunspots and sunspot groups. Scientists and many amateur radio operators keep close tabs on the sunspot number as a general indicator of radio propagation. The sunspot number and propagation conditions vary with two primary activities:

- **The sun's rotation on its axis causes HF propagation conditions to vary periodically in a 28-day cycle,** as the sunspots rotate into and out of the sun's earth-facing hemisphere. **G3A10**

- **The sunspot cycle (or solar cycle) in which sunspot activity varies over 11 year periods,** with a high activity peak called *solar maximum* and a low activity lull called *solar minimum*. **G3A11**

During the solar maximum, when sunspots are most prominent in the 11 year solar cycle, HF propagation is typically best and the higher frequency bands of 21 MHz (15m) and above *open* frequently for excellent long-distance skip ("*sky wave*") communications. During the solar minimum when sunspots are few these higher bands may remain ineffective for skip for long periods. **The significance of sunspot numbers with regard to HF propagation is that higher sunspot numbers generally indicate a greater probability of good propagation at higher frequencies.** **G3A01**

Solar Flux Index: A basic indicator of the sun's activity and radiated output. The solar flux is measured in units of... wait for it... *Solar Flux Units* (SFU). **The Solar Flux Index is a measure of solar radiation at 10.7 cm** wavelength (~2.8 GHz), and it is essentially a measure of radio frequency noise. The index is a good indicator of the amount of ionization in the earth's atmosphere, so it usually provides a good hint of the skip propagation conditions. The index values tend to vary between about 50 and 300 SFU, with the solar max consistently generating 200+ values. **G3A05**

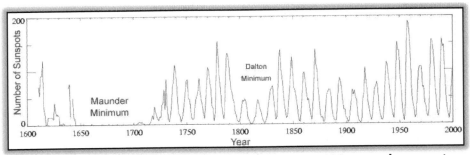

Figure 3.2: Historical observation of sunspots over 400 years shows variation in the 11-year solar cycle. Courtesy NASA/JPL-Caltech

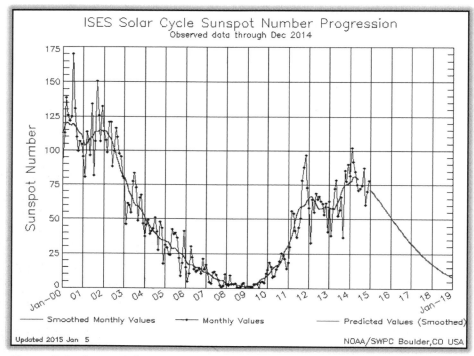

Figure 3.3: Sunspot history, 2000 to 2014. The current Solar Cycle 24 has been a low activity sunspot cycle by recent historical comparison.

Courtesy NOAA / SWPC Boulder, CO USA

Solar Flares: Occasionally the sun hiccups and produces a very intense projection of radiation called a solar flare. Solar flare emissions are electromagnetic radiation traveling at the speed of light. **This increased ultraviolet and X-ray radiation takes only about 8 minutes to reach the earth and affect radio wave propagation.** When a solar flare is directed toward the earth the very intense ionizing radiation can reach deeply into the atmosphere, disturbing the ionosphere layers and disrupting HF communications.

Coronal Holes: The sun's corona is an encircling layer of plasma gas that extends millions of miles into space around the sun. Occasionally the sun's magnetic field lines loop and "bubble" above the surface and into the corona, creating spectacular visual images of enormous glowing loops and coronal prominences. When these magnetic field lines sever and fail to close back upon themselves, an open channel is created called a *coronal hole.* The stream of proton and electron particles that the sun continually emits is called the solar wind, and a coronal hole allows these solar wind particles to really gust out in a torrent! **HF communications are disturbed by the charged particles that reach the earth from solar coronal holes due to the effects on the ionosphere.**

Coronal Mass Ejections (CME): Other, more violent eruptions in the sun's corona may eject massive amounts of matter into space. A CME will be largely comprised of protons and electrons like the normal solar wind, but heavier element particles may also be included such as helium, oxygen, and iron. These particles are ejected at high speeds, as much as 2000 miles per second. **Charged particles from a coronal mass ejection will reach earth and affect radio wave propagation in 20 to 40 hours** after solar ejection.

G3A15

Wow! The sun is rather violent, huh? Thermonuclear fusion spewing out charged particles and hurling mass in our general direction, even irradiating us constantly with deadly rays of high energy. Fortunately the earth protects us from most of this viciousness with the blankets of the ionosphere and the *magnetosphere.*

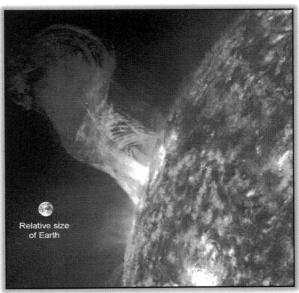

Relative size
of Earth

Each of these violent behaviors of the sun, from sunspot UV rays to solar flares to coronal holes and ejections, has an impact on the earth's protecting blankets. When those blankets become disturbed by absorbing and

Figure 3.4: A minor solar prominence erupts from the sun. Earth added for comparison.
Courtesy NASA/JPL-Caltech

redirecting the sun's impolite and dangerous belches, our HF radio propagation is disrupted. In the next section we'll consider the features of our ionosphere and magnetosphere in relation to radio propagation in order to better understand these solar impacts on operations.

But before we move on, why not click through the questions on solar activity!

HamRadioSchool.com/general_media

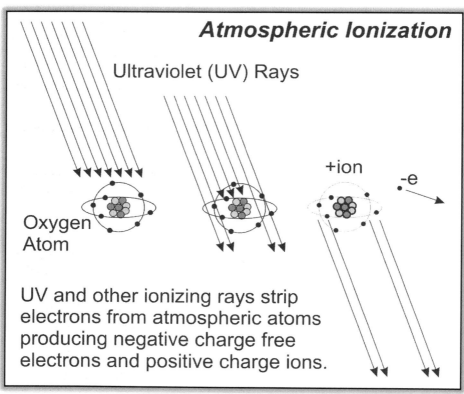

Figure 3.5: Atmospheric ionization creates the ionosphere.

Propagation

3.2 Ionosphere & Magnetosphere

" *Ogres have layers. Onions have layers.*
You get it? We both have layers. *– Shrek*

We've returned from the dangerous and violent environs of the sun's surface to the good earth. However, let's soar over land and sea for a while at great altitudes and investigate the ionosphere and the magnetosphere. They're both rather interesting and critical features of our planet, for both life support and for good HF propagation! Like an onion – or an ogre – they have layers.

Overview of Ionosphere and Magnetosphere: Let's make sure we have a good general understanding of what these two earthly planetary features are all about, and then we'll fly into some details.

The *ionosphere* is the name we give to four prominent layers of the atmosphere in which many electrically charged atomic particles exist – ions, we call them. Ions include negatively charged *free electrons* and positively charged ions. Usually, an atom will have an electron or two stripped from it to be set free, leaving a net positive charge on the remaining atom. High energy radiation from the sun, such as ultraviolet rays and X-rays, impact atoms in the atmosphere and kick out an electron with their energy, leaving the charged particles in their wake. This ability of high energy radiation to strip electrons from atoms is why it is referred to as *ionizing radiation* – it creates ions. These charged particles in the atmosphere can bend RF signals back to earth, providing over-the-horizon radio communications, especially on the HF bands.

The *magnetosphere* is a region around the earth where the earth's magnetic field is dominant, as compared to the magnetic field lines associated with the solar wind emanating from the sun. The charged particles of the solar wind – those protons and electrons constantly flying out of the sun – interact with the earth's magnetic field lines and help shape the magnetosphere. The solar wind effectively pushes on the earth's magnetic field lines, compressing and bending them on the sun-side and leaving a trailing magnetic tail on the leeward side. The magnetosphere ebbs, flows, and wavers with variations in the solar wind, but its magnetic lines tend to direct much of the solar wind's particles around the earth. Some of the particles flowing along the magnetosphere's lines of magnetic force are directed down into the earth's atmosphere near the magnetic polar regions, highly energizing atmospheric atoms and producing aurora. Measured variations in the magnetosphere can provide good clues about the solar wind intensity and, therefore, provide indications of the state of the ionosphere and RF propagation conditions.

Now let's cruise through the layers of the ionosphere, illuminate their characteristics, and define some related radio terms with which every General Class ham should be intimately familiar. Afterwards, we'll revisit the magnetosphere to examine its metrics and related radio effects.

Ionospheric Layers: The ionosphere is comprised of four prominent layers that result from several interacting factors. The increasing density of the atmosphere from space to the earth's surface affects the rates at which free electrons will recombine with positively charged ions to reform neutral atoms. This reduces the quantity and density of ions. The depth to which ionizing radiation will penetrate the atmosphere also comes into play, affecting the rates at which new ions are created. The net result is the set of ionosphere layers D, E, F1, and F2, each with unique ion densities and characteristics.

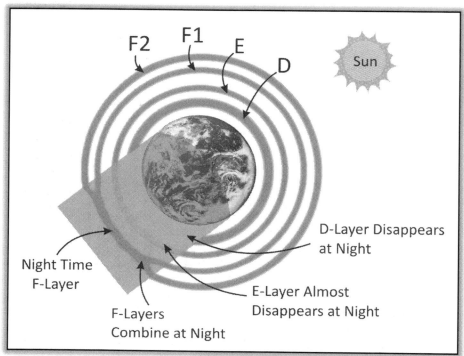

Figure 3.6: Layers of the Ionosphere.

The ionospheric layers exist from about 40 to 250+ miles above the earth's surface, and they **reach their maximum height where the sun is overhead.**

G3C02

D Layer: **The D Layer is closest to the surface of the earth,** roughly 40 to 55 miles in altitude. Because of relatively high atmospheric density the rate of recombination of ions into neutral atoms is high, resulting in the D Layer effectively dissipating at night. Unique electron effects in this band produce **daytime conditions in which lower frequency HF signals (below 10 MHz) are absorbed by the D Layer.** The amateur bands below 30m will be absorbed, significantly reducing or eliminating skip propagation with these bands during daylight hours. However, once the D Layer disappears at night these lower HF band signals are able to reach the higher ionospheric layers to be bent back to earth for effective over-the-horizon propagation. As a result, the lower frequency bands from 30m to 160m tend to be considered "night time bands" since their propagation is best after sundown.

G3C01

G3C12

During highly energetic solar events such as intense flares and CMEs, the D Layer may become ionized sufficiently to persist overnight and to absorb higher frequency signals, such as the 20m to 10m bands. This disruption of the normal D Layer condition degrades skip propagation and can even produce HF propagation blackout, in which HF skip communications are not possible.

E Layer: Roughly 55 to 75 miles in altitude, the E Layer is responsible for some of the most curious radio propagation behavior, sporadic E. Patchy clouds of ionization in the E Layer come and go sporadically, providing temporary over-the-horizon propagation that is effective for 10m, 6m, and occasionally 2m bands. The dynamic E Layer may provide skip in only one particular direction from your station and into a limited geographical area. That's part of the magic of sporadic E propagation – you never know exactly when it's going to happen or where it's going to take your signals! Although unpredictable and possible almost anytime, sporadic E does have some seasonal peaks of occurrence. In North America, the peak sporadic E occurs in mid- to late-June, and may persist through July or August. A less significant peak occurs from mid-December into January.

F1 and F2 Layers: The F1 Layer exists roughly 90 to 150 miles in altitude, while the F2 Layer is sky high at more than 200 miles up. **The F2 region is mainly responsible for the longest distance radio wave propagation because it is the highest ionospheric region.** Geometry dictates that the skip distance of a signal increases with the height of the reflecting layer (given equivalent earthly takeoff angles of the signal). The F1 and F2 Layers combine at night into a single F Layer approximately 180 miles

G3C03

altitude. However, the height of the F Layers varies significantly with solar activity, time of day, time of year, and even latitude.

Critical Angle: The ionosphere is not a perfect mirror for RF signals. It is not really a mirror at all. Rather than being a reflecting surface it is a refracting medium, meaning that it bends or curves the RF signal as the signal passes through it, much like a lens bends light. With strong enough bending action, thanks to lots of ions, an RF signal may be curved back toward earth. If the bending action is not strong enough the signal is instead directed off into space and is not receivable by earthly hams. The scenario is depicted in Figure 3.7.

As the figure depicts, low takeoff angle signals require the least severe bend angle to return to earth and travel the greatest distance, while higher takeoff angle signals travel shorter distances and must be bent at greater angles. As the takeoff angle increases an angle will be reached for which the ionosphere bending effect is insufficient to turn the signals back to earth, and they will fly off into space. The RF signal bending power of the ionosphere will change with atmospheric and solar conditions, as well as with the frequency being used. However, **under any specific ionospheric conditions the highest takeoff angle that will return a radio wave to the earth is the "critical angle."**

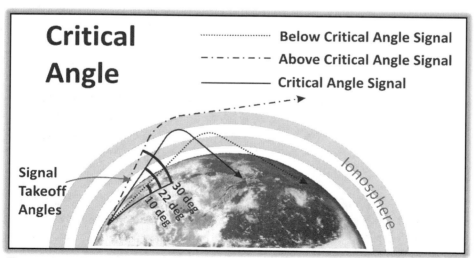

Figure 3.7: The Critical Angle – Signal takeoff angles above the critical angle will radiate into space, while takeoff angles at or below the critical angle will be returned to the earth's surface.

In the example of Figure 3.7 the critical angle is 22 degrees above the horizon – any greater takeoff angle (such as the 30 degree example), sends the signal into space. Takeoff angles lower than 22 degrees (such as the 10 degree example) are bent back to earth.

Maximum Usable Frequency (MUF): Consider that between your station and any other station over-the-horizon there is a takeoff angle that will result in a skip from the ionosphere such that the other station may receive your signal – the geometry is good. A higher skip angle will land your signals short of the other station, and a lower skip angle will land your signals beyond the other station. But that Goldie Locks takeoff angle is just right for the geometry to that specific station location.

Now consider that the ionosphere's bending effect weakens as frequency gets higher, as in Figure 3.8. Your 10m (28 MHz) signals will be bent less than your 15m, 20m, or lower band signals. What if the frequency you are using is a high one, perhaps in the 10m band, and it is not bent enough to achieve that Goldie Locks angle to the other station? You could choose a lower frequency for which the ionosphere will act more strongly and bend your signal at a greater angle, thereby achieving Goldie Locks and making your contact. You can imagine that there is a frequency that is just barely low enough for the ionosphere to provide enough bending to achieve that Goldie Locks angle to the other station. That is **the MUF, or the maximum usable frequency for communications between two points, and it is affected by factors of path distance and location, time of day and season, and solar radiation and ionospheric disturbances** that impact the ionosphere's bending performance.

Lowest Usable Frequency (LUF): **Similarly, the LUF is the lowest usable frequency for communications between two points.** The conditions of ionospheric absorption for a given time of day or solar condition determine the lowest frequency that will skip to another specific station location. **Radio waves with frequencies below the LUF are usually completely absorbed by the ionosphere.**

MUF & LUF Scenarios: In some circumstances **the lowest usable frequency (LUF) will exceed the maximum usable frequency (MUF) and no HF radio frequency will support ordinary skywave** (skip) **communications over the path** between stations. That is, for a given path the lowest frequency that will not be absorbed under the ionospheric conditions is a higher frequency than the ionosphere can bend down to the other station at the required Goldie Locks takeoff angle. This may occur during geomagnetic

G3B08 G3B12

G3B07

G3B06

G3B11

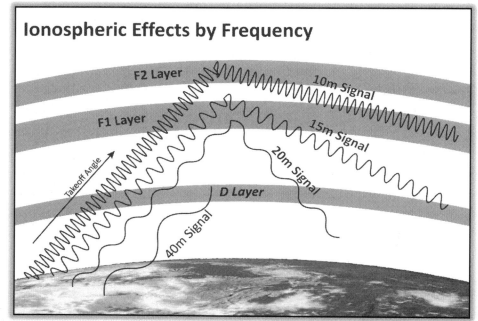

Ionospheric Effects by Frequency

Figure 3.8: The ionosphere's bending effect decreases with increased frequency, helping determine the MUF between two stations. Primarily D Layer absorption of lower frequencies helps determine the LUF. In this simplified example all takeoff angles are equivalent. The 40m band and lower signals are absorbed, while higher frequencies are variably refracted depending on frequency.

disturbances during which RF absorption effects are intensified. You're just out of luck for HF skip communications in this case.

However, **radio waves with frequencies below the MUF and above the LUF will be bent back to the earth when they are sent into the ionosphere.** That is, if your frequency is in between the two frequency limits of MUF and LUF you can make your contact.

The Magnetosphere: Given all the effects of the ionosphere, why do we even care about the magnetosphere? It is because the magnetosphere and the ionosphere are intimately linked, with the magnetosphere somewhat regulating how much of the sun's energy reaches the atmosphere to charge up the layers with ions. Further, measurement of some magnetosphere characteristics can provide indications of the ionosphere's conditions.

K-index: Magnetic observatories on earth use magnetometers to measure geomagnetic activity. Relative to an agreed reference condition, **the K-index indicates the short term stability of the earth's magnetic field.** The magnetometers detect fluctuations in the magnetosphere that may indicate changes in the solar wind impacting the earth's atmosphere. The K-index is collected every three hours for short term indications.

Figure 3.9: The earth's magnetosphere is shaped by the solar wind.

Courtesy NASA/JPL-Caltech

A-index: A daily average of the K-index is computed as the A-index. **The A-index indicates the long term stability of the earth's geomagnetic field.** By compiling the measured A-indices from around the world and over time, a long term picture of the magnetosphere's stability may be constructed, and impacts to the ionosphere inferred. The A-index reflects 24 hours of geomagnetic stability.

Geomagnetic Storms: **A temporary disturbance in the earth's magnetosphere is a geomagnetic storm.** When charged particles from a strong solar event reach the earth they may be trapped in the magnetosphere. This can cause some regions of the ionosphere to become highly charged with ions. For instance, such activation of the E Layer in the polar regions results in **degraded high-latitude HF propagation from a geomagnetic storm**, as well as aurora due to secondary photon emissions from energized atoms of nitrogen and oxygen. This phenomenon may also disrupt other layers of the ionosphere and cause poor propagation on the HF bands. The upper layers of the ionosphere tend to be most susceptible, resulting in higher HF frequency disruption first.

One possible benefit to radio communications that results from periods of high geomagnetic activity is aurora that can reflect VHF signals, particularly the 6m band signals. Aurora propagation tends to have a fluttery sound due to the rapidly fluctuating action of the particles bending the waves back to earth.

G3A12

G3A13

G3A06

G3A08

G3A16

That's all pretty cosmic! Lots of dynamic interaction between the sun and the earth, and it all has an impact on the ionospheric layers and our radio signal propagation. A general summary of the effects discussed in this section is provided in the table below, so that you may easily peel back the layers of the propagation onion.

In the next section we'll focus more on the operational impacts of these atmospheric characteristics. But for now, check your knowledge online with the quiz for this section.

HamRadioSchool.com/general_media

Summary Table of General Propagation Factors:

Factor	Ionospheric Impact	HF Propagation	VHF Propagation
Daylight	Dense F layers. D layer absorbs low frequencies.	Best above 30m band. Poor below 30m band.	Possible Sporadic E.
Night time	Combined F layer. D layer dissipates.	Good below 30m band. Higher bands may close.	Little / no Sporadic E.
Plentiful Sunspots	Denser ionospheric layers generally.	Good; higher bands 15m and 10m may open.	6m band may have F-layer skip
Sparse Sunspots	Weaker ionospheric layers generally.	Degraded propagation with higher HF bands.	
High A-index	Potential ionosphere disruption & D layer persistence	Poor.	Possible aurora propagation.
High K-index	Potential ionosphere disruption & D layer persistence	Poor.	Possible aurora propagation.
Geomagnetic Storm	Potential ionosphere disruption & D layer persistence	Poor.	Possible aurora propagation.

Propagation

3.3 | **Operational Impacts**

"" *The sun does not shine for a few trees and flowers, but for the wide world's joy.*
– Henry Ward Beecher

Indeed, the sun shines even for the joy of hams the world over! Without its ionizing rays our HF signals would simply race out into space and DX would cease to exist. The sun, its rays, and our ionosphere have enormous radio operational impacts.

So, let's now float back down to earth and crawl into the shack to consider how some of the factors of the sun and atmosphere affect our radio operations. How can we estimate the kind of propagation we'll get? Why are some signals weaker than others? How long of a skip distance can my signals achieve? When will the various bands work best, and what frequency should I use?

Sky-Wave Skip Paths & Distances: From what we've covered about ionospheric skip propagation, the critical angle, and MUF and LUF considerations, and ionosphere-magnetosphere disruptions, you're probably wondering just how far a typical skip will allow your signals to travel. It is a good question! But there is no single correct answer beyond, "It depends."

F2 Layer Skip: The F2 Layer is the highest ionosphere layer. As noted already, a higher signal reflection altitude will result in longer potential skip distances. The longest single skip from your station may be achieved by the lowest takeoff angle possible from your station – perhaps that signal ray skimming uninterrupted just along the earth right down at horizon level. Assuming that signal is of one of the higher HF frequencies that is best reflected by the F Layers, **the approximate maximum distance along the earth's surface that it will normally cover in one hop using the F2 region is 2,500 miles.** Depending on specific ion conditions, frequency used, and the impact of other ionosphere layers, your station's performance may vary, but a 2,500 mile hop with the 10m band during periods of high solar activity is not unusual.

G3B09

Pictured: James, KDØMFO

Figure 3.10: VHF contesters love to see the E Layer highly activated to rack up points with over-the-horizon distant contacts on VHF frequencies!

G3B10

G3B02

E Layer Skip: The E Layer, being significantly lower than the F Layers, will provide reduced skip distances when it is active. **The approximate maximum distance along the earth's surface that is normally covered in one hop using the E region is 1,200 miles.** And, of course, the E Layer skip opportunities are sporadic but commonly very effective up to the 6m VHF band. **A good indicator of the possibility of sky-wave propagation on the 6m band is short skip sky-wave propagation on the 10m band.** Since 10m signals are normally reflected from the F2 Layer with very long skip distances (roughly 2,000 miles or more), if you hear 10m signals from stations within 1,200 miles on the 10m band those signals are likely from lower E-Layer reflections, or sporadic E. If the E Layer is sufficiently energized you may achieve skip on 6m too! And if the 6m skywave propagation is short, check for sporadic E propagation on the 2m band. It's rare, but it happens occasionally.

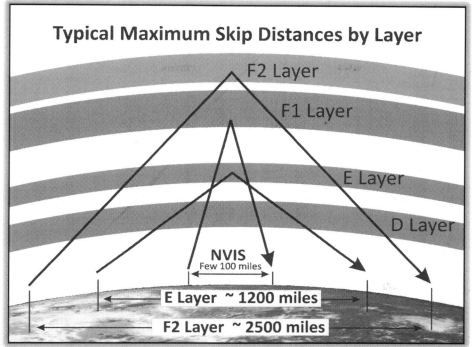

Figure 3.11: Longer skip distances occur with the higher ionosphere layers. NVIS is effective with 40m and lower bands for shorter distance HF communications of a few hundred miles.

Multiple Skips: Notice that the distances related above are for single skips. In good conditions it is common to achieve multiple hops between earth and sky with HF signals, each of an approximate maximum distance as stated above. In fact, under very good conditions it is even possible to skip a signal all the way around the planet! (Approximately 10 hops of 2,500 miles would be required, resulting in dramatically weakened signals, but feasible!) More common is the long path propagation as described in the *Operating Techniques* section of Chapter 2. Sometimes you may hear another **station's sky-wave (skip) signals arriving at your receiver by both short path and long path propagation, producing a well-defined echo effect** due to slightly different signal path propagation time. (An RF signal requires approximately 0.135 second to circumnavigate the earth, so echo delays on the order of 1/10 second are possible.)

NVIS: Near Vertical Incidence Sky-wave propagation is short distance HF propagation using high elevation angles. Consider the RF signals from an antenna that radiate not toward the horizon but rather more nearly vertical, almost straight up. If the ionospheric conditions and the selected frequency allow severe refraction of the signals back to earth, the propagation distance will be much less than the maximum values discussed here for F2 and E Layer skip. The angle of incidence up to any layer of the ionosphere is steep and so is the reflection angle back down to the ground. The result is HF propagation usually effective for a few hundred miles around your station. We will discuss how to generate effective NVIS signals with antenna techniques in Chapter 5.

Scatter: With HF skip propagation your signals can travel great distances, but unless NVIS is effective for the frequency you are using you will not be able to reach nearer stations *under the skip path*. This region that is outside of your station's ground wave (local) distance but closer than the nearest skip arrival is called the skip zone. However, HF signals may be randomly scattered into the skip zone due to occasional reflection of signals from particulate matter – dust or moisture – high in the atmosphere. So, **radio wave propagation that allows signals to be detected at a distance too far for ground wave propagation but too near for normal sky-wave propagation is scatter.** When these signals are reflected back toward the sending station they are known as *backscatter.*

HF scatter signals in the skip zone are usually weak because only a small part of the signal energy is scattered into the skip zone. Although very weak, scatter propagation can be very useful when sky-wave skip propagation is not available, or when getting signals into the skip zone is desired. **An indication that signals heard on the HF bands are being received via scatter propagation is the signal being on a frequency above the Maximum Usable Frequency (MUF).** Remember, skip is not possible on frequencies greater than the MUF because the ionosphere's bending effect is too weak for the frequency. Thus, hearing signals above the MUF is likely due to scatter.

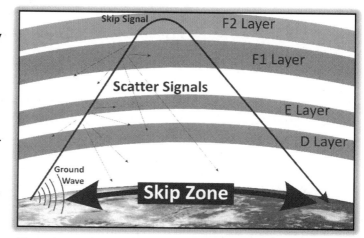

Figure 3.12: Scatter is weak signals reflected from atmospheric particles into the skip zone.

A characteristic of HF scatter signals is a wavering sound. This HF scatter signal distorted sound is due to the energy being scattered into the skip zone through several different radio wave paths, thereby producing multipath interference at your receiver.

G3C07 G3C06

Band and Frequency Considerations: Your selection of a band and even a frequency will be affected by many factors including the solar cycle and events, current ionospheric conditions, time of day, and desired propagation distance. Let's examine some of these factors in more detail

Solar Cycle: The 11-year solar cycle significantly changes ionospheric skip propagation. Near solar maximum when sunspot are plenty and the ionosphere is highly energized the higher HF bands will be open more frequently: the 10m through 15m bands will be busy with skip communications. During the solar minimum these bands may rarely open for skip beyond the occasional sporadic E occurrence – **21 MHz and higher frequencies are least reliable for long distance communication during periods of low solar activity.** Fortunately, **the 20m band usually supports worldwide propagation during daylight hours at any point in the solar cycle.** And the lower bands (40m – 160m) are usually effective throughout the cycle during nighttime hours.

G3A04 G3A07

Solar Eruptions: As noted in the *Solar Activity* section, the violence of our star directly impacts HF radio propagation here on earth. Solar eruptions can shut down HF communications. Geomagnetic disturbances from a harsh solar wind first diminish the higher bands (10m – 20m) that tend to be reflected from the outer F Layers, while **Sudden Ionospheric Disturbances** (solar flares) quickly increase the level of ionization in the low D Layer with UV and X-ray radiation, causing greater attenuating absorption of HF signals and **disrupting the lower frequencies** (40m – 160m) **more than the higher frequencies**.

G3A02

Time of Day: During daylight hours the higher HF bands (10m – 30m) will be more effective for skip. However, **long distance communication on the 40, 60, 80, and 160 meter bands is more difficult during the day because the D Layer absorbs signals at these frequencies during daylight hours.** At night the D Layer rapidly dissipates and these lower bands will open up for skip, being very effectively refracted by the higher E and combined F layers.

G3C05

MUF: Keep in mind that D Layer absorption attenuates (weakens) HF signals, and the attenuation is more severe as frequency lowers. Remember also that above the MUF the ionosphere cannot bend your signals

G3B03

sufficiently to return them to earth. Therefore, **when selecting a frequency for lowest attenuation when transmitting on HF, select a frequency just below the MUF.** This will help ensure skip propagation with the strongest possible signal for the attenuating conditions.

G3B04

So, you ask, **what is a reliable way to determine if the MUF is high enough to support skip propagation between your station and a distant location? On frequencies between 14 MHz and 30 MHz** (20m – 10m bands) **you can listen for signals from international beacons.** If you identify a beacon you can determine its location and frequency. By evaluating beacons that you can and cannot receive across the bands you may gauge whether the MUF is supporting skip into a distant area.

You can use other stations' reports and QSO success to gauge conditions as well. Further, online aids exist that evaluate propagation reports of operators and beacon reception around the world and conveniently summarize the MUF, LUF, and occurrences of sporadic E in various geographic regions.

So, how do you take stock of all the impacts of the sun and atmosphere on the operation you're about to try out? Most operators prefer to just get on the air and see what happens. The main way you'll realize the impact of the current conditions is simply by trying to initiate contacts and seeing what you get.

But you should be familiar with the solar and atmospheric science affecting your emissions, their paths, and propagation effectiveness so that you can intelligently operate your station and make well-informed decisions to keep your station going when the sun and the sky conspire against you.

Wrap up Chapter 3 with a review of this section's questions online, and when you come back we'll get into the inner workings of your transceiver!

HamRadioSchool.com/general_media

4.0   How Radio Works

" *Anyone who has had actual contact with the making of the inventions that built the radio art knows that these inventions have been the product of experiment and work based on physical reasoning, rather than on the mathematicians' calculations and formulae.*
— *Edwin Armstrong, inventor of FM radio*

I really like this perspective from Mr. Armstrong, and we will endeavor to adhere to its principle in this chapter. Let's undertake our contact with the inventions of the radio art with a little physical reasoning and leave most of the mathematics to the mathematicians.

Remember from your Technician studies that *modulation* is the process of encoding information into an RF signal by changing some characteristic of the signal. A modulating signal may be an audio signal from a microphone or other input. In brief review, the different types of modulation include:

Amplitude modulation (AM) encodes information by changing the power of the RF signal over time. Power is represented by the waveform amplitude, or height, of the wave. Section 4.1 discusses AM and its popular close cousin, *single sideband* (SSB) phone mode, along with some of the radio devices that are used to transmit and receive in these modes.

Frequency modulation (FM) encodes information by changing the frequency of the RF signal over time relative to a stable reference frequency, the *carrier frequency*. The change in frequency is called deviation, and Section 4.2 explores some details of FM and its inventions. We'll also touch on *phase modulation* here, encoding information with changes to the phase of the RF signal waveform.

Section 4.3 gets at methods of processing signals for enhanced operations. *Digital Signal Processing* is defined along with considerations for speech processors and for signal strength measurement.

Let's get on with the physical reasoning!

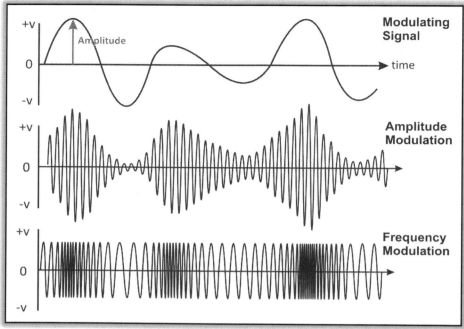

Figure 4.1: AM and FM radio signals relative to a modulating signal.

4.1 — How Radio Works — AM and SSB

> " *The brain is like a muscle. When it is in use we feel very good. Understanding is joyous.*
> *– Carl Sagan*

If Carl was right, understanding a bit about how radio generates signals to carry our voice or our codes across hundreds or thousands of miles should make for some mighty jolly hams. As an author there is no greater satisfaction than knowing that I have helped bring such joy into your life. Let's get happy with amplitude modulation.

By far the most popular voice mode on the HF bands is single sideband, a special form of amplitude modulation. **Single sideband has these advantages over other analog voice modes on the HF bands: Less bandwidth used and higher power efficiency.** You'll probably use SSB quite a lot with your General Class privileges so let's take a close look at it. We'll start with a review of amplitude modulation and then slide into the particulars of SSB.

G2A06

Amplitude modulation (AM) varies the instantaneous power level of the RF signal to encode information. In simple depictions of radio waves the amplitude, or height of the wave, is an indication of the signal power. The modulating signal, such as a voice signal from a microphone, determines the amplitude of the RF waves from instant to instant. This concept may be visualized as the relatively long audio wavelengths of the modulating signal forming mirror image upper and lower boundaries for the relatively very short RF wavelengths to oscillate within, as depicted in Figure 4.1.

G8A05

These upper and lower boundaries, envisioned as **the waveform connecting the peak values of the modulated signal, form the *modulation envelope* of an AM signal.** The process of changing the envelope of an RF wave to carry information is amplitude modulation. Any position along the axis of propagation (left-to-right in Figure 4.1) is the instantaneous amplitude, or power level, of the signal at the moment in time represented by that specific position in time along the axis.

G8A11

Sidebands: You may recall that true AM signals contain two sidebands, the upper sideband (USB) of frequencies greater than the *carrier frequency* (the tuned or displayed frequency value), and the lower sideband (LSB) of frequencies below the carrier frequency. Each sideband consumes approximately 3000 Hz of bandwidth. With AM phone transmissions each of these sidebands encodes information from approximately 3000 Hz of audio signals captured by the microphone. As a slightly simplified mental model you may consider each AM RF sideband as a collection of 3000 modulation envelopes, each 1 Hz wide. Each of those 3000 envelopes is formed by RF modulation with one of the 3000 audio frequencies of your voice, as captured by the microphone. Figure 4.2 depicts the scenario with a frequency domain view.

Notice that the two AM sidebands are mirror images of one another, with the carrier frequency to which you tune your transceiver mimicking the mirror. The distance away from the carrier, as measured in hertz, of any sideband RF frequency is equal to the audio frequency by which it is being modulated. For example, the RF frequency modulated by the 542 Hz audio waveform is both 542 Hz above the carrier and 542 hertz below the carrier frequency. The RF frequency encoding the 1263 Hz audio frequency is 1263 Hz above and below the carrier. So, if f is frequency, the AM sidebands extend as $f_{Carrier} + f_{Audio}$ and as $f_{Carrier} - f_{Audio}$ for the approximately 3000 Hz of audio frequencies modulating the RF signals.

SSB: The sideband above the carrier is called the *Upper Sideband*, or USB. The sideband below the carrier is called the *Lower Sideband*, or LSB. Each sideband consumes about 3 kHz of bandwidth. In a true AM signal both

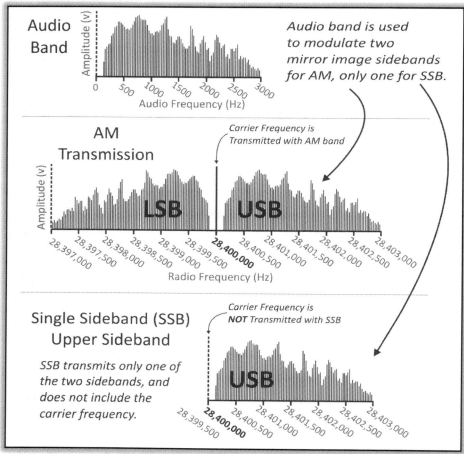

Figure 4.2: Frequency domain comparison of AM and SSB (USB) signals.

sidebands and the carrier frequency are transmitted, for approximately 6 kHz of total bandwidth. However, the AM signal is redundant, with each sideband carrying a complete set of audio information. **With the single sideband (SSB) voice mode only one sideband is transmitted; the other sideband and carrier are suppressed.** This leads to two primary benefits of SSB phone transmissions:

- **Single sideband phone emissions use the narrowest frequency bandwidth of any phone mode:** About 3 kHz.

- **Carrier suppression** (and opposite sideband suppression) **in single sideband phone transmissions allow the available power to be used more effectively.**

With narrower transmission bandwidth the applied power is distributed over a smaller band of frequencies, thereby giving the narrower band greater average amplitude. That is, the signal has more punch than when the same power is distribute across a wider band. With SSB, all the power is poured into just the one sideband that's a little less than half the bandwidth of AM. Thus, SSB uses the available power more efficiently. (Keep in mind that the typical CW transmission is only about 150 Hz wide, and some digital modes approach this same narrow bandwidth, so the power is squeezed into a very narrow band of frequencies making for great efficiency as compared to phone modes like AM or SSB! With narrow bandwidth a little power goes a long way… literally.)

Bandwidth Considerations: Let's consider some practical implications of the SSB bandwidth. First, there are two possible sidebands to use, the USB or the LSB. Which shall we select? The agreed convention by the amateur community is that the USB is used on the higher frequency bands of 20m (14 MHz) and above, while the LSB is used on the lower bands, 40m (7 MHz) to 160m (1.8 MHz). There is one exception to this on the five 60m band channels on which USB is always used.

So, given these conventions and your knowledge that a SSB signal is 3 kHz wide, consider the following practical scenarios, referring to Figure 4.3 on the next page:

- **When the displayed carrier frequency is set to 7.178 MHz, what frequency range is occupied by a 3 kHz LSB signal?** Remember, the LSB is below the carrier, so the frequency range will go from the carrier value to the carrier – 3 kHz. In this 40m band case the range occupied will be **7.175 to 7.178 MHz.**

- **When the displayed carrier frequency is set to 14.347 MHz, what frequency range is occupied by a 3 kHz USB signal?** The USB used for the 20m band transmission extends from the carrier up 3 kHz, so the range occupied will be **14.347 to 14.350 MHz.**

- **How close to the lower edge of the 40 meter General Class phone segment should your displayed carrier frequency be when using 3 kHz wide LSB?** Since the LSB will occupy 3 kHz below the carrier, and since you may not transmit any signal below the General Class lower edge phone frequency of 7.175 MHz, your displayed carrier should be at least **3 kHz above the edge of the segment at 7.178 MHz.** (Exactly as in the first case above.)

- **How close to the upper edge of the 20 meter General Class band should your displayed carrier frequency be when using 3 kHz wide USB?**

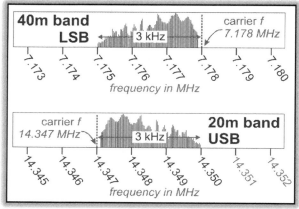

Figure 4.3: LSB and USB bandwidth examples.

Since the USB will occupy 3 kHz above the carrier, and since you may not transmit any signal above the General Class band edge at 14.350 MHz, your displayed carrier should be at least **3 kHz below the edge of the band** at 14.347 MHz. (Exactly as in the second case above.)

Regarding operations close to the edge of the bands as in these exam question scenarios, it is prudent to give your transmitter a little buffer zone beyond the 3 kHz SSB width. Transmitters may have inherent error in the displayed carrier frequency, they may not be calibrated perfectly, and transmitter frequency can drift over time. Another 500 Hz buffer is a good practical rule of thumb to add when near band edges. For instance, in the 20m band case immediately above you would keep your VFO tuned another 500 Hz lower in frequency to provide the additional margin from the band edge – you would not tune above 14.3465 MHz.

Transmitters: With the structure of a SSB signal now in mind, let's see how it is generated. We will take a functional approach to transmitters in this chapter, defining the components as blocks that perform tasks or functions with the waveforms or signals. We will put the blocks together in diagram form to illustrate the integrated functions of transmitters. (We will consider the electronic innards of some transceiver circuits later in Chapter 7.) Let's start with the simplest transmitter form, a single frequency CW transmitter, and then we will add component blocks to it in order to vary the frequency and finally to modulate a SSB voice transmission.

Simple CW Transmitter: Figure 4.4 shows a block diagram of a very simple CW transmitter. The signal flow direction in block diagrams is usually left-to-right, so we begin with the *oscillator*. An oscillator is an electronic circuit that produces a regular and unvarying sine wave signal – an alternating current (AC) swinging back and forth in the circuit with smoothly varying positive (+) and negative (-) voltage values. For this simple CW transmitter we will establish that the oscillator produces only a single frequency of the RF value to be transmitted. Let's just pick this fixed frequency oscillator's value to be 14.050 MHz, square in the 20m CW band.

The output signal of the oscillator is routed to amplifiers that boosts the amplitude (power) of the sine wave signal. A power amplifier boosts the signal to full power for transmission via the antenna.

The CW key (or electronic keyer) interrupts or completes the transmitter circuit as a switch so that the continuous wave transmission may be affected in

the *dit* and *dah* patterns of Morse Code. Beyond these "ON/OFF" patterns, no additional modification to the stable RF waveform is made – no other form of modulation is imposed.

With this transmitter you could happily make RF beeps to communicate with the world, if only on a single lonely frequency. But it is nice to be able to shift frequency, especially when a band is busy!

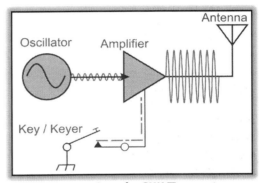

Figure 4.4: Simple CW Transmitter.

Variable Frequency Transmitter: The single frequency CW transmitter of Figure 4.4 can be made to emit other frequencies by simply varying the initial frequency created by the oscillator circuit. Assuming that the amplifier stages that follow are designed to accept and boost signals across a range of frequencies, a *variable frequency oscillator* (VFO) may be substituted for the fixed frequency oscillator with no other changes to the rest of the transmitter.

A VFO is an oscillator circuit containing electronic components that allow controlled variation in their values of electric *inductance* or *capacitance*. By changing these component values the oscillator's sine wave output frequency may be adjusted and the amplified and transmitted frequency follows right along. The result is a CW transmitter that may be tuned across a limited range of frequencies, usually within a single RF band. Thus, our transmitter may now be adjusted across a range of frequencies in the 20m band, perhaps from 14.000 to 14.150 MHz.

Now you can move to another frequency to avoid interference from nearby stations or chase others' signals across a range of the spectrum! But gee, wouldn't it be nice to select a whole other band when the ionospheric conditions make the current band unusable for skip?

Multiband Transmitter: The variable frequency transmitter can be upgraded to transmit across a similar range of frequencies in more than one frequency band. That is, we can punch up the design such that it transmits on any selected frequency within a range of perhaps:

15m Band	21.000 – 21.150 MHz
20m Band	14.000 – 14.150 MHz
40m Band	7.000 – 7.150 MHz

But in order to achieve this flexibility of band selection we will need a method by which the oscillator's frequency can be altered wholesale! Twiddling a few inductor or capacitor values is not usually sufficient to shift frequency by such a huge amount. How can we make a grand change in the oscillator's sine wave signal? One common way is by frequency mixing.

Mixers: A mixer is a special circuit that does just what its name implies: It mixes together a pair of frequencies. The result is almost magic! Mixing frequencies is a common method used to shift an oscillator's frequency into entirely different frequency bands. Mixers are used in both transmitters and receivers to affect frequency selections. **Another term for the mixing of two RF signals is heterodyning.** You can learn more about how heterodyning works to shift frequencies in the *HamRadioSchool.com* online learning media for this section, but the distilled bottom line concepts regarding frequency mixers and their heterodyning processes are as follows:

G8B03

1. Two new signals result from mixing a pair of frequencies – a higher frequency signal that is the sum of the two mixed frequencies ($f1 + f2$) and a lower frequency signal that is the difference of the two mixed frequencies ($f1 - f2$). [Example: 14.000 MHz + 7.000 MHz = 21.000 MHz; and 14.000 MHz - 7.000 MHz = 7.000 MHz]

2. If one of the two mixed signals is amplitude modulated (varies in amplitude due to a modulating envelope), this signal modulation is preserved in the amplitude variations of the sum and difference output frequencies.

"Aha!" you should now exclaim, because you have suddenly had a giant light bulb illuminate overhead due to outcome #1 listed above. By mixing the VFO

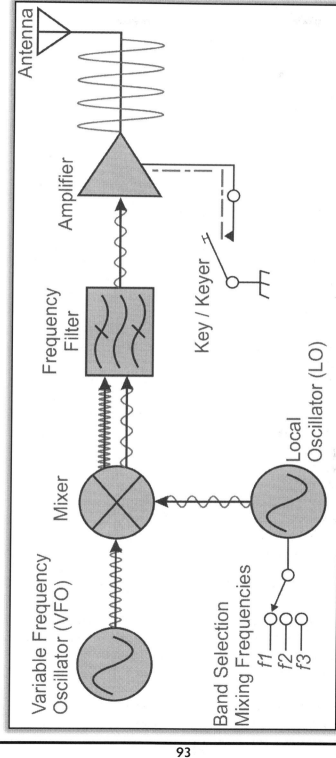

Figure 4.5: A multiband transmitter. VFO and LO frequencies are mixed to shift transmit frequencies into alternate RF bands. The LO frequency may be user-selected for band. The VFO affects a range of tuning within each selected band.

signal with a steady signal from a second oscillator, a much higher and a much lower frequency can both be generated, shifting the frequency for transmission into entirely other amateur radio bands. The small frequency range across which the VFO may be tuned is effectively shifted to become a small frequency range for tuning in other radio bands, as noted in the previous multiband transmitter range examples. In the example of mixing outcome #1 the original unmixed 14.000 MHz signal may be transmitted (20m band), or when mixed with 7.000 MHz either a 21.000 MHz (15m band) signal or a 7.000 MHz (40m band) signal may be selected, and the VFO will affect its smaller tuning range within the selected band.

In a transmitter the VFO signals are combined with signals from the *local oscillator* (LO) in the mixer. A *filter* allows only frequencies of the desired band to continue along the transmission path. You can imagine that frequency ranges in even more bands can be generated for transmission by providing different LO signal frequencies to the mixer. Keeping in mind mixing outcome #2 above, let's see what happens when the VFO signal is modulated by an audio signal envelope.

SSB Transmitter: Figure 4.6 depicts a typical SSB transmitter. Note that except for the deletion of the key the right half of the transmitter is identical to our multiband CW transmitter. However, we have inserted some additional components between the VFO and the mixer. Let's take a look at those.

> **Balanced Modulator:** No surprises here. The modulator does exactly what the name implies – it modulates the RF signal from the VFO. In this type of transmitter the VFO is also known as the *carrier oscillator*. The modulator accepts the carrier frequency from the VFO/Carrier Oscillator as well as the modulating signal from the microphone's speech amplifier. As described earlier, the modulator circuit combines the carrier frequency with each audio frequency to create the AM sidebands, enclosing the sidebands' RF waveforms within the modulating envelope of the audio frequencies' waveforms, varying the RF amplitude moment to moment.
>
> A balanced modulator is a special type of mixer producing sum and difference products of the 3 kHz wide audio band mixed with the carrier frequency. The output of a properly adjusted balanced modulator is a *double sideband* (DSB) signal – both the upper and lower sidebands – but *without* the carrier. This DSB signal with the carrier frequency added back in its unmodulated form is a true AM signal: Carrier, USB, and LSB altogether at 6 kHz of bandwidth. (A special technique allows the carrier to be generated in the modulator output, and this is referred to as an *unbalanced modulator.*)

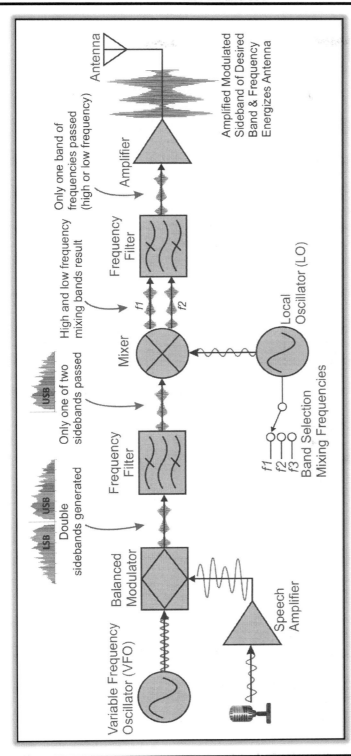

Figure 4.6: A SSB transmitter and signal processing stream. The balanced modulator creates dual AM sidebands, but only one is passed by the filter onto the mixer. The mixer also receives the LO signal that has been adjusted for a specific band-selecting frequency. The sum and difference mixer products are filtered to select the desired mixer product for amplification and transmission.

SSB Signal Generation: Starting with a DSB signal from a balanced modulator, an undesired sideband can be filtered out of the signal leaving only a single sideband, either USB or LSB. (Other methods of generating SSB signals are more complex, but this filter method is commonly used in SSB transmitters.) The filter depicted in Figure 4.6 between the balanced modulator and the mixer is used to remove one of the sidebands, leaving a single sideband modulated signal to be mixed with the LO signal and ultimately amplified and transmitted. **The balanced modulator is the circuit used to combine signals from the carrier oscillator** (the VFO) **and speech amplifier and to send the results to the filter in some single sideband phone transmitters. The filter is used to process signals from the balanced modulator and send them to the mixer in a SSB phone transmitter.**

AM Overmodulation: Sometimes you may get a little excited on the air and talk too loud. It's a natural reaction when we're struggling to communicate with someone in a noisy environment like a crowded room or on a noisy RF band, or when we really feel passionately about the point we're making! Occasionally these characteristics of human nature will slip into our radio operations and cause a little overmodulation. Having the microphone gain set too high for your voice can cause the same issue.

Overmodulation of AM or SSB signals means that our driving signals (the audio signal of the microphone) is varying the RF amplitude too much for a proper signal. Those envelope mirror image waveforms will meet and distort the envelope shape as depicted in Figure 4.7. Additionally, if your audio drive level results in your speech amplifier exceeding its maximum output power level, the tops (and bottoms) of your modulating audio waveforms may get *clipped* into a flattened

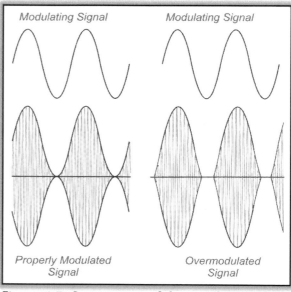

Figure 4.7: Comparison of the envelopes of a properly modulated and an overmodulated AM signal.

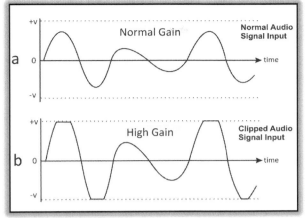

Figure 4.8: Clipping (flat-topping) of the modulating audio signal is caused by excessive drive or mic gain.

shape, as in Figure 4.8. **This SSB distortion caused by excessive drive is also called flat-topping** due to the characteristic shape of the resulting waveform.

When overmodulation happens, additional frequency components are created in the frequency domain view of your transmission, spreading out the signal well beyond the normal 3 kHz wide SSB signal. That means you may create *splatter*, or RF frequencies beyond the desired bandwidth for good amateur practice with SSB transmissions. Fortunately most transmitters have a technological solution to this problem.

ALC: *Automatic Level Control* is a special type of circuit in a transmitter that reduces the drive power when it becomes too great for a properly modulated signal. The ALC will usually kick in during natural peaks in voice loudness. Most transceivers will require adjustments for proper ALC adaptation to your voice characteristics. In particular, **the transmit audio or microphone gain is a control that is typically adjusted for proper ALC setting on an amateur SSB transceiver.** While monitoring the ALC, adjust these settings so that ALC is activated only during your natural voice peaks. Additionally, **if the ALC is not set properly when transmitting AFSK digital signals using SSB mode, improper action of ALC distorts signals and may cause spurious emissions.** (See Section 6.9 *Avoiding Interference* regarding spurious emissions.)

Superheterodyne Receivers: With all those SSB signals flying around, bouncing from the ionosphere, and getting all jumbled up in your receiving antenna, your receiver faces a daunting task: Select only a small band of frequencies of interest, rejecting all the rest of the RF jumble, and demodulate those RF signals to reconstruct the audio waveforms that ride on them as the envelope in order to recreate the sound of the transmitting operator's voice. That's a tall order, but the superheterodyne receiver is up to the chore!

The superheterodyne receiver is a widely used type of receiver for demodulating AM and SSB signals. As you may have surmised from the name containing that "heterodyne" term, this receiver uses the principle of mixing to shift received frequencies while retaining modulated information. Let's take a look at a block diagram of a superheterodyne receiver and consider the general signal processing steps that it undertakes. Then we will elaborate on a couple of the steps in greater detail. Again, the signal flow is left-to-right in the diagram of Figure 4.9 on the adjacent page.

1. Modulated RF weak signals create alternating currents on the receiving antenna. These signals are routed to an RF amplifier that boosts the weak signals' strength (increased amplitude or power).

2. **The amplified RF signals are routed to a mixer where they are mixed with a local oscillator (LO) signal.** The mixer output is the sum and difference products of the LO frequency mixed with received signal frequencies.

    a. The LO in the receiver is a variable frequency oscillator (VFO) that may be adjusted by an operating control on the receiver.
    b. The LO frequency is selected to produce a specific, desired mixing product frequency (the difference product) of a lower frequency value called the *intermediate frequency* (IF).
    c. The IF is a much lower RF frequency than the received signals, and the audio modulation is preserved in the IF. But the IF is not yet at the much lower audio frequencies necessary for sound reproduction.

3. **The mixer's output products** (sum and difference) **are routed to the IF filter.** The IF filter eliminates the sum frequency product (and other undesired signals) and passes only the specified (difference product) intermediate frequency.

4. The IF amplifier strengthens the isolated IF signal and then routes it to the product detector. **The product detector** is another specialized mixer circuit that **combines signals from the IF amplifier and the beat frequency oscillator (BFO), and sends the result to the audio frequency (AF) amplifier.**

    a. The IF is a static, unchanging reference value, and the BFO frequency is engineered to mix with the IF and generate a difference product (a lower frequency than the IF) that recovers the audio frequency modulating signal from the IF. The originally transmitted modulating audio signals have finally been liberated from their RF hosts!

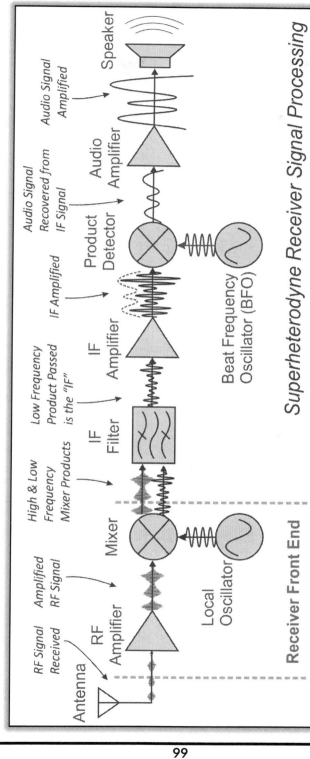

Figure 4.9: Basic signal processing of the superheterodyne receiver. The receiver front end shifts received signals to the intermediate frequency (IF) by mixing. The product detector shifts the IF lower, recovering the original modulating audio waveform.

5.   The audio frequency output signal of the product detector is amplified further by an audio frequency (AF) amplifier in order to drive a speaker that reproduces the voice sound of the transmitting operator.

(Although the received RF and the IF are referred to as lone frequencies, realize that the entire 3 kHz band of SSB signal frequencies is being dragged through these steps simultaneously. The audio-value offsets from the RF carrier frequency are preserved as offsets from the IF value, and ultimately as a range of audio frequency values representing the original modulating signals.)

These steps represent a single conversion superheterodyne. It is referred to as single conversion because only a single mixing step is used to convert from the received RF to the IF. Most modern receivers having multiple broad frequency band demodulation requirements or high signal selectivity capability will use multiple mixing stages to achieve such high performance. **The absolute simplest combination of stages that implement a superheterodyne receiver would be an HF oscillator** (the local oscillator) **linked to a mixer** (that is also receiving antenna signals) **and the mixer products routed to a detector circuit.**

Intermediate Frequency: In step 2 of the superheterodyne signal processing a specific IF is a product of the mixing process of received RF signals with the LO. Further, as noted in step 4a, the IF is a single, unchanging frequency value that the IF filter passes on for additional processing into audio by the product detector. What exactly is going on here?

As noted, the LO in this case is a VFO with operator-selectable frequency values. This is the VFO control by which you tune your transceiver to a desired frequency. When you alter the LO frequency you select an oscillator frequency to be mixed with every RF signal received by the antenna – lots and lots of different frequency signals pulled from the air. Every one of those myriad mixes between a received RF signal and the selected LO signal results in a sum and difference product out of the mixer. So, in reality, there are myriad x 2 mixer products! Of course, only one received RF signal frequency value mixed with the LO signal will result in a difference product that is exactly the unchanging IF value. And if you change the LO frequency you change the received RF signal frequency that mixes to the IF value. Perhaps a numerical example will help drive home the point.

IF Example: Suppose we are operating in the 20m band with a superheterodyne receiver. The receiver uses one of the standard IF values of 455 kHz. That IF value never changes, and that is the only frequency value that the IF filter will pass for further processing into audio signals. That value of 455 kHz, or

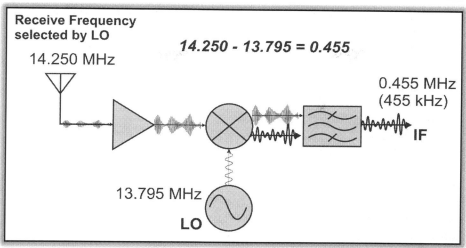

Figure 4.10: The received signal frequency is selected from all other frequencies by changes to the LO mixing frequency since the IF is unchanging at 455 kHz.

0.455 MHz, is the desired difference product of the mixer circuit.

Let's say that the LO is providing a mixing signal of 13.795 MHz. **In order for the IF of 455 kHz** (0.455 MHz) **to be the difference product of the mixer, the mixer must combine the 13.795 MHz local oscillator signal with a received input signal of 14.250 MHz.** This is true because

14.250 MHz – 13.795 MHz = 0.455 MHz (or 455 kHz)

If the LO is altered to generate a signal of 13.820 MHz, it can produce a difference product of 0.455 MHz only by mixing with a received signal of 14.275 MHz:

14.275 MHz – 13.820 MHz = 0.455 MHz (or 455 kHz)

Thus, by adjusting the LO frequency to the mixer a received RF frequency is selected for continued processing into the IF. Even though there are uncountable other mixing products resulting from the mixing process, the only product that is passed along by the IF filter is the singular difference product resulting from the LO signal mixing with a received signal that produces that exact 455 kHz IF. This is how the VFO control tunes your transceiver to the desired frequency.

Image Response: You may have considered already that another RF frequency besides the desired receive frequency may result in the 455 kHz intermediate frequency. For example, **if a receiver mixes a 13.800 MHz VFO (LO) signal with a 14.255 MHz received signal to produce a 455 kHz intermediate frequency signal, a 13.345 MHz received signal will produce the same IF due to its difference from the 13.800 MHz VFO signal:**

G4A11

14.255 MHz – 13.800 MHz = 0.455 MHz, and

13.800 MHz – 13.345 MHz = 0.455 MHz

So, if a signal exists on 13.345 MHz it will produce interference known as *image response*. In this example the IF of 455 KHz will contain signals derived from both 14.255 MHz and from 13.345 MHz received RF. If this occurs there is no convenient method of eliminating or filtering the undesired image signals.

However, most modern receivers will have *front end filters* or *image filters* that eliminate the signals that may cause undesired images like this. The *receiver front end* is considered the combination of RF amplifier, mixer, and local oscillator (LO or VFO) at the beginning of the receiver's signal processing stream, and filters added to these components would never allow the 13.345 MHz signals from our example into the mixer processing stream and IF.

G8B02

IF Shift: In a case **when another station very close to the receive frequency is interfering, the IF shift control on a receiver may help to avoid the interference.** The IF shift control changes the IF passband higher or lower without changing the IF itself. In some cases this can help reduce interference from stations near the VFO-selected receive frequency by moving the passband of frequencies such that it no longer includes the interfering signal, but while maintaining proper audio demodulation of the IF passband.

There. Aren't you overjoyed? Isn't your brain muscle good and exercised, producing cognitive bliss? That is the exultant world of amplitude modulation and single sideband transmitting and receiving! Not so terribly complicated, huh? And boy, does it just radiate joy! Review the questions for this section and then we'll tackle a few concepts of Frequency Modulation.

HamRadioSchool.com/general_media

How Radio Works

4.2

FM

> ❝ *...atoms emit light waves of a specific length or oscillation frequency - their familiar characteristic spectra - and these can come in the form of electromagnetic waves only from accelerated electric quanta.*
> — *Johannes Stark*

Accelerated electric quanta – accelerated electric charge, such as electrons flowing back and forth in an antenna – is a fundamental concept in the production of radio frequencies. The frequency of alternation in the AC signal energizing an antenna will determine the frequency of emitted electromagnetic waves. Frequency modulation (FM) takes advantage of Stark's insight by encoding information in AC frequency variations that are mirrored in the antenna's EM radio frequency emissions.

Let's consider some of the characteristics of FM and contrast them with what we've learned about AM and SSB. Just because you earn your General Class ticket doesn't mean you will abandon the local VHF and UHF FM repeaters and simplex communications. In fact, you may be inspired to explore FM digital mode operations and other related facets of amateur radio. So, it pays to be knowledgeable of FM as a General Class operator.

Frequency modulation changes the instantaneous frequency of an RF wave to convey information. The audio signals generated by your transmitter's microphone and speech amplifier drive the modulation with FM just as with AM or SSB, but instead of an amplitude envelope encoding the audio signal a frequency shift encodes the audio signal. When a modulating audio signal is applied to an FM transmitter the RF carrier frequency changes proportionally to the instantaneous amplitude of the modulating signal.

Figure 4.11 depicts the FM scenario. Note how the frequency is increased when the audio amplitude is positive and the frequency is decreased when the audio amplitude is negative. The greater the driving power (amplitude) of the audio signal, positive or negative voltage, the greater the deviation from the *carrier frequency* value. The carrier frequency is a stable or *resting* value that manifests when no modulating audio signal is present or when the audio

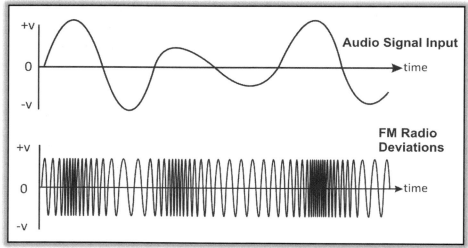

Figure 4.11: FM deviations with audio signal modulation.

signal is zero volts. All frequency deviations are relative to the carrier frequency, and the carrier frequency is what is depicted on your radio's tuning display (VFO display).

Spring Model: A simplified way to think of the FM scenario is to imagine the RF carrier waveform as a spring with a preferred extension (resting state frequency). Think of the spring coils as the RF waveforms. The spring may be compressed tighter than its preferred extension (higher frequency) or it may be stretched out greater than its preferred extension (lower frequency). When the modulating waveform is of relatively low power (weak audio signals from a soft voice), the spring oscillates back and forth at a frequency equivalent to the audio signal and to only a mild compression and a mild extension – a small *deviation* from its preferred extension, or resting state. When the driving audio amplitude is great (strong audio signals from a loud voice), the spring oscillates back and forth at the same audio frequency rate, but the deviations are much larger – very tight compressions and very stretched out extensions. In this way the amplitude of an audio signal is encoded into the frequency deviations of the RF transmission.

As with AM and SSB, there is a band of audio frequencies that must be encoded this way in order to reproduce voice audio. Imagine a unique spring for each 1 Hz audio frequency in the band. You might imagine a set of a few thousand such "RF springs," each one compressing-and-extending at a rate equal to that of a single, unique audio frequency in the band, and each one representing the amplitude of its modulating audio frequency with the magnitude of its deviation from a standard resting state. In this way the entire audio band of frequencies is represented by the commensurate band of spring deviation rates (the rate of frequency deviations), and the amplitude of each audio frequency is represented by the extent of the spring deviations (the magnitude of the frequency deviations from the carrier frequency reference). This multi-spring model is depicted in Figure 4.12. *However…*

Caution: This spring model image is an oversimplified view of real FM and it should not be taken as an accurate physical depiction, but it provides a good mental tool for describing the essence of FM. In a real FM transmission the full set of "spring oscillations" (frequency deviations) is an incredibly complex behavior of the RF carrier waveform that is adequately defined only by advanced statistical mathematics. It's sort of

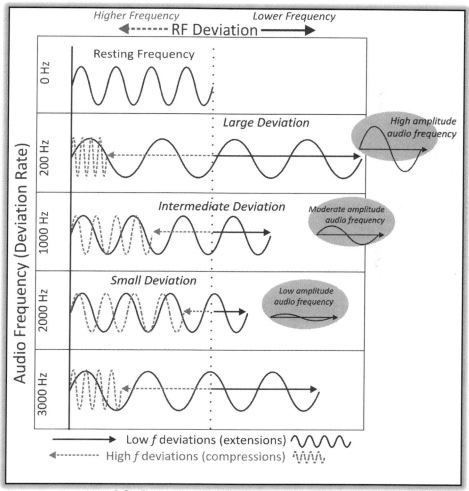

Figure 4.12: Simplified spring model of FM. Spring deviation rates represent audio band frequency encoding. Spring deviation magnitudes represent each audio band frequency's instantaneous amplitude.

like having all those jittering springs' dynamics crammed together in one really crazy dancing spring. Specifically, FM signals are characterized by *Bessel functions* that offer a solution to a differential equation describing the complex dynamics of frequency modulated waveforms. The exploration of this topic is left as an exercise for the advanced student. No exam questions test your knowledge of Bessel functions or differential equations. (Whew!)

FM Bandwidth: You may recall from your Technician Class studies that the bandwidth of FM phone signals depends upon the frequency deviation described above. As the frequency deviates to greater extents a larger band of frequencies must be used by the FM signal. Since deviation is determined by the amplitude of the modulating audio signal, louder audio results in greater FM bandwidth. Thus, FM bandwidth changes constantly with the driving audio signal. The Technician Class question pool indicates 5 – 15 kHz as typical FM bandwidth, although in practice signals may be of somewhat wider bandwidth.

Most FM transmitters have limiting circuits that keep FM deviation within the bounds of good amateur practice. The limiter circuit's maximum allowed deviation (or a lower maximum driving signal amplitude) may determine the *peak carrier deviation* value for a transmission. The peak deviation, along with the highest modulating frequency, influences the bandwidth of the FM signal.

Carson's Rule: A good approximation of FM signal bandwidth may be calculated using Carson's Rule:

Bandwidth = 2 x (peak deviation + highest modulating frequency)

Let's consider an example from the question pool: **What is the total bandwidth of an FM phone transmission having a 5 kHz deviation and a 3 kHz modulating frequency?** Let's plug in the values for peak deviation and highest modulating frequency per the Carson's Rule formula:

Bandwidth = 2 x (5 kHz + 3 kHz) = 2 x 8 kHz = **16 kHz**

Notice this example provides an estimated bandwidth for FM about five times greater than the 3 kHz bandwidth of SSB. Many regions utilize 15 kHz to 25 kHz spacing of designated VHF and UHF FM channels. This spacing may not always be sufficient to avoid interference between adjacent FM channels, depending on operating practices and transmitter characteristics.

Note, you can over-modulate FM, too. Usually this is referred to as *over-devi-*

ation with FM, where the limiter circuit will kick-in. But just as with amplitude modulation **one effect of over-modulation is excessive bandwidth** since the resultant deformed waveforms will generate frequency components beyond the desired bandwidth limits. However, if the transmitter's limiter circuit is functioning correctly, overdeviation of RF should never get transmitted – that's the whole point of having a limiter in an FM transmitter.

Frequency modulated (FM) phone is not used below 29.5 MHz (10m band) because the wide bandwidth is prohibited by the FCC rules. With the bandwidth of FM phone signals several times greater than SSB, a simple bandwidth analysis makes it clear why the FCC limits FM operations in the lower HF bands. The available spectrum in the amateur phone bands below 10m is relatively narrow: 400 kHz on 80m band to just 58 kHz on 17m band, and intermediate values on the other HF bands. Compare this to the 1.4 MHz of 10m band, the 3.9 MHz of 2m band, and 30 MHz of 70 cm band where FM is allowed. The 17m phone band would support only about four simultaneously detectable FM QSOs with an average bandwidth of 15 kHz. This really illustrates the squeeze that would result if wide bandwidth FM were permitted on the lower HF bands!

FM Transmitters: Two significant signal production techniques differentiate FM phone transmitters from SSB transmitters:

1. FM uses a *reactance modulator* instead of a balanced modulator. A reactance modulator uses a special circuit that varies capacitance values in electronic components in order to rapidly shift the frequency of a resonating circuit (oscillator). The FM oscillator initially produces a relatively low frequency signal, well below the desired operating frequency.

2. **FM transmitters shift the oscillator's frequency to the higher operating frequency using a multiplier stage that generates a harmonic of the lower frequency signal.** A *harmonic multiplier* is a circuit that produces signals that are integer frequency multiples of the input signal. Many multiples may be produced – 2x, 3x, ... 12x the input and higher – and a filter is used to select the particular frequency multiple needed for a transmitter design.

Figure 4.13 is a block diagram of a simple FM transmitter showing the left-to-right signal processing with the reactance modulator and harmonic multiplier components. The reactance modulator accepts the speech signals of the microphone and amplifier to affect frequency modulation with the oscillator. The output signal of the oscillator is a low RF frequency: For example, a 2m band transmitter oscillator will output about a 12.21 MHz frequency modulated signal. The filter eliminates undesired harmonics generated by the multiplier. For the 2m transmitter only the 12th harmonic is passed on to the amplifier:

12 MHz x 12 = 144.00 MHz.

In order to generate the 2m calling frequency of 146.52 MHz the oscillator must generate a 12.21 MHz signal:

12.21 MHz x 12 = 146.52 MHz.

The amplifier then boosts this signal for transmission by the antenna.

Transmitter Design Considerations: Interestingly, the harmonic multiplier not only multiplies the oscillator's frequency by 12 (or other desired values for other bands), but it multiplies the *frequency deviations* that are output by the oscillator as well. That is, the "spring oscillations" created by the reactance modulator and oscillator are magnified 12 times, too. The compressions are 12 times tighter and the expansions are 12 times longer!

Let's use our 2m band FM example above and the 5 kHz deviation from the Carson's Rule discussion for an example of the implications for transmitter design: **For a pure 146.52 MHz signal in a 5 kHz deviation the reactance modulated oscillator (before the multiplier) must deviate its frequency by 416.7 Hz.** That is, an initial oscillator deviation of 416.7 Hz is going to be multiplied by 12 in the harmonic multiplier for this 2m transmitter case:

416.7 Hz x 12 = 5000 Hz (5 kHz) transmitted deviation.

Or, of course, the calculation may be inverted to:

5000 Hz ÷ 12 = 416.7 Hz oscillator deviation.

You may wonder why harmonic multipliers are not implemented in AM and SSB transmitters instead of mixers to shift frequencies higher or lower. The multiplier is usually simpler and cheaper to use. However, a harmonic multiplier is not linear, meaning that it will distort the amplitude of the signal. In fact, it is a feature of this purposeful distortion that results in the generation of harmonic frequency multiples. An AM or SSB signal would not survive these distortions intact. However, since the FM information is encoded in the undistorted frequency deviations and not in an amplitude signal, the information is properly preserved, allowing FM use of the harmonic multiplier.

G8B07

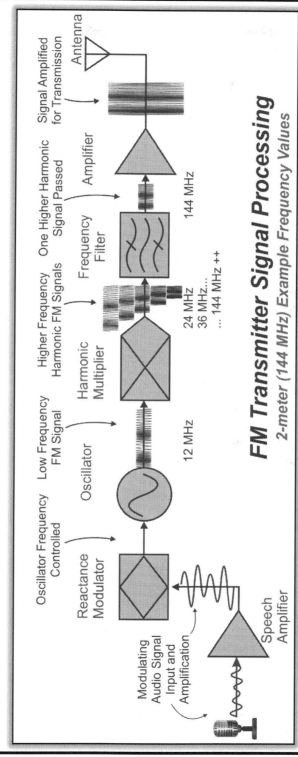

FM Transmitter Signal Processing
2-meter (144 MHz) Example Frequency Values

Figure 4.13: FM transmitter signal processing. The harmonic multiplier receives a relatively low frequency FM signal from the oscillator and outputs multiple higher frequency harmonic signals in which frequency deviations are preserved. The frequency filter allows only one of the harmonic frequencies to pass for transmission.

FM Receivers: The front end of the FM receiver is identical to the superheterodyne SSB receiver, but following the IF generation (by mixing and filtering) a different set of components is used to recover the audio information. As depicted in Figure 4.14 the FM receiver employs a *limiter*. The limiter removes any amplitude variation, and only the frequency deviations remain in a constant-amplitude square wave signal. Following the limiter is **a circuit called the discriminator, used to convert signals coming from the IF amplifier to audio.** The discriminator circuit output is amplified for sound reproduction.

G7C08

Phase Modulation (PM): Phase modulation is a process that changes the phase angle of an RF wave to convey information. Phase angle changes are illustrated in Figure 4.15. A continuous range of phase angle changes from 0 to 360 degrees can be used to encode a modulating signal with PM, just as a continuous range of amplitude changes or of frequency deviations are used in AM and FM.

G8A02

A slight difference in the FM transmitter's reactance modulator connection will result instead in PM. FM results when the reactance modulator is connected to an oscillator tuned circuit, as shown previously in Figure 4.13; **Phase modulation results when the reactance modulator is connected to an RF power amplifier** instead.

G8A04

Phase modulation is less commonly used in amateur radio than either FM or SSB, but it is a viable modulating technique for

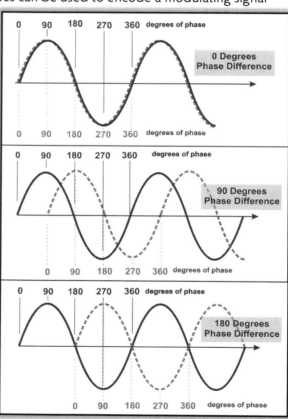

Figure 4.15: Example phase shifts of a waveform (dashed) relative to a reference waveform (solid).

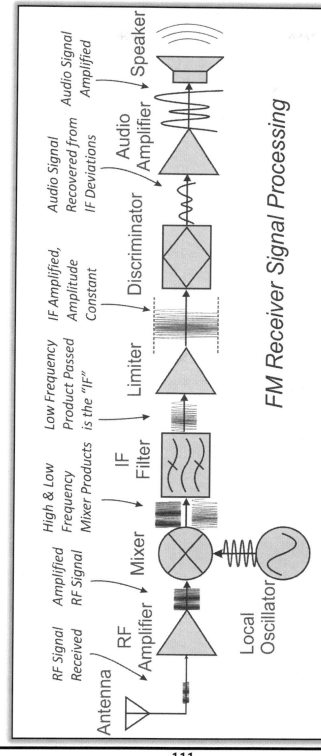

FM Receiver Signal Processing

Figure 4.14: The FM receiver signal processing begins the same as the SSB superheterodyne, but a limiter circuit ensures a constant IF amplitude and a discriminator circuit recovers the audio signal from the IF deviations.

voice transmissions. Recall that *phase shifting* is used with the popular PSK31 digital mode described in Section 2.4 *Digital Modes*. The PSK31 mode uses the presence or absence of a 180-degree phase shift of a narrow bandwidth tone transmission within rigidly specified time intervals to convey 1s and 0s of digitally coded characters.

No matter how advanced you get in amateur radio license class, you will likely always enjoy the clear sound of FM and the convenience of FM repeaters for day-to-day local communications. There's just nothing like a good net on a repeater with a sizable group of hams participating from across the experience spectrum, and FM promotes that interaction like no other mode. Enjoy it, but understand it too!

Section questions wait for you at: *HamRadioSchool.com/general_media*

How Radio Works

4.3 Signal Processing

> ❝ *All physical systems can be thought of as registering and processing information ...*
> *— Seth Lloyd*

I'm certain that Professor Lloyd would agree that ham radio constitutes a physical system. We can generate and receive signals. We can make waveforms bolt across vast distances, bounce them from the ionosphere, modulating and demodulating information in electromagnetic dialog with our fellow hams – we can register a lot of information flying around as RF!

But what about the quality of those signals? Even if we are able to modulate, transmit, receive, and demodulate, we will not necessarily communicate if the quality of signals is poor due to weak signal strength, an improperly configured transceiver, or failure to take advantage of all the technological marvels available in modern transceivers.

Let's consider some of the ways that our RF signals can be analyzed and enhanced so that our RF communications capabilities are optimized. How can we gauge signal strengths? How can we enhance signals carrying our modulated voice and reduce signals carrying noise? How can digital technology improve our analog RF signals? The amazing capabilities of the modern amateur radio transceiver provide help with each of these questions. Let's see how our ham system can process the information it registers.

Signal Strength: No matter if you are operating QRP (low power) or blasting out a kilowatt, signal strength is a critical factor for communication success. Many different factors influence the strength of your signal at a receiving station including transmitter output power, atmospheric conditions, operating mode, and signal path. Signal strength is also one of the most commonly exchanged metrics of performance between operators during contacts. How is signal strength determined?

S Meter: **Received signal strength is measured with an S meter** (S = signal). **An S meter will be found in virtually every receiver.** Figure 4.16 shows various styles of S meters on modern receivers. Notice

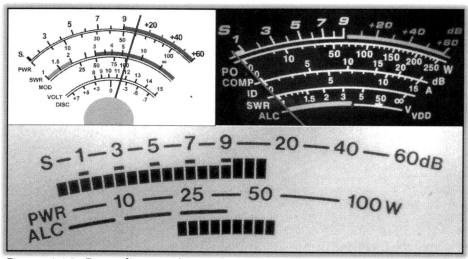

Figure 4.16: Example typical S meters. Top scale is the S meter scale in each example. Needle readouts and LCD segmented displays are common.

that they share some common features, and often will have multiple scales for various functions other than signal strength. The S meter scale is the top scale in each depicted example.

S Units: An S meter will usually depict *S units* on the left half of the scale, from S=0 to S=9. One S unit change in signal strength usually indicates a 6 dB change in received signal strength. As we reviewed in Chapter 0, *Before We Begin*, a 6 dB change is about a 4X change in power. **So, to change the S meter reading on a distant receiver by one S unit, say from S8 to S9, the transmitter power output must be raised approximately 4 times.** (Note: S meters scaling and accuracy may vary depending upon receiver manufacturer and quality, and automatic gain control [AGC] may also affect how the S meter responds to signal strength. Check your transceiver users manual.)

Strong Signal Comparisons: A reading of S9 is considered to be a strong signal, and most S meters will depict S9 centered on the scale. To the right, or *above* S9, the S meter scale will typically depict values of +20, +40, and +60 dB. You will hear very strong signals reported on the air such as *"20 over S9,"* or *"S9 + 20,"* or simply *"20 over,"* or other indicated levels above S9. **Assuming a properly calibrated S meter, a reading of 20 dB over S9 means the signal is 100 times stronger than an S9 signal** (20 dB = 100X change). A signal of S9 + 40 dB would be 10,000 times stronger than S9, and S9 + 60 dB means a 1,000,000 times increase!

G4D07

G4D05

Attenuation: Signal strength varies over a very great range, hence the use of the logarithmic decibel unit for comparisons. When signals approach S9 + 60 dB strength and stronger your received signal may sound distorted. The amplifiers in the receiver produce linearly amplified signals in the normal signal strength range, but very strong signals can overdrive the circuit. That is, the amplifier cannot handle the extreme signal strength and it cannot accurately reproduce the amplitude modulated waveform or envelope signals being received. This effect may occur in the RF amplifier of the receiver front-end or in the IF amplifier following the mixing process. This effect is called *overload*, or *front-end overload*. **To reduce signal overload due to strong incoming signals use the attenuator function present on many HF transceivers.** The attenuator circuit will reduce overall signal strength from the front end through the IF amplifier, improving the receiver's ability to handle very strong signals such as those from a strong, nearby station. But the attenuator will diminish your ability to receive weak signals, so you do not want to leave it on permanently.

G4A13

Speech Processors: **The purpose of a speech processor used in a modern transceiver is to increase the intelligibility of transmitted phone signals during poor conditions.** This is accomplished by boosting the signal strengths of some frequency components of the transmitted AM or SSB signal. Let's take a closer look at how a speech processor works in your transceiver. Let's start with just a smidgen of simple engineering-speak wrapped in common experience.

G4D01

Signal detection is a common engineering task across many domains. Your receiver endeavors to detect RF signals among a chaotic sea of RF noise. A submariner strives to detect a whisper of the sound reflection from the sonar against the ocean's eerie background sound track. With my poorly functioning ears I endeavor to detect my wife's voice among the noise of screaming kids, loud music, barking dogs, and ringing tinnitus… OK, maybe sometimes I'm not endeavoring too hard, but let's use this example.

If the kids, their music, the dogs, and my tinnitus are all fussing and thumping and barking and ringing, generating a cacophony of noise, I will not hear the wife's stated orders even if she shouts them at the top of her lungs, per normal. Why not? Because I cannot detect her commanding verbal signals among all the noise signals in the environment. The *ratio of signal to noise* is too low for the signal to be detected by my faulty ears. (A low signal-to-noise ratio could also result if she tried to sweetly whisper through only my ringing tinnitus, hence low noise but also a very low signal, but that would be a very rare scenario in my home.)

Low Signal to Noise Ratio

High Signal to Noise Ratio

In contrast, once the kids are at school, the electronics are turned off, and the dog is asleep, I am left in peace with only the persistent mild ringing in my ears to interfere with my darling's mellifluously squawked signals. With a large *signal-to-noise ratio* (SNR) like that it is difficult to get out of honey-do chores no matter how bad the ears may be.

Back to radio now, before I get into trouble: In poor conditions a receiving operator has a similar problem – lots of noise and perhaps a weak signal imbedded in it. A voice signal may be heard but not clearly distinguished or understood. This is because some of the frequencies in typical voice audio are relatively weak while others are strong. For instance, lower frequency vowel sounds are usually bellowed with relative strength of sound pressure, while many higher frequency consonant sounds are relatively weak in sound pressure, such as those of the letters c, f, n, s, v, or w. As a result the audio band signals and their modulated RF sideband signals will have greatly varying signal strengths across the band's frequency range. It's like trying to hear a friend from across a crowded room at a party – you may hear the words but not understand them because too much of the detailed sound information is lost in the noise of many conversations.

A speech processor boosts the power of those relatively weak signals while leaving the relatively stronger signals at normal levels. (Other techniques may also be implemented, but this is a common arrangement.) The SNR is increased, particularly for those lower power, higher frequencies in the voice band, enhancing signal detection by the receiv-

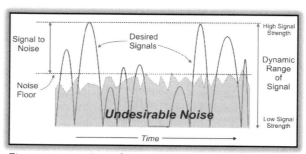

Figure 4.17: Signal-to-noise ratio. Noise (gray) can mask a desired signal if the signal-to-noise ratio is low, making detection of the desired signal difficult. Strong signals exceed the noise, producing a high signal-to-noise ratio, and are more easily detected by a receiver.

ing operator. For instance, the speech processor may amplify many of those consonant sounds by several decibels but leave all vowel sounds unchanged. By doing this **the speech processor affects a transmitted sideband phone signal in a couple of ways:**

G4D02

- **It increases the average power of the transmitted signal** (relative to the unprocessed signal and within the limits of the transmitter output).

- It ultimately increases the receiver's sound output for audio frequencies that may otherwise have been lost in the noise.

The typical use of a speech processor is called *compression*, as depicted in Figure 4.18: The range of power levels across the frequency band has been reduced or compressed, keeping all frequencies closer to a consistent peak power level and improving speech intelligibility – the weaker signals have been boosted out of the noise level with a greater SNR.

However, take care in making manual adjustments to your transceiver's speech processor. **An incorrectly adjusted speech processor can result in distorted speech, pickup of excessive background noise, and even splatter** caused by overmodulation or amplified frequencies outside the normal audio bandwidth.

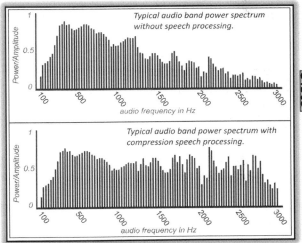

G4D03

If you use a speech processor, start by trying the typical pre-programmed options. In most instances one of those configurations will improve your signal quality and keep you out of trouble. Follow the directions in your transceiver users manual, but also ask for on-air signal reports to check for audio quality.

Figure 4.18: Example of compression of an audio band. The distribution of power across frequencies is adjusted for greater consistency, boosting weaker frequencies.

Digital Signal Processor (DSP): The transmitters and receivers described earlier in this chapter are analog devices, meaning they work with continuous electrical signals and waveforms. However, many modern transceivers now utilize a *Digital Signal Processor* (DSP) to enhance received signals and, in some cases, to generate signals for transmission by digital methods. After a simple illustration of the nature of digital signals we will examine some typical applications of DSP in amateur radio.

Sampling: A smooth and continuous signal waveform may be approximately represented by *sampling* its values in regular intervals of time. Sampling means simply measuring a characteristic instantaneously with regularity and recording the measurements. For an AC signal in an electrical circuit we may measure the instantaneous voltage in equally timed intervals. We could represent our sampled waveform in a table that relates time to measured voltages, and we could plot the waveform according to the table as in Figure 4.19. (We will suppose the use of an oscilloscope to depict and measure the waveform voltages for illustration, and you will learn more about measurement with oscilloscopes in Chapter 6.)

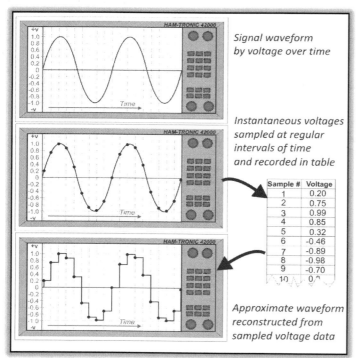

Signal waveform by voltage over time

Instantaneous voltages sampled at regular intervals of time and recorded in table

Sample #	Voltage
1	0.20
2	0.75
3	0.99
4	0.85
5	0.32
6	-0.46
7	-0.89
8	-0.98
9	-0.70
10	0.?

Approximate waveform reconstructed from sampled voltage data

Notice that the reconstructed waveform is not a smoothed shape, but rather a squared distribution of points on a graph. If we sampled more frequently we would have more complete and accurate information to store, and if we sample less frequently we have to do more guesswork with less information. Even if we do not have all the information required to accurately recreate the waveform we can make intelligent guesses

Figure 4.19: Digital sampling and storage of a signal's waveform voltages. The sampling interval trades accuracy with data quantity. Sampled data may be stored electronically and operated upon with mathematical functions to alter the reconstructed signal.

about its shape and fill-in between the plotted points. This is particularly easy with a typical sine wave RF signal.

With DSP, RF signals are converted into digital representations through a sampling process. A digital microprocessor, programmed with appropriate software algorithms, may then be used to perform mathematical operations on the digitized signal data. These digital methods can affect many common functions such as signal filtering, audio equalizing, and more. **One use for a DSP in an amateur station is to remove noise from received signals,** thereby improving the signal-to-noise ratio and signal intelligibility.

G4C11

ADC and DAC: The sampling process described above is a method of *analog-to-digital conversion*, or ADC. Following the ADC process the signals may be manipulated by the digital processor. Following digital processing, the digital signal representations must go through a reverse *digital-to-analog conversion*, or DAC, so that audio waveforms can produce sound from a speaker. **Any Digital Signal Processor function, such as an IF filter, requires an analog to digital converter, a digital processing chip, and a digital to analog converter,** as depicted in Figure 4.20. **All Digital Signal Processor filtering is accomplished this way, by converting the signal from analog to digital and using digital processing,** and then converting back to analog waveforms.

G7C09

G7C10

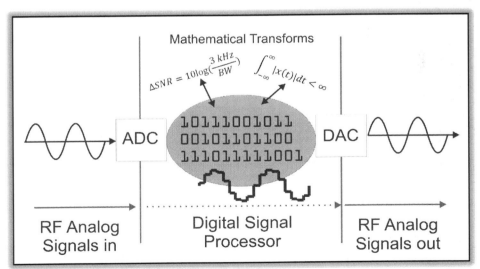

Figure 4.20: ADC produces digital data by sampling. DSP operates on the digital data to modify the signal representation. DAC converts the modified data into an altered analog signal.

Digital Filtering: A filter is a circuit that is designed to transmit, or pass, some frequencies applied to it and to attenuate, or reject, other frequencies applied to it. For example, the IF filter in a receiver is designed to transmit only a small band of frequencies near the intermediate frequency value and attenuate all others. Filtering in modern transceivers is often accomplished with a DSP. To help understand how this is accomplished let's first review some basics about RF filtering that apply to analog as well as digital methods, and we'll compare the analog methods with the digital.

Filter Types: It is typical for a filter circuit to be defined by the *passband* of frequencies it will transmit, or alternatively by the *stop band* of frequencies it will attenuate or reject. A filter's *cut-off frequency* is a frequency value beyond which the filter will attenuate signals. For instance, a *high pass filter* will allow the passage of frequencies higher than the cut-off value, and it will attenuate frequencies below the cut-off value. Conversely, a low-pass filter passes frequencies lower than the cut-off value and rejects higher frequencies. A bandpass filter has two cut-off values, passing only the frequencies between the two cut-off values. A *notch filter* is a vary narrow bandpass filter, and it will transmit all frequencies except a narrow band either side of a defined *center frequency*. **The purpose of the notch filter on a transceiver is to reduce**

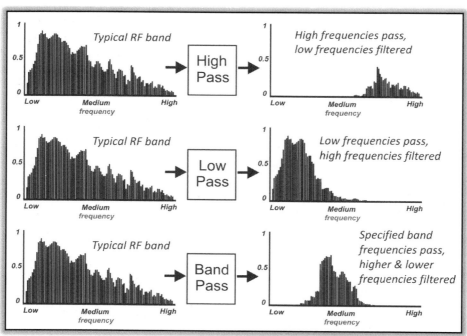

Figure 4.21: High Pass, Low Pass, and Band Pass filtering effects.

interference from carriers in the receiver passband. (See notch example described below and Figure 4.22 on the next page.)

Selectivity: Most of a superheterodyne receiver's frequency *selectivity* (the ability to reject undesired signals) is achieved with IF filtering in which the mixer products resulting from nearby receive frequencies are rejected and only the desired band of signals is passed to the product detector. **It is good to match receiver bandwidth to the bandwidth of the operating mode because it results in the best signal-to-noise ratio.** For instance, use a 3kHz wide filter with SSB and perhaps a 400 Hz wide filter for CW. A close matching of filter width to signal bandwidth enhances receiver selectivity by passing precisely the desired intermediate frequency band and rejecting all others, thereby eliminating noise from those rejected adjacent frequencies.

G8B09

In a purely analog receiver filtering must be affected with filter circuits that are designed with specific characteristics that are not readily changed or manipulated. Filter circuits may be physically swapped out when the available selections are inadequate for the desired operation or conditions, but this is not always a convenient or swift modification to make, as it usually requires opening the chassis of the transceiver and mucking about its innards. Digital filtering makes things much easier!

An advantage of a receiver Digital Signal Processor IF filter as compared to an analog filter is that a wide range of filter bandwidths and shapes can be created. For example, the DSP can be programmed through simple receiver controls to implement an IF of 2.4 kHz for a narrow SSB filter, or it can be configured for a comfortable 300 Hz CW filter. The DSP filters out the unwanted frequencies and passes the desired signal band, just like the band pass filtering illustrated in Figure 4.21. Other types of filtering can also be digitally accomplished, including *notching* and *noise reduction*, all without the hassle of mechanically substituting filter modules!

G4C12

Notching: **The DSP filter can also perform automatic notching of interfering carriers.** By performing an analysis of the receive passband frequencies and their relative power, the DSP can identify any narrow signal *spike* that indicates an interfering carrier signal. A notch filter can be defined and implemented to reduce interference from carriers in the receiver passband, as in Figure 4.22 on the following page.

G4C13

Noise Reduction: With other filtering techniques the DSP can perform other filtering functions. Noise reduction is one of the primary functions offered by DSP, and there are multiple noise reduction techniques that

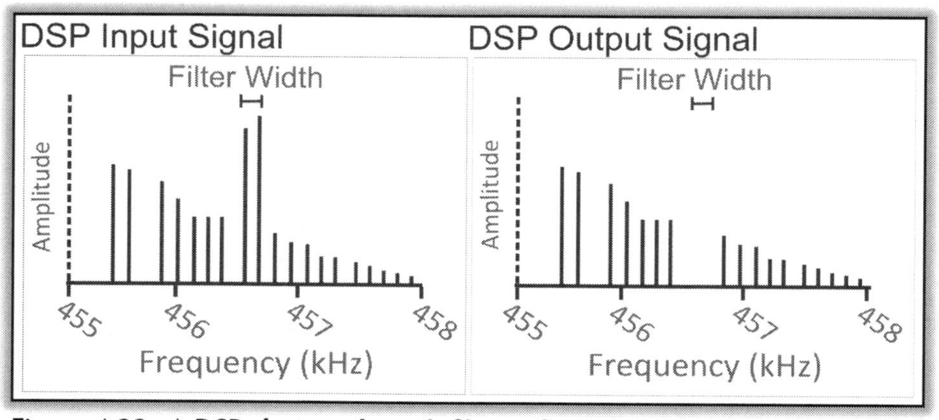

Figure 4.22: A DSP-designed notch filter effect, eliminating an offending narrow carrier signal from the IF pass band.

may be used singularly or in combination. Random noise reduction and mode-specific adaptive algorithms for notching or bandpass are common.

Software Defined Radio (SDR): SDR is a radio in which most major signal processing functions are performed by software. Although various configurations are possible, the SDR receiver typically uses an analog heterodyning front end and digitizes mixing products for software processing of all signals via a high performance computer. Many common desktop or PC computers are sufficient for use as an SDR processing platform. The spectrum display, signal analysis, filtering, selectivity, and other signal processing capabilities of the SDR are impressive. The SDR leverages the power of a PC to perform a lot of DSP.

DDS: Additionally, the SDR may also use a *direct digital synthesizer* (DDS) to create signals for modulation and transmission. The DDS utilizes a stable digital clocking reference coupled with a numerically controlled oscillator and DAC to generate RF waveforms. The DDS provides great agility for variable frequency signal production under digital control. **One advantage of a transceiver controlled by a direct digital synthesizer is variable frequency with the stability of a crystal oscillator** – the signals produced are typically rock solid and very clean, with almost no noise artifacts.

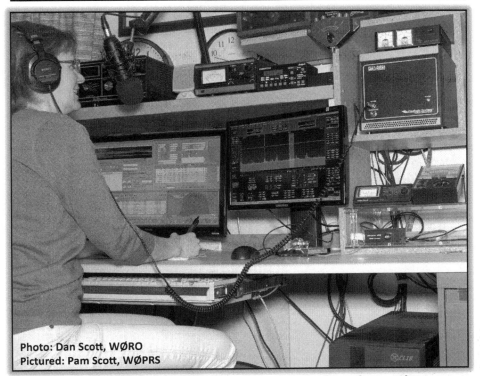

Photo: Dan Scott, WØRO
Pictured: Pam Scott, WØPRS

Figure 4.23: The Flex 5000 Software Defined Radio has a heterodyning receiver (upper right black box) and leverages the digital processing power of a PC (lower right). Detailed receive spectrum analyses can be conducted and graphically displayed.

There is a whole world's worth of signal processing methods, components, devices, and configuration choices! It can be overwhelming and confusing. But most modern HF-capable transceivers are marketed with good features and ready-to-operate configurations, so you can get started without a lot of anxiety over the vastness of the signal processing universe. Start with a basic rig, learn its inherent signal processing features, try them out, and then grow your shack's accoutrements as you learn more and as your needs and interests drive you.

Go receive the passband of questions on signal processing, avoid any notch filtering of topics in the passband, and perform your own internal processing necessary to demodulate these signals into intelligible communications!

HamRadioSchool.com/general_media

Waterton Amateur Radio Society, NØLM

5.0   Antennas

> **" I'm the antenna**
> **Catching vibration**
> **You're the transmitter**
> **Give information!**   *- Kraftwerk, Antenna*

I am convinced that almost one half of the people who get involved in ham radio were drawn to it by antennas. Really. Antennas gleam and radiate and fascinate, and they readily facilitate rewarding hands-on projects for even the beginner. Of course, a well-implemented antenna system that both *catches and dispatches RF vibration* is critical to the success of your station, too.

We will begin our climb into antennas with some review of basic concepts and definitions from Technician material. Section 5.1 will elaborate on the basics with some antenna theory and principles that have big operational impacts, especially for work on the HF bands. Section 5.2 is all about feedlines, connectors, and SWR, and getting them all to agree with one another in *giving information* to the antenna. Lastly, we'll take a look at a variety of directional antennas in Section 5.3 with particular focus on the popular Yagi design.

Gather up your copper wire and aluminum tubing, your coax and connectors, your analyzer and tuner… Let's catch some vibration!

Review Definitions and Concepts: Just in case your brain is a little rusty from your last Technician Class studies, let's refresh on a few key definitions and concepts about antennas, and perhaps a few new concepts. These will come in handy in the forward sections.

Impedance: The opposition to the flow of alternating current in an electric circuit. Impedance matching is very important in an antenna system to achieve high performance. Impedance should match from the transceiver to the feedline and connectors to the antenna feed point. Impedance mismatches cause power reflections back toward the transmitter and drive up SWR… and usually that's a bad thing.

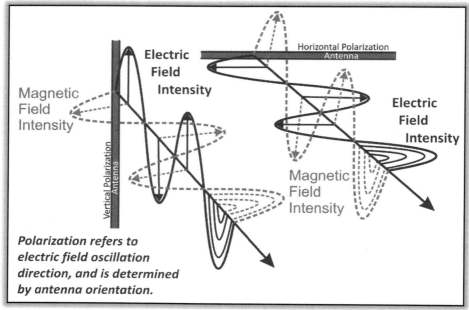

Figure 5.0a: Vertically and horizontally polarized RF signals.

Feed Point: The position at which the feedline connects to the antenna. Optimally, feed point impedance should be matched with the feedline, and feed point impedance is the ratio of RF voltage to current at the feed point.

Element: The components of an antenna that radiate and receive radio frequencies. The *driven element* is an element directly connected to the feedline. *Passive* or *parasitic* elements are not connected to the feedline, but they will interact with the driven element to help shape the antenna's radiating and receiving pattern.

Polarization: The orientation of the electric field oscillations radiated from an antenna, as determined by the orientation of the antenna elements. *Horizontal polarization* results from horizontally arranged elements, resulting in electric field oscillations that are parallel with the surface of the earth. *Vertical polarization* results from vertically arranged elements, resulting in electric field oscillations that are perpendicular to the surface of the earth.

Radiation Pattern: A graphical depiction of the relative strength of emitted signals from an antenna by direction. Two pattern graphs are typical: 1) *Elevation Pattern* – a side viewpoint of the antenna pattern, as if you are standing on earth some distance from the antenna. The elevation pattern shows the relative strengths of signals as radiated at angles above the horizon, or in the vertical.

2) *Azimuthal Pattern* – a viewpoint from directly above the antenna, looking down onto its horizontal signal pattern.

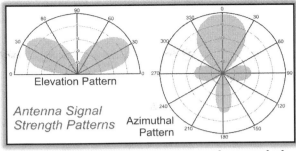

Isotropic Antenna: An antenna that radiates equally in all directions. The radiation pattern would appear as a sphere

Figure 5.0b: Antenna elevation and azimuthal signal strength pattern examples.

around the antenna indicating equal vertical and horizontal signal strength in every direction. The isotropic antenna is a theoretical model for comparisons.

Omnidirectional Antenna: An antenna that radiates equally in horizontal radial directions. The azimuthal pattern will appear circular.

Directional Antenna: An antenna that radiates more strongly in one (or more) direction. The azimuthal pattern will usually contain *lobes* of signal strength to indicate stronger signals in the antenna's pointing direction.

Antenna Gain: The increase in signal strength for the antenna's pointing direction as compared to a reference antenna such as the isotropic model or an ideal dipole antenna. The unit of gain is the decibel (dB). **Antenna gain compared to the isotropic model is referred to as *dBi*, while the comparison with a dipole is referred to as *dbd*. Gain figures in dBi are 2.15 dB higher than dBd gain figures** since a dipole exhibits 2.15 dB of gain over the isotropic model.

Antenna Analyzer: A device connected to an antenna-feedline system to measure SWR or impedance across bands and frequencies. The analyzer generates its own signals and no connection to a transceiver is made.

SWR Meter / Directional Wattmeter: A device inserted in the feedline between the transmitter and antenna to measure the power in both directions for determination of standing wave ratio (SWR). The SWR meter typically displays SWR directly, while the directional wattmeter requires dual measurements (one in each direction of the feedline) and a manual computation of SWR. (See Figure 5.0c SWR meter, next page.)

Antenna Tuner / Transmatch: A device that presents a matching impedance (usually 50 ohms) to the transceiver for a feedline and antenna system that does not have a matching impedance. The impedance of the antenna system is not altered, but only that presented to the transceiver.

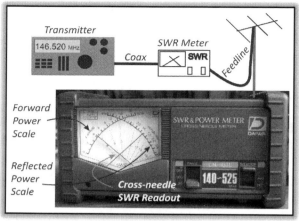

Field Strength Meter: A device that measures relative strength of received RF signals at a distance from the antenna. A field strength meter is useful for measuring the radiation pattern of an antenna.

Figure 5.0c: SWR meter feedline insertion and cross-needle readout example meter.

Feedline Loss: Any feedline, such as coaxial cable or twin lead wire, will attenuate the signal strength directed through it, dissipating some of the energy as heat. Generally, feedline loss will increase with increasing operating frequency. Different types of feedlines and coaxial cable will exhibit different loss characteristics due to variations in materials and physical features.

Antenna Tradeoffs: There is no perfect antenna; every antenna represents tradeoffs among performance, design, convenience, environment, arrangement, materials, and other factors. A compelling reason to understand antenna theory and practice is to accurately judge your station situation and the related antenna tradeoffs for the creation of a well performing antenna system that fits your communications goals.

Radiating EM: Thanks to some basic laws of physics an electromagnetic wave is emitted from any electric charge that is accelerated through space. An electron with a negative charge, or a positively charged ion, may be accelerated by applying a voltage. As electrons are accelerated back-and-forth in a conductor by an AC voltage, they radiate a tiny EM wave. The frequency of the EM wave is determined by the frequency of alternating current accelerations. Amass a gazillion charged particles all zipping back and forth at RF rates in perpetual acceleration along a wire and you have an antenna emitting an RF signal.

With that little review out of the way we can now consider some General Class antenna theory and principles!

5.1   Antennas   Theory & Principles

❝ *In theory there is no difference between theory and practice. In practice there is.*
— *Yogi Berra*

With your General Class license and much greater access to the HF bands, you will surely want to erect antennas for some of those bands. Of course, the HF band wavelengths are quite long compared to the VHF and UHF wavelengths you have been most accustomed to as a Technician Class operator, and so the HF antenna elements are necessarily much longer, too. This section will help you scheme on some simple antennas with which you can readily begin making some of those long wavelength signals. You really do not need a giant, complex antenna farm to get started on the HF bands.

First, we will consider a couple of basic antenna types in discussing some fundamental theory and principles of antennas: The half-wave dipole and the ¼ wave vertical antenna. Then we will briefly explore some more specialized antennas and their unique characteristics. At no point in this section will we challenge the *theory of practice*, but we will certainly engage in the *practice of theory*.

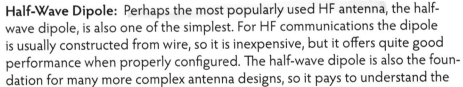

Half-Wave Dipole: Perhaps the most popularly used HF antenna, the half-wave dipole, is also one of the simplest. For HF communications the dipole is usually constructed from wire, so it is inexpensive, but it offers quite good performance when properly configured. The half-wave dipole is also the foundation for many more complex antenna designs, so it pays to understand the workings of this basic radiator.

Radiation Pattern: The dipole's basic electrical configuration and radiating pattern are depicted in Figure 5.1. The feed point is at the center of two wires of equal length extending in opposite directions. The dipole's two halves are each approximately ¼ wavelength long for the frequency of operation. **The radiation pattern of a dipole antenna in free space** (far away from the ground or any conductors) **is a figure-eight at right angles to the antenna in the plane of the conductor.** The strongest signals radiate broadside to the antenna wire axis and the weakest signals radiate out the ends of the wire axis. When installed about ½ wavelength high and parallel to

G9B04

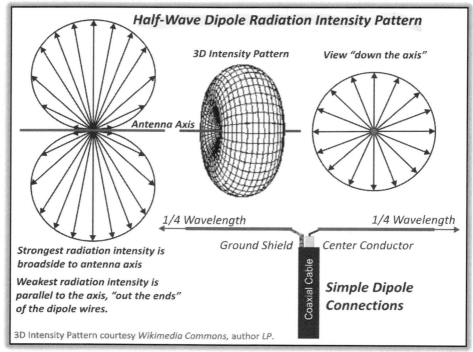

Half-Wave Dipole Radiation Intensity Pattern

3D Intensity Pattern

View "down the axis"

Antenna Axis

1/4 Wavelength

1/4 Wavelength

Ground Shield

Center Conductor

Strongest radiation intensity is broadside to antenna axis

Weakest radiation intensity is parallel to the axis, "out the ends" of the dipole wires.

Coaxial Cable

Simple Dipole Connections

3D Intensity Pattern courtesy *Wikimedia Commons*, author *LP*.

Figure 5.1: Radiation pattern of a dipole antenna in free space.

the earth (horizontally polarized), the elevation pattern of a half-wave dipole tends to direct strong signals low to the horizon, promoting long distance ionospheric skip. We will examine this phenomenon more in a moment.

Length Calculation: Although covered in your Technician Class studies, computing the length of a half-wave dipole is even more important for HF operations since this type of antenna is so often deployed by amateurs to operate on those lower frequency bands. The approximate length in feet of a wire half-wave dipole may be computed as:

Length (ft) = 468 ÷ frequency (MHz)

G9B10
For example, suppose you wish to construct a half-wave dipole antenna for 14.250 MHz. What is the approximate total length?

Length (ft) = 468 ÷ 14.250 MHz = 32 feet

G9B11
Just to thrash the deceased equine: What is the approximate length for a half-wave dipole antenna cut for 3.550 MHz?

Length (ft) = 468 ÷ 3.550 MHz = 131 feet

This formula will result in an *approximate* total dipole length, keeping in mind that each half segment of the antenna will be one-half of this length. You might notice that this estimated total length is a little shorter than the half-wavelength of the frequencies denoted. For instance, calculating the total wavelength for 14.250 MHz yields 21.05 meters [300 ÷ 14.250 = 21.05], or about 69 feet. One half of 69 feet (for one half wavelength) is 34.5 feet, so the half-wavelength dipole total length of 32 feet indicated by our construction formula is a little shy of the actual RF half wavelength values. A practical half-wave wire antenna will usually be roughly 5% shorter than the length of the actual half RF wave. Why?

The ends of the antenna wire (along with insulators and/or wire loops used to anchor them) add a little capacitance to the antenna circuit. As we will explore a bit later, adding capacitance to an antenna (or any circuit) has the effect of lowering its resonant frequency. This is called *end effect*. So, the wavelength for the frequency of resonance of the antenna will be longer (lower frequency) than the physical antenna length. The added capacitance increases with thicker antenna wire or radiating elements, so antennas with thicker elements will (within extreme limits) require shorter elements for a given target resonant frequency. In almost all cases the antenna will require trimming of the length to obtain the best matched feed point impedance for the desired operating frequency. [*See the HamRadioSchool.com Technician License Course*, Section 7.2 *SWR*, for a review of trimming and SWR curves.]

Feed Point Impedance: Consistent with Ohm's Law, electrical impedance may be computed as the ratio of voltage (E) to current (I) in a circuit, including an antenna circuit. For a half-wave dipole cut to length for its driving frequency, the voltage and current along the antenna wire will ideally look like Figure 5.2 on the next page.

Notice that the voltage is of greatest magnitude (either positive or negative in value) at the ends of the antenna's length, and a minimum (but not zero) at the center feed point position. The current, however, is greatest in the center and drops to zero at the ends. Let's consider a few things about this voltage/current scenario:

- The impedance will be lowest at the center (E/I is the smallest value here).
- Typical feed point impedance of a center fed half-wave dipole is about 72 Ω (ohms).
- With each AC cycle the voltage values and the current direction reverses, at the RF frequency.
- As the current of charges surge back and forth across the antenna's

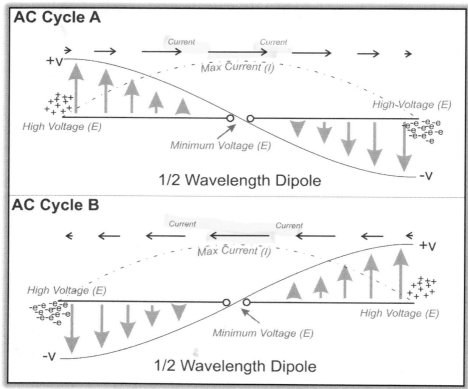

Figure 5.2: Half-wave Dipole Voltage and Current Relationship.

length, there is no place for them to go at the end points, so a charge of high voltage piles up on alternating ends each AC cycle.

- With a high voltage and low current near the antenna ends, the impedance (E/I) increases to become very large as compared to the center position impedance.

- **If the feed point location were moved from the center toward an end the feed point impedance would steadily increase** with distance away from the center.

Height Above Ground Impedance Effects: Many half-wave dipole antennas will be fed with coaxial cable of 50 Ω or 75 Ω impedance. The center feed point impedance of the free space dipole is about 72 Ω, which results in a 1.44 SWR with a 50 Ω feedline, so not a bad match. However, dipoles in free space don't really exist and the antenna's impedance will be affected by objects in the environment and especially by that giant conductor called *the earth.*

The ground affects the antenna's characteristic impedance because it is a conductor, although sometimes a very poor one. The ground's conductance creates an inverse electrical image of the antenna. If the antenna and the image are close enough to one another they will interact. Since the image is like a mirror reversal of the real antenna, the interaction affect is a canceling or *shorting* one. The net result is that the center feed point impedance

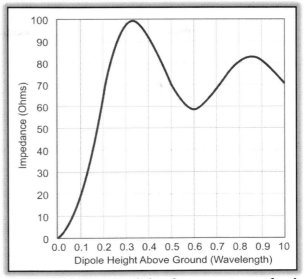

Figure 5.3: **Horizontal dipole approximate feed point impedance for height above ground.**

will vary with height above the ground. **As a half-wavelength dipole is lowered from ¼ wave above the ground the feed point impedance steadily decreases** and will reach zero at ground level. At greater heights the impedance increases and decreases in an oscillatory manner above and below its free space value, ultimately becoming stable at several wavelengths above ground level, as in Figure 5.3. The feed point impedance tends to be approximately the free space value at ½ wave and at one wave above ground level. Many wire dipoles are erected to be about ½ wavelength or slightly higher above the ground in order to achieve a good feed point impedance match, but also to achieve low elevation pattern angles of radiation.

Height Above Ground Radiation Pattern Effects: The nice *fat donut* pattern of the free space dipole changes significantly when the dipole is within a few wavelengths of the ground. The antenna's radiation is reflected by the ground, so the pattern of signal strength at a distance from the antenna is a combination of the radiating element's emissions and those emissions reflected from the ground. But the path distance of a directly radiated signal and that of a ground-reflected signal are somewhat different, so the propagation time to any given location will also vary somewhat for the different waves. As a result the waves may add together *in phase* with one another (wave crests and troughs lined up to make a stronger signal), or they may cancel one another *out of phase* (wave crests and troughs exactly opposite one another, nulling the signal strength), or they may interact with some intermediate phase alignment and various intermediate signal strengths.

The upshot of this wave combining effect is that a half-wave dipole's elevation pattern exhibits *lobes* and *nulls* – strong signals at some angles of elevation and weak or non-existent signals at other elevation angles – that vary with the antenna's height above ground. Some typical elevation patterns for a dipole are shown in Figure 5.4.

Notice that when the antenna is ½ and 1 wavelength above the ground that most of the lobes of high signal strength are directed at relatively low angles. This will be most effective for long distance skip propagation, helping to keep take-off angles below the critical angle and affecting the longest distance for a single ionospheric skip. (See Chapter 3, *Propagation.*) One-half wavelength high dipoles are popular for long distance contacts.

When the dipole is less than ½ wavelength above the ground its azimuthal pattern is essentially omnidirectional and a great amount of energy is also directed vertically rather than horizontally, as indicated by the elevation pattern. If the desire is for long distance skip this vertically directed energy is essentially wasted since these high take-off angle may be above the critical angle for the frequency used, and even if they are returned to earth the skip distance will be short. If the ionosphere will reflect a dipole's near-vertically radiated signals (usually 40m band or lower), such a low-to-the-ground antenna can be used for shorter range communications as an *NVIS antenna.*

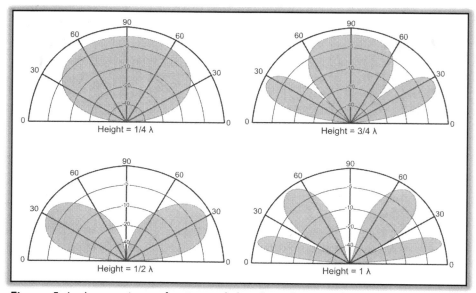

Figure 5.4: Approximate horizontal dipole radiation elevation patterns (gray) for various heights above ground.

NVIS: Near Vertical Incidence Sky wave. Intentionally placing a dipole low to the ground to generate **high vertical angle radiation can be advantageous for short distance HF communications of up to a few hundred kilometers. An NVIS antenna is typically installed between 1/10 and 1/4 wavelength height above ground.** For example, installing a **40m band** (7 MHz) **horizontal half-wave dipole at a height above ground of** about 5 to 10 meters **(1/8 to 1/4 wavelength) will likely be most effective for NVIS skip communications during the day.** (Because the high incidence angle path through the ionosphere's D layer is relatively short and direct, D layer absorption during daylight hours is less severe than for the low angle paths and daytime NVIS skip is feasible, particularly during winter months with weakened sunlight and D layer.)

Configuration: The simple dipole is usually configured in one of three ways: 1) Flattop, 2) Inverted V, or 3) Sloper. Figure 5.5 illustrates these three typical arrangements. The inverted V configuration is perhaps the most common since it requires less horizontal space to erect and requires only a center high support. The peak gain of the flattop is generally slightly more than the inverted V, but the downward sloping elements of the inverted V will provide greater radiation strength in the two directions off the ends of the flattop's axis, thereby improving the omnidirectional characteristics. The sloper configuration provides a similar omnidirectional advantage. More compromises!

In any configuration the best results will be obtained with the feedline running away at a right angle to the flattop or sloper, and directly down between the sloping elements of the inverted V. Feedpoint impedance can be affected by having the feedline running close to, or parallel with, the radiating elements.

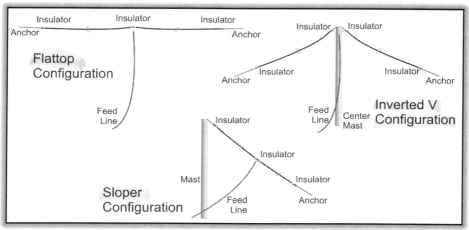

Figure 5.5: Three common dipole configurations.

The dipole is a terrific option for those seeking an inexpensive and simple way to get started on the HF bands. Many hams string them up in trees, using a high tree center support for an inverted v configuration, or pulling just one end high into a sloper. A flattop may be configured using two trees, pulling both ends up and allowing the feedline to dangle in the middle or run down a third, centered bark-covered mast. Of course, if you have the luxury of erecting dead masts such as fiberglass or aluminum poles, that works too!

Variations on the simple, single-band dipole are common for multi-band operations. We will come back to the beloved dipole shortly to examine these modifications on its basic theme, but for now let's chop that dipole in half and hold a mirror up to one end.

¼-Wave Vertical Antenna (Ground Plane Antenna): Another very popular HF antenna arrangement is the ¼-wave vertical antenna, usually coupled with a *ground plane*. This antenna may be considered to be one half of a dipole in which the other half is represented by a mirror electric image resulting from the ground plane, as in Figure 5.6. The real portion of the element is ¼ wavelength long, typically mounted above a ground plane conductive material. The feed point is where the real element meets the ground plane. The voltage-current dynamics for the ¼-wave ground plane antenna are similar to that of the dipole, with the ¼-wave voltage signal being minimum at the feed point and maximum at the element end. Of course, the orientation of the element is usually vertical rather than horizontal, so this antenna is often referred to simply as a "vertical."

Ground Plane:
The ground plane is simply a conductor arranged at an angle to the vertical element. The ground plane may be a solid metal surface, a screen, or an array of *radials*. Ground planes are commonly comprised of radial elements extending from

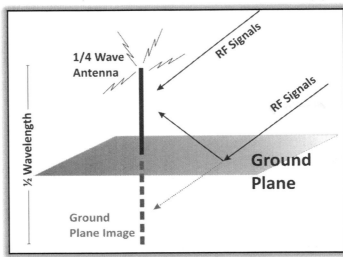

Figure 5.6: ¼-Wave Vertical Antenna with ground plane.

the base of the vertical element, and they may be perpendicular to the vertical or sloped downward from the vertical. **Verticals** designed for the low frequencies of the HF bands **are often ground-mounted with radial wires distributed along the surface or buried a few inches below the ground.**

Ground planes for HF verticals may be comprised of copper wire radials numbering from only a few to many dozens to over 200! Gener-ally, the ground

Photo: Jürg, KØPOP

Figure 5.7: Laying ground radials just under the sur-face for a flag pole ¼-wave HF multi-band .

plane image is enhanced with greater numbers of radials, essentially allow-ing more ground current to flow in the antenna. However, the performance enhancement of more radials is coupled with their length: Greater numbers of radials may be made longer for greater current flow and enhanced antenna performance, while fewer radials do not benefit from great lengths. A rough guideline is to make ground radials about the same length as the height of the ¼-wave antenna, but be aware that actual performance will vary some-what depending upon the earth's conductivity in your area and other factors, including the frequency band used. For multi-band verticals it is prudent to in-stall ¼-wave radial lengths for the lowest band on which you wish to operate.

Feed Point Impedance: The feed point impedance of the ¼-wavelength vertical with a horizontal ground plane is about one-half that of the dipole, near 35 Ω. However, the orientation of the ground plane affects the feed point impedance. **As the ground plane radials are changed from horizontal to downward sloping the feed point impedance increases.** Since the most commonly used feedlines have impedance of 50Ω, **sloping the radial downward is a common way of adjusting the feed point impedance of a quarter wave ground plane vertical antenna to be approximately 50 ohms.** If you were to continue to lower the ground plane radials' angles the impedance would continue to increase until the radials merged and physically formed the other half of a dipole configuration! At that point the impedance should, in theory, reach about 72 Ω. (See Figure 5.8.) In practice it may not be feasible to slope an HF antenna's radials at all, but the mild impedance mismatch of a perpendicular ground plane usually does not have a significant performance impact.

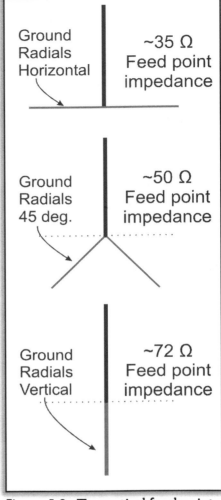

Figure 5.8: Theoretical feed point impedance changes with ground radial angles to the vertical. Most large verticals will have horizontal radials.

Length Calculation: If you can remember the calculation for the length of a half-wave dipole, you can simply divide by 2 to get the approximate length of the ¼-wave vertical. Of course, another way of viewing the calculation is to halve the 468 value used for dipole length calculations in units of feet to 234 and proceed identically to the dipole computation, as follows:

$$\text{Length (ft)} = 234 \div \text{frequency (MHz)}$$

For example, what is the approximate length for a ¼-wave vertical antenna cut for 28.5 MHz?

$$\text{Length (ft)} = 234 \div 28.5\,\text{MHz} = 8\,\text{feet}$$

As with the half-wave dipole, expect that some trimming will be required to get the lowest SWR.

Radiation Pattern: The vertical antenna radiates strongest broadside to its element, much like the dipole. The vertical will be an omnidirectional antenna, radiating equally around the azimuthal angles. Thus, no worries about weak signals along the axis of the antenna and missing out on contacts in those directions. The vertical is often preferred for long distance skip contacts due to the low takeoff angles it can generate. However, like the horizontal dipole, the vertical antenna does suffer from ground reflection losses and generally these are somewhat greater than the horizontal antenna. As such, **an advantage of the horizontally polarized dipole as compared to the vertically polarized HF antenna is lower ground reflection losses.**

The vertical antenna can be a good option for getting started on the HF bands for many hams. They are simple and relatively easy to install. Particularly for the higher HF bands from 10m to 20m, portable or temporary verticals are feasible that can be erected and taken down in a matter of minutes for good HF operations in a covenant restricted area or for the camp site. See *HamRadioSchool.com* features and learning media for more ideas and details.

Multiband and Wide Band Antennas: A simple antenna design tends to work well on a single RF band. You can trim a half-wave dipole or a ¼ wave vertical to length for a frequency and in most cases the feed point impedance will be matched well enough and the related SWR will remain sufficiently low across a range of frequencies on the band. A common metric is the bandwidth for which the antenna system provides a 2:1 SWR or lower. (See SWR in Section 5.3 and in the *HamRadioSchool.com Technician License Course*, Section 7.2.) However, many simple dipoles or verticals will not be well matched across all of a single wide band such as 10m, much less across multiple bands without an antenna tuner to provide matching impedance at the transceiver.

Some antennas are designed to be *wide band* antennas, usable across a very wide bandwidth of spectrum including more than one band. Other antennas are designed to use more complex designs or electrical techniques to achieve good impedance matches on multiple bands. As you may already suspect there are tradeoffs with wideband and multiband antennas, but the convenience of operating on multiple bands via a single feedline and a single antenna is a most desirable characteristic for which to trade!

Random Wire: One of the simplest multiband antennas is the *random wire*, and it's just what the name implies: A random length of wire erected or configured in any way feasible and compatible with the environmental constraints. For example, I have seen a random wire run all around the interior perimeter of an apartment near the ceiling, in and out of bedrooms and living area, and even one end draped off the balcony. The random wire can typically be used on several bands and it does not pretend to be resonant on any particular one of them. So, what's the catch? What are the tradeoffs?

> **Tradeoffs:** A random wire can be directly connected to the transmitter, but a significant impedance mismatch is likely. The random wire is not resonant and feedpoint impedance mismatch is almost guaranteed. So, a high quality antenna tuner is usually a *must.* Because of the unusual physical configuration that some random wire arrangements may assume, the lobes and nulls of the transmitting patterns are usually unpredictable and chaotic. **A major league disadvantage of the directly fed random wire antenna is that you may experience RF burns when touching metal objects in your station!** Unless you can affect a very good RF ground for the antenna it may induce significant RF currents in your shack that can give you a nasty bite. Still, if you just take what you get with lobes and nulls, if you can avoid the RF burn hazard, and if your antenna tuner can handle the impedance on a couple of bands or more, you can actually get some interesting and good performance with the random wire.

G9B01

Trap Antennas: A multiband antenna may be created using traps placed in the antenna elements. A trap is a simple parallel circuit placed in-line with a radiating element, as depicted in Figure 5.9. **The primary purpose of antenna traps is to permit multiband operation.** Notice that the trap antenna has radiating element segments between the two traps and additional segments outside of the two traps.

G9D04

The parallel circuits added into the antenna element are LC circuits. We will discuss LC circuits more in Chapter 6 *Hamtronics*, but you should recall from your Technician Class studies that an LC circuit has both inductance (L), usually from an inductor component, and capacitance (C), usually from a capacitor element. An LC circuit will *resonate* with an AC frequency, and the specific frequency of resonance is determined by the values of inductance and capacitance selected for the circuit. When in resonance the electrical energy is very efficiently traded back and forth between the inductor and capacitor in alternating cycles, with the inductor temporarily storing energy in a magnetic field and the capacitor storing it in an electric field.

High Band Function: When the traps are resonant they present very high impedance and do not allow current flow beyond them into the outer segments of the radiating element. In essence the traps become insulators when at resonance, electrically terminating the radiating element. With proper selection of L and C values, the trap may be made to resonate at the frequencies of a relatively high RF band for which the inner segment of the antenna is trimmed. For instance, the dipole length between the traps may be about 16 feet for 10 meter band operation (28 MHz) and the LC components would be selected for the trap to resonate at about 28 MHz.

Low Band Function: However, when AC frequencies much lower than the trap's resonant frequency are fed to the antenna the trap behaves differently. The trap is not resonant and no longer acts as an insulator. The capacitors will not pass the lower frequencies, but the inductors will, allowing the full length of the radiating element to be energized by the lower frequency. Fortunately, a lower frequency signal needs a longer radiating element to remain a half-wave antenna. So, if our example antenna were fed with a 20 meter band (14 MHz) signal, the traps allow the outer segments of the radiating element to be added to the antenna length and the overall antenna length is properly trimmed for 20m band operation.

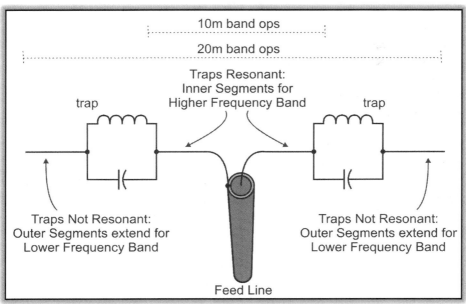

Figure 5.9: Trap dipole antenna configuration.

Voila! Two bands with one trap antenna! By including two traps on each side of the dipole an effective tri-band antenna for 10m, 15m, and 20m bands may be created. Three bands with one antenna! This seems like a terrific technique to use, right? So, what are the tradeoffs?

Tradeoffs: You should understand that the inductor in the trap has the effect of electrically lengthening the antenna. With the inductor the antenna will trim to a shorter length for the desired operating band than an antenna without a trap or other inductive *loading coil*. A physically shortened antenna will have somewhat reduced efficiency – it will not transmit as well as a physically full length antenna, and some receive signal loss will be imposed by the traps. Further, since the antenna is designed to operate on multiple bands it may also strongly radiate any undesirable, out of band harmonic frequencies produced by your station. Harmonics are frequency multiples of the fundamental, or desired frequency. For instance, transmissions in the 40m band (7 MHz) may produce 3rd harmonics on the 15m band (21 MHz), as the two bands' frequencies are harmonically related. If your multiband antenna is designed for both 15m and 40m bands, you might radiate harmonics on the 15m band inadvertently when transmitting a 40m band signal. Similar harmonic relationships exist among other bands as well. While most modern transceivers will have good harmonic filters to avoid this as a significant issue, **the multiband antenna has the disadvantage of poor harmonic rejection.**

G9D11

Fan Dipole: A popular multiband variation on the dipole is the *fan dipole* (also called multi-element or parallel wire dipole). A fan dipole has multiple half-wave dipoles of different lengths, each trimmed for operation on a different band and all fed from a single feedline as depicted in Figure 5.10. The various dipole wires are separated from one another using insulating spreaders or stand-offs. As compared to the trap dipole the fan dipole will usually be slightly more efficient. Fan dipoles are generally more easily constructed than the trap antenna, but it is tedious and sometimes impossible to trim all elements for a low SWR value due to the electrical interactions among the multiple parallel dipole elements. As a result, some bands may necessarily be operated with an SWR higher than others, and an antenna tuner is usually necessary. The interaction among elements can be reduced by placing some at right angles to others and also by placing some in a flattop configuration with others in an inverted V configuration. Fan dipoles of three or four separate half-wave dipoles are common. The fan dipole is often a good choice for a beginning HF antenna, offering the advantages of a single feedline, good multiband operation, and a low visual profile.

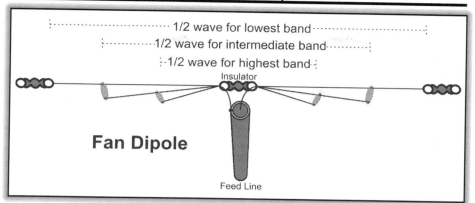

Figure 5.10: Typical fan dipole antenna configuration.

Beverage Antenna: Used only for receiving signals. **The Beverage antenna** (named for its inventor, Harold Beverage) **is a very long and low directional receiving antenna used across the lower HF bands** of 40m and below. **The Beverage** is a very inefficient radiator, **having high losses compared to other types of antennas, and so is not used for transmitting.**

Usually erected less than 20 feet above ground level, the Beverage is a long wire, usually between 1 and 4 wavelengths long, with a resistor terminating one end and the feedpoint on the opposite end. It receives directionally in the orientation of the terminated end and is excellent at noise rejection, hence its utility as a receiving antenna in spite of its poor efficiency or gain. This is a *traveling wave antenna,* meaning that it receives well only when the RF wave is aligned with the axis of the wire (the inverse of a dipole's broadside signal preference). Signals arriving from other directions do not create significant voltages on the wire and this reduces noise and reception in all but the direction of the wire's length. Because of its length and unique receiving dynamic it may be used across several low bands. Note that a one wavelength Beverage for the 160m band is over 500 feet long!

Mobile HF Antennas: In recent years amateur transceiver manufacturers have marketed very compact "all mode, all band" transceivers that make HF installation in vehicles relatively painless. One of the chief remaining challenges in taking the low frequencies on the road is the antenna. Because you can't readily mount a full length HF antenna on a vehicle, **the antenna system most limits the effectiveness of an HF mobile transceiver, particularly when operating on the low bands such as 75m**/80m or 160m band.

Again, antenna compromises are necessary. Shortened mobile antennas are very popular and use *loading techniques* to electrically lengthen the antenna in a manner similar to that described for trap antennas in this section. While loading works to achieve feed point impedance matching with very short antennas (relative to the operating wavelength), **one significant disadvantage of using a shortened mobile antenna as opposed to a full size antenna is that the operating bandwidth may be very limited.** The range of frequencies for which acceptable impedance match is achieved can be extremely narrow. But there are ways of getting around that common problem, too!

Loading Techniques: In order that a shortened antenna present an acceptable feedpoint impedance it must be made to resonate on the desired frequency using electrical methods. Inserting an inductive component in the antenna element is one method of making the antenna seem longer electrically than it is physically. Further, as with a simple tuned circuit, adding a capacitive element can further help achieve resonance of the antenna circuit.

Loading Coil: You have probably seen loading coils on mobile antennas before. A loading coil is a coil of wire or conductor connected in the antenna circuit and commonly positioned at the base of a vertical whip antenna or near the center of the antenna. Again, this inductor makes the antenna seem electrically longer so that resonance can be achieved in a desired frequency range much lower than that provided by the physical length of the antenna alone. Some single band antennas may utilize a loading coil wrapped around all or part of the antenna element and typically sealed onto the vertical with a coating or wrapper material.

Tapped Coil: A tapped coil is a loading coil that has a variable *tap point* along the coil that allows the inductance to be varied with operating frequency selected. This technique provides a method for the operator to change the resonant frequency of the antenna by adjusting the number of inductive turns or loops to be included in the antenna circuit. Even though any given adjustment provides a very narrow bandwidth with matching feed

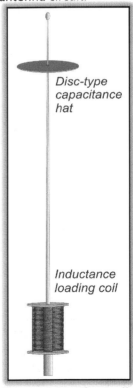

Disc-type capacitance hat

Inductance loading coil

Figure 5.11: Physically shortened antenna with loading coil and capacitance hat.

Photo: Paul, AAØK
Hi-Q-Antennas

Figure 5.12: A coil-loaded mobile antenna for the HF bands.

point impedance, the frequency of resonance may itself be readily varied by moving the tap point up or down along the coil to alter the affected inductance loading. In this way a broad band of frequencies may be used, bypassing the extremely narrow bandwidth limitation of the physically shortened antenna. The tapped coil is incorporated into many commercial HF mobile antenna designs, many of which use an SWR meter to help display and select the proper tap position for a chosen frequency of operation, and many implementing automatic tuning circuits to quickly achieve the proper tap position without manual adjustment. The popular "screwdriver" type of mobile antenna takes advantage of a slight variation on the tapped coil concept to tune across a broad bandwidth and operate on multiple bands.

Capacitance Hat: Typically used in concert with a loading coil, a **capacitance hat** helps to achieve resonant frequency with a shortened antenna. It is another **device to electrically lengthen a physically short antenna.** As noted in the trap antenna discussion, the inductance coil imposes signal loss when it is used to electrically lengthen an antenna. The more turns in a loading coil the greater the loss. By adding a capacitive element to the antenna (the capacitance hat), resonance can be achieved with fewer inductive turns and with less signal loss. A capacitance hat will usually take the form of a solid disc or a wheel with spokes placed about the vertical antenna element above the loading coil section. The larger the hat, the greater the capacitance, and the less number of inductive turns required to achieve resonance on a selected operating frequency.

Corona: As a mobile antenna moves through the airstream it develops static charge due to dust, moisture, and other statically charged particles in the air.

G4E01

Like the voltages that build up on the ends of the antenna due to RF energy, the static charge builds at the tip of a mobile vertical antenna. When the

charge reaches severe voltage levels it can discharge to a ground level voltage like a little bolt of lightning! This *coronal discharge* can be dangerous and the build up of static will deteriorate your antenna's receive performance, inducing static noise on the audio. A common means of reducing these effects is to broaden the tip of the antenna so that the charge is spread out over a larger surface area, thereby alleviating a very high voltage pinpoint charge and reducing the chance of

Figure 5.13: Corona "balls" come in many forms, usually a simple broadened antenna tip.

coronal discharge. **A corona ball on an HF antenna will reduce the high voltage discharge from the tip of the antenna.** Most corona balls are simple teardrop or spherical add-ons to expand the antenna tip surface area.

Zap! Mental corona! You now have covered the fundamentals of HF antenna theory, and I can see the little lightning bolts bouncing around inside your head ready to put theory into practice. But we're not done yet. There are more electrifying concepts coming up regarding *directional antennas* that will point most of your radiated signal in one direction. That has some operational advantages! First, trap the questions for this section inside your mind.

HamRadioSchool.com/general_media

5.2 Directional Antennas

Antennas

❝ *Beam me up Scotty!*
– James Tiberius Kirk
(a.k.a. William Shatner)

"Captain, we're receiving strong starboard interference! And now from port, too! And aft!"

"Shields up! Arm photon torpedoes! Phasers at the ready! Rotate the directional antenna and beam a concentrated RF signal to zero mark two seven zero. Transmit at will! Now! Push to talk!"

Yea, that'll show those pesky interfering Klingon stations. We'll just directionalize our signal.

There's no need to get up in arms over a little RF interference on a busy HF band, and if your station is equipped with a directional, or "beam," antenna, you can help minimize interference by aiming the bulk of your signal energy in a preferred direction. That way your signal will be strongest for only those stations in the preferred direction, and you'll receive signals most strongly from that direction, too. Those port, starboard, and aft interfering stations will fade into insignificance and you won't interfere with their communications either. It's almost like having a station cloaking device!

No question about it, Captain: Directional antennas can reduce tensions, avoid interference, improve your station's communications, and generally help promote peace and harmony across the Ham Galaxy. It's time to get your station beamed up.

In this section we will examine beam antennas with a laser focus on the very popular Yagi (Uda-Yagi) design. We'll also note two types of directionals based upon loop antennas, the quad and delta loops, and wrap up with a look at the log periodic wide band directional.

Uda-Yagi Antenna: Although originally designed by two Japanese inventors, Shintaro Uda and Hidetsugu Yagi, this antenna is popularly known as simply a

Figure 5.14: A three element Yagi antenna for HF bands.

Yagi. The Yagi is simple to construct, it provides ample gain or directionality, and it is therefore the most popular directional antenna for hams.

Yagi Structure and Radiation: The Yagi is based on the half-wave dipole. The radiating element (*driven element*) is a dipole arrangement, but other parallel elements are added to it and all mounted along a boom to hold the elements in proper configuration. Figure 5.15 illustrates three typical arrangements of simple Yagi designs, but many others are feasible with different numbers and spacings of elements. As with the half-wave dipole, **the length of the driven element of a Yagi antenna will be approximately ½ wavelength.**

G9C02

The additional elements that are not connected to the feedline are called *parasitic elements*. The two types of parasitic elements are *reflectors* and *directors*. When the driven element radiates RF, a nearby parasitic element will receive part of the energy, inducing a current flow in the element. The current flow then produces RF re-radiation of the energy from the parasitic element. The re-radiated RF signal will interact with the signal from the driven element, with waveforms reinforcing or cancelling one another in a similar manner as the ground reflections discussed in Section 5.1 that produce lobes and nulls. With clever arrangement of the parasitic elements relative to the driven element, a radiating pattern can be generated that produces a single large lobe of great signal strength – a directional signal propagation pattern. **The direction of maximum radiated field strength from a directive antenna is called the *main lobe.*** Generally, the main lobe will be more directional and the antenna will exhibit more gain with additional elements on a longer boom, as depicted in Figure 5.15.

G9C08

Reflector: A Yagi will usually have a single reflector parasitic element positioned on the boom in the direction opposite the main lobe. The simplest Yagi design consists of just two elements, the driven element and a reflector element, as in the left side of Figure 5.15. The reflector will be approximately 5% longer than the driven element and positioned about 0.15 to 0.20 wavelength aft of the driven element. When the reflector element re-radiates its RF energy the waveforms in the direction of the main lobe (forward) will be in phase and reinforce one another, while the waveforms in the opposite (rearward) direction will be out of phase and cancel one another. In this way a main lobe of signal strength is created in the forward direction. **A ratio comparison of the power radiated in the major radiation lobe with the power radiated in exactly the opposite direction is called the "front-to-back ratio" of the Yagi.** A simple two-element Yagi provides gain in the main lobe direction of about 5 dBi (comparison with isotropic pattern), or about 3 dBd (comparison with a dipole). Adding more reflectors does not significantly improve the main lobe strength or front-to-back ratio.

G9C07

Director: In a three element Yagi (center of Figure 5.15) the parasitic element on the boom forward of the driven element is called the director. The director will be approximately 5% shorter than the driven element, and this shortening helps to shift the re-radiated signal's phase slightly so that it further reinforces forward propagation and boosts main lobe strength. **In a simple three-element, single band Yagi the director is normally the shortest parasitic element (and the reflector is normally the longest element).** The inclusion of a director increases the front-to-back ratio and main lobe gain. The approximate theoretical forward gain of a three-element, single band Yagi antenna is 9.7 dBi. A Yagi may have multiple directors to increase the antenna's gain further, as illustrated in the right side of Figure 5.15.

G9C03 G9C04

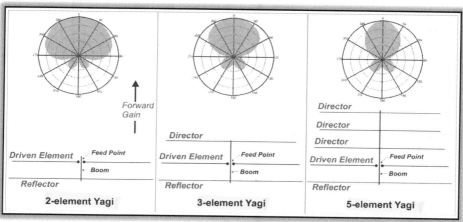

Figure 5.15: Three different Yagi antenna designs and approximate main lobe effects. *(Yagi dimensions not to scale.)*

Yagi Enhancements: The basic Yagi designs described above can be modified to provide enhancements in gain and bandwidth. Some general principles for modification and enhancement include the following:

- **Adding directors (the number of elements on the boom) increases gain and front-to-back ratio.**

- **The spacing of elements along the boom influences gain, front-to-back ratio, and SWR bandwidth.**

- **Increasing boom length (with added directors) increases gain.**

- **Larger diameter elements increase the bandwidth**

- **Vertical stacking of horizontally polarized Yagis narrows the main lobe in elevation pattern, increasing gain**

Stacked Yagis placed approximately ½ wavelength apart vertically reinforces signals in the horizontal (azimuthal) plane while canceling or nulling signals vertically. The net effect is to narrow the elevation pattern as compared to a single Yagi and improve forward gain. **Two 3-element horizontally polarized Yagi antennas spaced vertically ½ wavelength apart typically increase gain over a single 3-element Yagi by approximately 3 dB.**

Yagi Impedance Matching: The feedpoint impedance of a typical Yagi design is usually much lower than the 50 Ω value to match most common coaxial feedlines. The parasitic elements of the Yagi influence the voltage and current of the driven element dipole and alter the impedance value of the feedpoint. Yagi impedance values under 25 Ω are common and will result in undesirable SWR values of 2:1 or greater. Usually some type of impedance matching technique is required for the Yagi to get a matching impedance closer to 50 Ω.

While multiple techniques are feasible, **the gamma match is very common on Yagis for the purpose of matching the relatively low feedpoint impedance to 50 Ω.** As depicted in Figure 5.16, the gamma match extends a short, *unshielded* section of the feedline. The ground side or shield of the coaxial feedline extends to the driven element center point. The conductive center wire of the coaxial feedline is routed parallel to the driven element, and electrical interaction between the driven element and the unshielded parallel feedline increases the feedpoint impedance closer to 50 Ω.

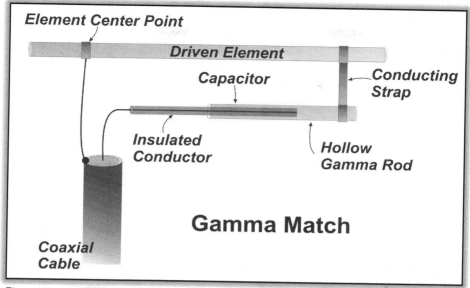

Figure 5.16: The gamma match uses a parallel capacitive element to achieve a near-50 Ω impedance match.

However, this arrangement also creates *inductive reactance,* causing an un-desirable shift in the phase relationship of voltage and current, as compared to the simple dipole case described in Section 5.1. To offset this phase shift a capacitor is inserted into the conductive parallel feedline to create *capacitive reactance.* As noted in Chapter Ø *Before We Begin,* and as we will discuss more in Chapter 6, these two types of reactance counter one another, shifting the phases of current and voltage with opposite effect. The capacitor effectively nulls out the phase shifting of the inductive feedline element, but the antenna's feedpoint impedance remains elevated at the matching value near 50 Ω.

The capacitive element may be implemented either by inserting a capacitor into the unshielded parallel feedline section or by insulating the feedline conductor from direct contact and inserting it into a metal tube that is a portion of the parallel feedline section (Figure 5.16). The metal tube is supported by a conductive *shorting strap* attached to the driven element. This arrangement effectively creates a linearly oriented capacitor (capacitance between center conductor wire and metal tube) that may be adjusted in capacitance value by adjusting the length of center wire and tube overlap. In practice the shorting strap position and capacitor value are adjusted until the lowest SWR is achieved, indicating closely matching feedpoint impedance. These two adjustments will interact, and getting things just right can be a delicate trial and error operation that requires some patience!

G9C12 **A further advantage of using a gamma match for impedance matching of a Yagi antenna to 50 Ω coax feed line is that this technique does not require that the elements be insulated from the boom,** assuming the boom is itself conductive. Non-conductive boom material is used with some Yagi designs, but aluminum or other conductive metal is more common. The gamma match allows the antenna elements to be mounted without concern of insulating the driven element from the boom. This can simplify the Yagi design and fabrication substantially!

Yagi Design Considerations: The design of Yagi antennas blends science and art. The spacing, number, and sizing of elements for desired performance, combined with impedance matching techniques and intended implementation can make design and execution challenging. Software packages are commercially available to aid with custom designing, but even with computer-aided design the implementation of impedance matching with a gamma match or other popular techniques can be tedious. Many proven Yagi designs are available from online and printed sources, and these are probably the best way for the beginner Yagi home-brewer to start.

And the payoff for a job well done is enormous! As alluded to in this section's spacey introduction, the Yagi is often used for radio communications on crowded bands like the 20 meter band because it helps reduce interference from other stations to the side or behind the antenna. Any directional can do the same, but the Yagi is simple elegance that many hams appreciate.

The Quad Antenna: A quad is a directional antenna constructed very similarly to a Yagi except that the elements are square loops of about one wavelength instead of linear ½-wavelength elements. Example quad antenna arrangements are depicted in Figure 5.17. The quad functions on the same principles as the Yagi, with driven element waveform reinforcement and cancellation by re-radiated emissions from the parasitic elements.

G9C13 G9C15 G9C06 G9C14 Since elements are approximately one wavelength long, **each side of the quad antenna driven element is approximately ¼ wavelength.** Like the Yagi, the reflector element is longer than the driven element, so **each side of the quad antenna reflector element is slightly more than ¼ wavelength. The configuration of the loops of a two-element quad antenna (a driven element and a reflector) operating as a beam antenna must have a reflector element approximately 5% longer than the driven element. The forward gain of a two-element quad antenna will be about the same as a three-element Yagi antenna.**

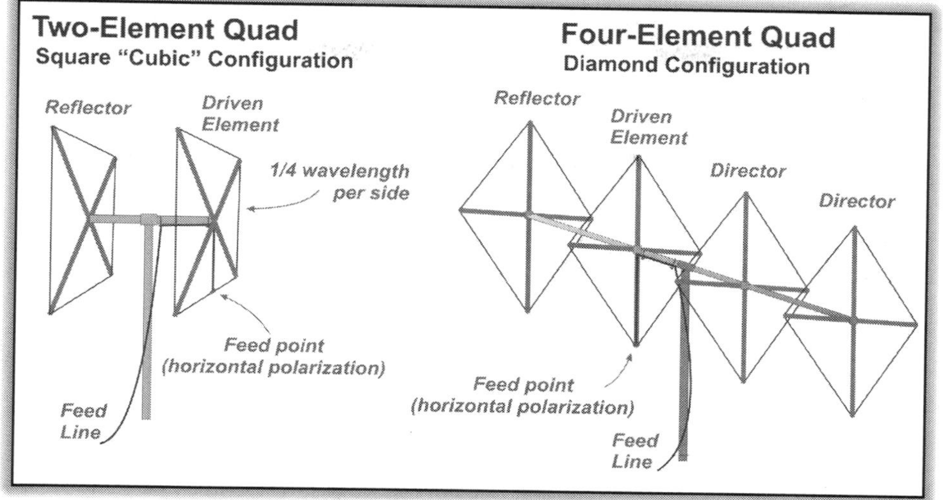

Figure 5.17: Example quad configurations.

So, although somewhat more difficult to construct than a typical Yagi, the quad offers improved gain with fewer elements.

The quad may be erected as a "square" or as a "diamond," as in Figure 5.17. Interestingly, the polarization is determined by the feedpoint selection. The polarization is summed up as follows:

	Square Config	Diamond Config
Horizontally Polarized	Bottom center feedpoint Top center feedpoint	Bottom corner feedpoint Top corner feedpoint
Vertically Polarized	Either side center feedpoint	Either side corner feedpoint

Examples: For a square configuration, **if the feedpoint of a quad antenna is changed from the midpoint of the top or bottom to the midpoint of either side, the polarization of the radiated signal changes from horizontal to vertical.** For a diamond configuration, if the feedpoint is changed from a side corner to the bottom corner, the signal polarization changes from vertical to horizontal.

The Delta Loop Antenna: Another beam antenna based upon one wavelength loop elements is the multi-element delta loop. The concept is nearly identical to the quad antenna except that each element loop is formed as a triangle instead of as a square. **Each leg of a symmetrical delta loop antenna will be approximately 1/3 wavelength. The gain of a two-element delta loop is about the same as a two-element quad.**

G9C18

G9C17 G9C16

A common configuration for the delta loop is to have one corner at the bottom and one side of the triangular element shape across the top horizontally. Feeding the loop at the bottom corner provides horizontal polarization. If instead the triangle element is oriented with a horizontal bottom side and an apex up, vertical polarization is affected with a bottom corner feedpoint. Other side feedpoints may also be used, and impedance matching techniques such as a gamma match may be required in some cases. As with the Yagi, a proven design and assistance for the new beam antenna home brewer is recommended!

Be aware also that loop antennas as single elements – just the driven element – may be used as a more omnidirectional radiator similar to the dipole. Quad loops or delta loops without parasitic elements are very effective and tend to offer somewhat better noise rejection than other single element designs.

Log Periodic Antenna: The log periodic antenna (Figure 5.18) has a general appearance much like a multi-element Yagi, but its characteristic design details and performance are significantly different. The log periodic's boom-mounted array of dipole elements will provide moderate directionality (signal gain), but not as much as the Yagi. Rather, **the primary advantage of the log periodic antenna is wide bandwidth.** It may operate over several bands while maintaining low SWR values on each band.

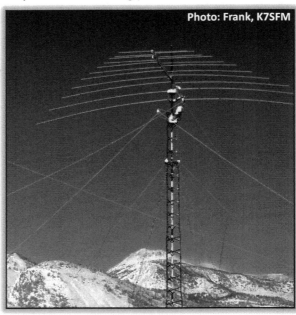

Photo: Frank, K7SFM

Figure 5.18: A log periodic antenna for HF bands.

The log periodic will typically array multiple half-wave dipole elements together along a boom in a unique pattern. **The length and spacing of log periodic elements increases logarithmically from one end of the boom to the other,** as depicted in Figure 5.19. Elements on each side of the boom are fed alternatively by

G9D06

G9D07

the electrically opposite sides of the feedline. The result of this unique arrangement is that different elements along the boom are *activated* to become the radiating elements as the feeding frequency changes. Lower frequencies are radiated by

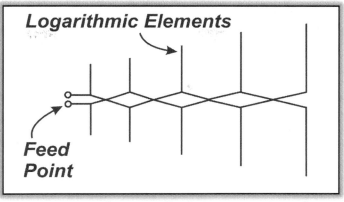

Figure 5.19: The log periodic design is an array of dipoles with alternating feed polarity.

the longer elements and higher frequencies by the shorter elements. The log periodic is another good option for multi-band performance from a single antenna-feedline system, although its mechanical and mounting requirements are substantially more demanding than those associated with the horizontal wire multi-band antennas discussed in Section 5.1.

You'll encounter even more varieties of directional antennas, but the Yagi, the quad, the multi-element delta loop, and the wide band log periodic are four of the most common in amateur radio. Many hams enjoy the challenge and reward of fabricating their own antennas. Give it a try! You'll learn even more and perhaps open up an entirely new hobby enterprise to enjoy.

Captain: "Status report, Technician?"

Technician: "All hands beamed up, Captain. Ready for questions."

Captain: "Very good, Technician. You're well on your way to a promotion to General!"

HamRadioSchool.com/general_media

Waterton Amateur Radio Society, NØLM

5.3	Antennas SWR & Impedance Matching

> **"**
> *... what we are concerned with here is the fundamental interconnectedness of all things.*
> *— Dirk Gently*

While he may have been just another offbeat character from the depths of Douglas Adams' warped sense of humor, Detective Gently's words apply equally well to ham radio antenna systems as to his uncommon investigations. Indeed, from the transceiver to coaxial feedline to cable connectors to characteristic impedances to reflected power to standing wave ratios... All these things are bound together, affecting one another. All fundamentally interconnected. Let's see how.

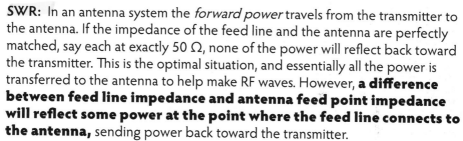

SWR: In an antenna system the *forward power* travels from the transmitter to the antenna. If the impedance of the feed line and the antenna are perfectly matched, say each at exactly 50 Ω, none of the power will reflect back toward the transmitter. This is the optimal situation, and essentially all the power is transferred to the antenna to help make RF waves. However, **a difference between feed line impedance and antenna feed point impedance will reflect some power at the point where the feed line connects to the antenna,** sending power back toward the transmitter.

The signal waveforms of *reflected power* will superimpose with the waveforms of forward power in the feed line as the waveforms travel in opposite directions. The superimposition of the oppositely traveling waves of equal wavelength set up a *standing wave* in the feed line, as depicted in Figure 5.20. As the oppositely traveling waveforms' amplitudes combine, the resulting summation waveform seems to remain stationary, unmoving, but with amplitude rising and falling in place due to the cycle of variably reinforcing and nulling combining waves.

Typically, the power (amplitude) of the forward traveling wave is greater than the power of the reflected wave. The peaks of the standing wave will rise and fall between two extreme conditions: 1) the two traveling waves will constructively superimpose, adding together their momentarily in-phase waveforms to produce a high peak amplitude, and 2) the two traveling waves will be exactly

G9A04

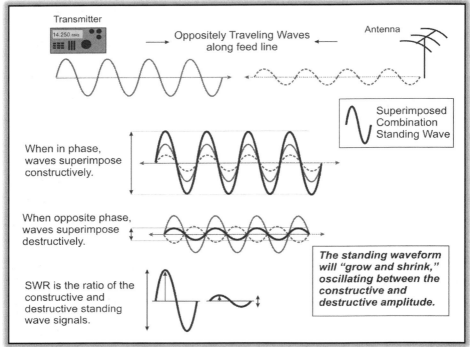

Figure 5.20: Standing waves result from the constructive and destructive superimposition of oppositely traveling waves of equal frequency, as in a feed line. SWR is the simple ratio of the maximum and minimum standing wave voltage amplitudes as the waves interact in passing.

out-of-phase, superimposing destructively to produce a momentary low peak amplitude.

SWR is the ratio of these two alternating standing wave voltage peaks, hence the name standing wave ratio. SWR can be computed from a measure of the power in each direction in the feed line, like this:

$$SWR = \frac{\sqrt{Fwd\ Pwr} + \sqrt{Refl\ Pwr}}{\sqrt{Fwd\ Pwr} - \sqrt{Refl\ Pwr}}$$

Measuring SWR: An *SWR meter* placed in the feed line will measure the signal in each direction simultaneously and display the computed SWR as a digital value or, more commonly, via a scale on which SWR values are read at the position where two indicator needles cross – one needle is driven by the forward power and the other by the reflected power, with crossing position indicating SWR. A cross-needle SWR meter is depicted in Figure 5.0c on page 128. These types of meters most often measure feed line *voltages* in each direction and derive SWR from the comparative values. Alternatively, **standing wave ratio may be determined with a directional wattmeter,** measuring the forward and reflected power separately and then manually calculating with the preceding formula. With each of these instruments the antenna system must be connected to a transmitter to provide power for measurement.

An *antenna analyzer* provides its own signals for measurement, eliminating the need to connect the antenna system to a transmitter. Rather, **the antenna and feed line must be connected to the antenna analyzer when it is being used for SWR measurement.** An antenna analyzer will generate signal frequencies of known power, measure the reflected power, and then compute and display the SWR value. Most popular analyzers provide user controls for selecting the desired frequency band and for "dialing through frequencies." The SWR may be observed on a display as the bands and specific frequencies are changed. Some newer analyzers generate a rapid sequence of signals across a frequency band, storing a whole set of measures and displaying the graphical function of SWR by frequency ("SWR curve") on an LCD display.

Figure 5.21: Antenna analyzer examining 20m band SWR.

Strong signals from nearby transmitters can affect the accuracy of measurements made on an antenna system with an antenna analyzer, so some caution should be taken to avoid this problem. [Note: **Other than measuring the SWR of an antenna system, an antenna analyzer may also be used to determine the impedance of an unknown or unmarked coaxial cable.**]

Impedance Ratios and SWR: The SWR of an antenna system will also be equivalent to the ratio of the impedance mismatch between feed line and antenna feed point. For example, **the connection of a 50 Ω feed line to a**

non-reactive load (antenna feed point) **having a 50 Ω impedance will result in an SWR of 1:1** (50 Ω ÷ 50 Ω = 1/1). **The SWR resulting from feeding a vertical antenna with a 25 Ω feed point impedance with a 50 Ω coaxial cable will be 2:1** (50 Ω ÷ 25 Ω = 2/1). **A 50 Ω coaxial cable feeding an antenna with a 300 Ω feed point impedance will result in an SWR of 6:1** (300 Ω ÷ 50 Ω = 6/1). Notice that regardless of the orientation of the impedance mismatch – high coax with low feed point, or low coax with high feed point – the SWR ratio is always expressed as a ratio greater than or equal to one (i.e. 3:1, never 1:3). Further, since SWR is always a ratio comparing with unity (1), many hams will drop the ratio terminology and simply state the SWR as the higher number in the ratio – "The SWR is 2.5."

Additional question pool items on this topic are:

50 Ω feed line and 200 Ω non-reactive load = 200/50 = 4/1 or 4:1 SWR

50 Ω feedline and 10 Ω non-reactive load = 50/10 = 5/1 or 5:1 SWR

Common Feedlines: **To prevent standing waves on an antenna feed line the antenna feed point impedance must be matched to the characteristic impedance of the feed line.** Let's take a look at the two most common feedline types and their characteristics to which we must match:

Coaxial Cable: "Coax" [kō' aks] is used more often than any other feed line for amateur radio antenna systems because it is easy to use and requires few special installation considerations. **The typical characteristic impedances of coaxial cables used for antenna feed lines at amateur stations are 50 and 75 ohms.** The characteristic impedance of coax is determined primarily by the diameters of the center conductor and the surrounding shield, as well as the type of insulating dielectric material that separates the two.

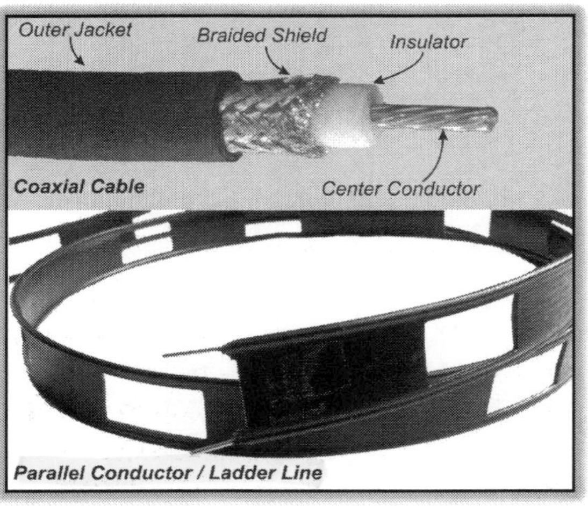

Figure 5.22: Typical coaxial cable and parallel conductor feedline.

Coaxial cable will impose some loss, or *attenuation,* of signal power over its length. **Feed line losses are usually expressed in decibels per 100 feet. The attenuation of coaxial cable increases as the frequency of the signal it is carrying increases.** Hence, coaxial feed line losses are generally low on the HF bands but may become quite significant into the UHF range, especially for long runs of 100 feet or more. Some typical loss values are summarized in the following table, depicting the greater loss with higher frequency in each type.

Cable Type	Frequency (MHz)	Loss (dB / 100 ft.)
RG-8/U	50	1.2
	100	1.7
	200	2.6
	400	3.9
RG-58/U	50	2.5
	100	3.8
	200	5.6
	400	8.4
RG-8/U Low Loss	50	0.9
	100	1.3
	200	1.8
	400	2.7
Twin Lead / Ladder	50	0.7
	100	1.1
	200	1.6
	400	2.5

SWR and Loss: Consider that a feedline imposes signal loss as the signal travels along a length of the feedline. With high SWR a significant portion of the signal will be reflected back-and-forth through the feedline, effectively increasing the length of feedline through which it travels. Thus, **if a transmission line is lossy, high SWR will increase the loss.** Additionally, **the higher the transmission line loss, the more SWR measured at the input to the line will read artificially low.** This is because signal reflections traveling back down the feedline from the antenna will be attenuated over the double-length of the lossy feedline.

Parallel Conductor, TV Twinlead, and Ladder Line: These types of feed lines have the advantage of lower loss than coax, and they are used by amateurs in many situations where feed line shielding is unnecessary or undesirable for the operation of the antenna. **Flat ribbon TV type twinlead has a characteristic impedance of 300 Ω,** while other parallel conductor feed lines have impedances of 300, 450, or 600 Ω. These are also called *ladder line, window line,* or *open wire* feed lines. **The characteristic impedance of a parallel conductor antenna feed line is determined by the distance between the centers of the conductors and the radius of the conductors.** Parallel conductors often exhibit very low signal loss values, and they are excellent feedlines for some antenna types and scenarios.

Impedance Matching: As discussed in Sections 5.1 and 5.2, achieving an antenna feed point impedance to match the feed line as closely as possible will result in reduced power reflections and greater power transfer to the antenna. A close natural match is achieved with some systems such as a 50 Ω coaxial feed line coupled with a vertical antenna with downward sloping radials. The implementation of matching techniques like the gamma match described in Section 5.2 with Yagi antennas also help achieve antenna feed point match to the feed line impedance. Trimming antenna length can also impact the match.

Trimming: Dipoles and other antennas may be trimmed in length to obtain closely matching feedpoint impedance as indicated by the measured SWR curve. A common antenna metric is the bandwidth with SWR of 2:1 or less, as depicted in Figure 5.23. The SWR curve, and hence the 2:1 SWR band, may be moved to a higher frequency range by shortening the antenna or moved to a lower frequency range by lengthening the antenna.

Q Factor: Notice that the SWR curves of Figure 5.23 do not indicate 2:1 SWR or less across the entire 20m band from 14.000 to 14.350 MHz. This is a common scenario with many antennas, particularly physically shortened, loaded antennas as described in Section 5.1. This operating bandwidth of an antenna is called the *quality factor,* or "Q." High Q antennas have narrow SWR bandwidth, such as the physically shortened, loaded case. Wide SWR bandwidth antennas, such as a full sized dipole, are *low Q* antennas.

Most modern transceivers will begin to reduce transmit power when SWR exceeds 2:1. While trimming the antenna length can move the 2:1 band higher or lower as preferred, this is not an activity you'll want to undertake every time you wish to dial to another portion of the band! An *antenna tuner* or *coupler* can help with this scenario.

Antenna Coupler or Tuner: **An antenna coupler is a device often used to enable matching the transmitter output to an impedance other than 50 Ω. Also known as a *tuner*,** *impedance matcher,* or *transmatch,* antenna couplers use circuits or networks of adjustable value capacitors and inductors to present a 50 Ω impedance to the transmitter while maintaining the coupling to the antenna system, no matter its characteristic impedance (within extreme limits). The device is placed between the transceiver and feed line to affect this coupling. Higher quality couplers will be able to handle larger impedance mismatches, while others may match only up to a limited SWR value of perhaps 3:1 or 4:1.

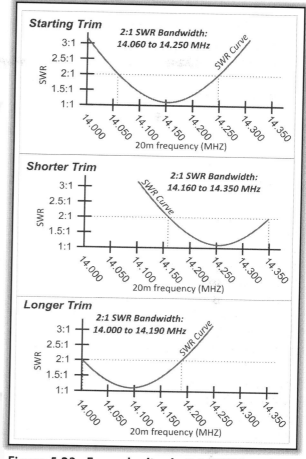

G4A06

Figure 5.23: Example dipole 2:1 SWR bandwidth and trimming effects.

However, just because the transceiver "sees" 50 Ω from the antenna tuner does not mean that the antenna system characteristics have changed! Only the matching impedance at the transceiver has been altered – *an antenna tuner does not actually tune the antenna!* So, **if the SWR on an antenna feed line is 5:1 and a matching network at the transmitter end of the feed line is adjusted to 1:1 SWR, the feed line SWR will remain 5:1.** That means that you will still get reflections back toward the transmitter and the power transfer to the antenna will not be optimal. So, what's the point in doing it? A couple of fine points…

G9A08

First, remember that most modern transmitters are designed to begin reducing transmit power at a detected SWR of 2:1. As the SWR increases the transmitter power decreases. This is done to avoid any chance of harming transmitter circuits with high power reflections. So, with the poor impedance match you get the reflections and the imposed loss in the feed line plus the double-whammy of your transmitter reducing output power! Rats!

But the antenna coupler and its nicely presented 50 Ω impedance comes to the rescue and avoids the power shutdown! The transmitter knows no difference, seeing only the desired matching 50 Ω impedance from the tuner, so it does not power down. Further, the coupler will handle those nasty power reflections and not allow them through to the transmitter.

Secondly, even when you have a mismatched impedance you can have a very usable antenna system. Even with a poor match some of the power is going to be transferred to the antenna and get your signal out. Yes, there will be reflected power and it will essentially bounce to the antenna coupler and then back again to the antenna. On this second trip a portion of it will be transferred to the antenna and a portion reflected yet again. Repeat, repeat, repeat. Granted, each time a reflection travels back down the feed line and up again to the antenna it will be subjected to feed line loss and diminished somewhat in strength. But quite a lot of the power will ultimately be transferred to the antenna, albeit in perhaps several back-and-forth reflection cycles before the signal is completely diminished. The upshot is that even with a significant impedance mismatch you can radiate and communicate, even if not with optimal efficiency, and the antenna coupler keeps your power up and your transmitter happy!

Feed Line Components: Transceivers and feed line cables and couplers and antenna feed points are not the end of the story! You should probably now realize that anything placed in the antenna system has the potential to cause power reflections and drive up SWR. That includes things like moisture (a common coaxial cable problem!), a power amplifier, or an in-line filter. Any intentional component of a feed line should have matching impedance to avoid reflections. For instance, **as**

Figure 5.24: Common amateur radio connector types.

compared to the impedance of the transmission line into which it is inserted, the impedance of a low-pass filter should be about the same as the transmission line. That goes for any component in a feed line or antenna system through which the transmission signals must pass.

Coaxial Connectors: Connectors, too, have characteristics that can impose losses or reflections. While the loss values for most common connectors at HF frequencies is not significant, a poorly attached or faulty connector can create reflections and cause SWR values to go up or to be erratic.

- **N-Connector: Moisture resistant RF connector useful up to 10 GHz.**
- **PL-259 (and SO-239) Connector: Commonly used for RF service up to 150 MHz.**
- **SMA Connector: Small, threaded connector suitable for signals up to several GHz.**

Most transceivers will use the PL-259/SO-239 connector. An HF station antenna system will typically use the PL-259/SO-239 connectors throughout the feed line, soldered solidly onto coaxial cable, or directly welded connections of parallel line to an antenna feed point component or line adapter. Many amateurs prefer to use N-Connectors throughout a coaxial feed line in lieu of the PL-259/SO-239. In either case, make certain that your connectors are protected from moisture if they are exposed to the elements, and make sure your solder welds are solid to avoid SWR problems.

Yep, make sure that *all your things are interconnected…* all bound together, as Dirk suggested, and do it in an effective way. Now you have some idea of how your antenna system's performance is measured and how many different characteristics and components must bind together in a harmonious, fundamental interconnectedness to effectively connect you with the amateur world…

Wow. It's the circle of antenna systems.

OK, don't get too deep. The questions….
Just hit the online questions. *HamRadioSchool.com/general_media*

6.0   Hamtronics

> **" I am an expert of electricity. My father occupied the chair of applied electricity at the state prison.**   *– W. C. Fields*

You don't have to be an expert in electricity to be an amateur radio operator. You also don't want to accidentally experience what it was like to hold the honorable position of Mr. Fields' father! So, let's acquire enough expertise in electrical principles and electronics to set up an advanced ham station and to do it very safely.

This chapter has nine sections, and that should provide an indication of how important electrical concepts are to ham radio. At least, that provides insight into how many exam pool questions are related to hamtronics.

- We'll start our electrifying discussion with fundamental principles of electricity and of electrical power in 6.1.
- In 6.2 we will examine many electronic components and their functions in electric circuits.
- Section 6.3 introduces combinations of multiple components in series and parallel circuit arrangements and how to compute equivalent single components.
- Impedance and reactance in electric circuits is covered in 6.4, with practical application to power transfer to loads like antennas.
- Sources of power are discussed in 6.5, and we will learn the details of how an AC power supply works.
- Section 6.6 is all about vacuum tube amplifiers and how to safely operate them.
- Integrated circuits and computers go well with ham radio, especially with digital operating modes, and we'll explore this connection in 6.7.
- Electrical measurements are critical to ensuring your station's proper operations, and this topic is covered in 6.8.
- Finally, Section 6.9 considers issues of radio interference and how to resolve them using simple electrical techniques.

It's a big chapter, so let's waste no more time... Have a chair and apply yourself to electricity.

6.1 Hamtronics
Power and Principles

    The measure of a man is what he does with power.
            — Plato

How will you measure up? What will you do with power? Most likely you'll radiate your message to the world, and maybe even include a few words from Plato. He would likely be rather amazed at what a ham radio operator can do with merely a few watts of power.

Since electrical power is fundamental to radio operations – in transceiver electrical circuits and RF emissions – it is prudent for the General Class license holder to have a more advanced understanding of the principles by which power is applied and controlled. You'll need your middle school math skills, so grab your calculator and let's see what we can do with power.

Ohm's Law Reprised: Unlike the Technician Class exam pool there is not a single question in the General Class pool directly derived from Ohm's Law. However, it will help us to relate to some newly introduced power principles, so let's review Mr. Ohm's insight. [You may want to review the Technician Class introduction to Ohm's Law and Power Law in the *HamRadioSchool.com Technician License Course*, Section 8.2.] First, the quantities represented within Ohm's Law:

     E: Electromotive Force (EMF) in units of volts
     I: Current in units of amperes, or amps
     R: Resistance in units of ohms

     Ohm's Law: $E = I \times R$

     Also: $I = E/R$ and $R = E/I$

The triangle representation of Ohm's Law helps to keep these relationships easily in mind. Cover the quantity you wish to find and the relationship of the other two defines the calculation to be made – the side-by-side remaining quantities are to be multiplied together, while top-over-bottom remaining quantities are to be divided. For example, to find E (cover E) you multiply I x R. Or to find I (cover I) you divide E÷R.

Power Law: Power Law also embodies a simple relationship among quantities:

P: Power in units of watts
E: Electromotive Force (EMF) in units of volts
I: Current in units of amperes, or amps

Power Law: P = E x I

Also: E = P/I and I = P/E

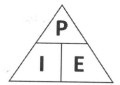

In an identical manner to the Ohm's Law triangle, the power law triangle can help you keep straight this simple relationship. Again, cover the quantity you seek to compute and the remaining two quantities will either multiply (side-by-side) or divide (top-over-bottom).

Example: **How many watts of electrical power are used by a 12 VDC light bulb that draws 0.2 amperes?**

P = E x I = 12 volts x 0.2 amps = **2.4 watts**

Power and Resistance: Now let's combine Ohm's Law and the Power Law to forge a new equation that broadens our computational repertoire. Since by Ohm's Law E = I x R, and also I = E/R, we can substitute the right side definition of both E and I from these equations into the Power Law equation, like this:

P = E x I
E = I x R
I = E/R

Thus,

P = (I x R) x (E/R), and substituting again for E
P = (I x R) x (I x R)/R, simplifying to
$P = I^2 \times R$

Example: A resister opposes the flow of current in a circuit, and it dissipates power as heat when a current flows through it. How much power? Let's use $P = I^2 \times R$ and find out:

7.0 milliamperes flowing through 1.25 kilohms resistance?

First let's convert to standard measures of amps and ohms:

0.007 amps flowing through 1250 ohms resistance...

Now we'll calculate with our derived equation:

$P = I^2 \times R$ = $(0.007 \text{ amps})^2 \times 1250 \text{ ohms}$ = **0.06125 watts,**
or about **61 milliwatts**

Power and EMF: With a little more algebraic wizardry we can derive another relationship for power that uses EMF, or voltage. Beginning with the basic Power Law once again:

$P = E \times I$; and $I = E/R$, thus
$P = E \times (E/R)$, or
$P = E^2 / R$

Example: An appliance, like a light bulb, a fan, or a radiating antenna is called a load on the circuit. Loads offer resistance, much like a resistor. A load may convert electrical power into work. How much power does it convert? Let's use $P = E^2/R$ to find out:

400 VDC supplied to an 800 ohm load

We are already in the standard units of volts and ohms, with no pesky math prefixes attached this time. So...

$P = E^2/R$ = $(400 \text{ volts})^2 \div 800 \text{ ohms}$ = **200 watts**

Pretty simple, huh? Just be sure to keep these three formulas in mind for the exam, or better yet be sure you can derive them as we've done here. And be sure to bring a calculator. OK, let's take it up a notch now.

Decibels (dB): The Technician Class materials provided a solid foundation on decibels, the logarithmic unit of measure used to compare two power values. Remember, the decibel is not a conventional unit of measure, but rather a tool for relative comparisons. Because power can vary over such a broad range, the logarithmic scale makes comparisons a little easier to handle than giant, multi-digit numbers that would be necessary otherwise. You should recall a couple of easy shortcuts when using decibels:

A two-times (2X) increase or decrease in power results in a change of approximately 3 dB.

A ten-times (10X) increase or decrease in power results in a change of 10 dB.

Those two Technician Class rules will get you through 90% of practical application of decibels and one of only two questions on this topic in the General Class pool. The remaining 10% of application and the other potential exam question require only a little more cognitive consideration, in lieu of a bunch of ugly equation manipulations.

A change in power may also be considered as a percentage relative to the initial power level that is always considered to be 100%. For instance, in the rules listed above, the "2X increase or decrease in power" could instead be characterized as "200% power" or "50% power," each referring to a 2X change. So, we might ask the question, "What percentage of power results from a 3 dB decrease?" We can confidently answer that a 3 dB decrease equates to power about 50% of the starting value. Here is how decibels and relative percentages line up, with percentage values rounded:

Resulting Power (Relative to 100% Starting Power)		Resulting Power (Relative to 100% Starting Power)	
dB change	% of starting power	dB change	% of starting power
-1 dB	-20%	1 dB	125%
-2 dB	-37%	2 dB	160%
-3 dB	-50%	3 dB	200% (2X)
-4 dB	-60%	4 dB	251%
-5 db	-68%	5 dB	316%
-6 dB	-75%	6 dB	398%
-7 dB	-80%	7 dB	500%
-8 dB	-84%	8 dB	630%
-9 dB	-87%	9 dB	794%
-10 dB	-90%	10 dB	1000% (10X)

Example 1: Suppose you wish to know what percentage of transmitter power is reaching your antenna given a coaxial feedline loss value in decibels: **What percentage of power loss would result from a transmission line loss of 1 dB?** Since we are interested in the percentage of loss, this is a decrease in power, specifically a decrease of 1 dB. A decrease of 1 dB (or -1 dB change) is equivalent to about a 20% decrease (-20%). Among the responses to this example exam pool item, **20.5%** is easily identified as the correct one.

Example 2: What percentage of power loss would result from a transmission line loss of 2.4 dB? This is not an exam pool item, and from our table of dB and percentages we can interpolate that the percentage of loss is roughly 43%. For those who have ample math skills, this may be precisely calculated with the following equation:

$$\%P = 100\% \ anti \ log \frac{dB}{10} = 100\% \ anti \ log \frac{-2.4}{10}$$

$$= 100\% \ x \ 0.575 = 57.5\%$$

100% - 57.5% = 42.5% decrease

(Note: Antilog is computed as 10^x where x is the value following "antilog.")

Power and AC Waveforms: By now you've seen your share of the simple sine waveforms used to represent both the electric field oscillations of an RF electromagnetic wave and the back-and-forth oscillations of voltage in an AC circuit. When representing AC voltage the positive voltage (+v) part of the wave means the voltage is providing potential in one direction in the circuit, thereby pushing the electric current that way. The negative voltage (-v) means the voltage is pushing in the opposite direction in the circuit. The up and down undulation of the sine wave from +v to –v represents the voltage revers-ing back-and-forth in the circuit over time. The am-plitude, or height of the wave relative to the zero voltage line is a represen-tation of the magnitude of the voltage over time.

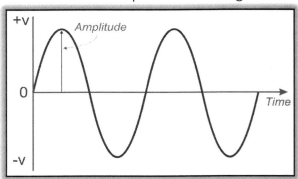

The AC voltage is not like DC voltage when it comes to measurements. DC voltage does not oscillate

Figure 6.1: AC waveform time domain view.

from one direction to the other, changing value constantly. Rather, DC remains steadily in a single direction in the circuit with a constant value for conditions. Our previously derived equations for power, such as $P = E^2/R$ work beautifully for DC because the EMF is a non-changing voltage value. But what voltage are you going to use in this formula with an AC circuit?

- Will you use the peak amplitude voltage as determined above or below the zero line?
- Will you use the total voltage change from the +v peak to the –v peak?
- Will you use the average voltage? (That would equal zero, wouldn't it?)
- Will you use some other value of voltage?

You see the point. How do we define AC voltage? Do not fret. There is an answer!

Root Mean Square Voltage: A rather convoluted computation may be made to determine a statistical average of a varying signal value such as an AC voltage signal. It is called the Root Mean Square, or RMS. The RMS may be determined for the +v portion of the waveform or for the –v portion. To compute the RMS of an AC signal across one-half wavelength (all above or all below the zero line) you would follow these steps:

1. Measure the amplitude of every voltage point along the wave.
2. Square each of the measured amplitude values.
3. Find the average (the mean) of all the squared values.
4. Take the square root of this average.

Wow, that's a pain, huh? Well, fortunately for a nice sine wave form with a peak amplitude normalized to 1, this calculation always yields the same value: 0.707. The E_{RMS} is different for differently shaped voltage waveforms, but it always equals 0.707 for our AC voltage sine waves of amplitude unity (1). Memorize that number!

Figure 6.2 depicts the E_{RMS} value on an AC sine waveform for both +v and –v, relative to peak voltages. **The RMS value of an AC signal results in the same power dissipation as a DC voltage of the same value.** Thus, E_{RMS} may be used in the $P = E^2/R$ calculations for AC circuits.

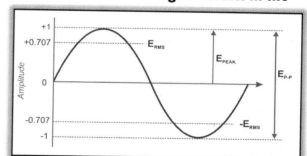

Example: **What is the RMS voltage across a 50 ohm dummy load (resistor) dissipating 1200 watts?**

Figure 6.2: Root Mean Square voltage is 0.707 x peak voltage, and is the AC voltage used for power calculations.

$P = E_{RMS}{}^2/R$, and rearranging this with a little algebra yields

$$E_{RMS} = \sqrt{P \text{ x } R}$$

$$E_{RMS} = \sqrt{P \text{ x } R} = \sqrt{1200 \text{ x } 50} = 245 \text{ } volts$$

You can compute E_{RMS} if you know the peak voltage, and you can compute the peak voltage if you know E_{RMS}, like this:

$$E_{RMS} = E_{Peak} \text{ x } 0.707$$

And by computing the inverse $1 / 0.707 = 1.414$ you may compute:

$$E_{Peak} = E_{RMS} \text{ x } 1.414$$

Example: **What is the RMS voltage of a sine wave with a value of 17 volts peak?**

$$E_{RMS} = E_{Peak} \text{ x } 0.707 = 17 \text{ x } 0.707 = \textbf{12 volts}$$

Example: What is the peak voltage of a sine wave with E_{RMS} of 50 volts?

$$E_{Peak} = E_{RMS} \text{ x } 1.414 = 50 \text{ x } 1.414 = 70.7 \text{ volts peak}$$

Peak-to-Peak Voltage: It is sometimes important to work with the peak-to-peak voltages of a waveform, designated $V_{p\text{-}p}$ or $E_{p\text{-}p}$. The peak-to-peak value is also indicated in Figure 6.2. For the sine waveform the peak-to-peak voltage will be twice the peak voltage. Thus, peak-to-peak voltage is also calculated using E_{RMS}, and E_{RMS} is calculated using $E_{p\text{-}p}$, as follows:

$$E_{(P\text{-}P)} = 2 \text{ x } E_{RMS} \text{ x } 1.414$$

$$E_{RMS} = (E_{P\text{-}P} \text{ x } 0.707) / 2$$

Example: **What is the peak-to-peak voltage of a sine wave that has an RMS voltage of 120 volts?**

$$E_{P\text{-}P} = 2 \text{ x } E_{RMS} \text{ x } 1.414 = 2 \text{ x } 120 \text{ x } 1.414 = \textbf{339.4 volts}$$

Example: What is the RMS voltage of a sine wave with measured peak-to-peak voltage of 339.4 volts?

$$E_{RMS} = (E_{P\text{-}P} \text{ x } 0.707) / 2 = (339.4 \text{ x } 0.707) / 2 = 120 \text{ volts}$$

Peak Envelope Power (PEP): The formulas discussed so far are fine for a very simple signal, but that's not the typical practical case. Most commonly hams will be more concerned with a complex modulated signal. Given an amplitude modulated signal as described in Section 4.1, an envelope will shape the peaks of the carrier frequency sine waveform, resulting in continuous change of the peak voltages and associated power over time. For instance, with phone mode the modulation envelope will expand and contract with the ebb and flow of our voices, creating frequent *high power peaks* of modulation as our voice rises interspersed with vocal pauses of almost no modulation at all, and many levels in between.

How can we characterize the power of a varying amplitude envelope of signals like this in a practical and useful manner?

Peak envelope power (PEP) is the average power (RMS) supplied to the antenna transmission line by a transmitter during one radio frequency cycle at the crest of the modulation envelope. As depicted in Figure 6.3, PEP is the average power of the signal calculated where the envelope peaks to its highest voltage (*Peak Envelope Voltage*). The PEP is an index of the highest power peaks to be expected for given conditions of the transmitter, load, and modulating signal – a *practical* measure!

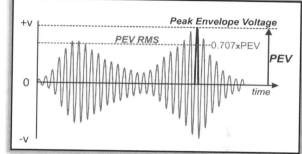

Figure 6.3: In amplitude modulated signals the RMS of the Peak Envelope Voltage is used to compute the Peak Envelope Power (PEP).

The FCC uses PEP to set maximum power standards for amateur radio transmitters. An averaging wattmeter will display a time averaged value for PEP (usually across many envelope peaks in its averaging time) for adjustments of transmitter or amplifier drive levels. A signal PEP may also be calculated using the previously derived equations for power, remembering that it is the *average power at the envelope peak.* So, the *RMS voltage* of the peak cycle must be used for calculation of PEP. And if the RMS voltage is not provided it may be calculated from the peak-to-peak voltage of the envelope peak measurement. Let's drive this home with a couple of examples:

Example 1: **What is the output PEP from a transmitter if an oscilloscope measures 200 volts peak-to-peak across a 50 ohm dummy load connect-**

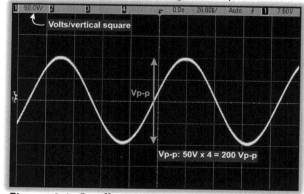

Figure 6.4: Oscilloscope screen measurement of 200 volts peak-to-peak, at 50V per vertical scale unit. *Compliments Agilent Technologies*

ed to the transmitter output? (Don't let the oscilloscope or dummy load mentions confuse you… that's just a measurement technique scenario that is irrelevant to the numerical facts provided.) So, we're asked for PEP, and we are given $E_{p\text{-}p}$ and R.

$P_{PEP} = (E_{RMS})^2 / R$ at the envelope peak. This is the same $P = E^2 / R$ equation used earlier for the sine waveform power calculation, only changed to use the RMS voltage.

Recall: $E_{RMS} = 0.707 \times E_{p\text{-}p} / 2 = 0.707 \times (200 \text{ v}) / 2 = 70.7 \text{ v}$

Again, this is the same method of computing RMS voltage already introduced in which we must use only the peak voltage, or one-half of peak-to-peak voltage ($E_{p\text{-}p} \div 2$).

Plugging E_{RMS} into the P_{PEP} formulas then gives:

$P_{PEP} = (70.7 \text{ v})^2/(50 \ \Omega) = (4998.5)/50 = \textbf{100 watts}$ (rounded)

Example 2: **What is the output PEP from a transmitter if an oscilloscope measures 500 volts peak-to-peak across a 50 ohm resistor connected to the transmitter output?** Exactly the same equation applies since we are asked for PEP and given $E_{p\text{-}p}$ and R.

$$P_{PEP} = \frac{(0.707 \times \frac{E_{P-P}}{2})^2}{R} = \frac{(0.707 \times \frac{500}{2})^2}{50} = 625 \ watts \ \text{(rounded)}$$

Unmodulated Carrier PEP: One last PEP consideration: What if the carrier is unmodulated? That is, what if there are no peaks and valleys of amplitude on the envelope, but only a steady carrier frequency of some given power?

In such a case the PEP is equal to the steady carrier power. The peak voltage of the signal is unchanging so any calculated RMS voltage equals the steady RMS voltage value, as depicted in Figure 6.5. Further, the PEP will be equal to the average power of the steady carrier signal at any point in time since an "envelope" is non-existent without modulation. Put another way, **the ratio of PEP to average power for an unmodulated carrier is 1.00.**

Example: **What is the output PEP of an unmodulated carrier if an average reading wattmeter connected to the transmitter output indicates 1060 watts?**

Since the PEP to average power for an unmodulated carrier is 1:1, the output PEP is equal to the wattmeter's average power reading of **1060 watts.**

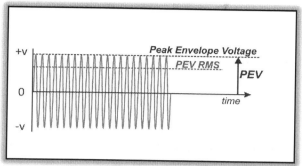

Figure 6.5: An unmodulated carrier's Peak Envelope Power will equal the carrier RMS power, since the PEV is equal to the carrier peak voltage (V$_{PEAK}$).

As you can see, there's a lot to be done with power! If you didn't quite measure up, check out the next page summary table of equations used in this section and review each of those areas representing question pool items. It may require a little practice, but you'll be powering up in no time!

Review questions: *HamRadioSchool.com/general_media*

Section 6.1 Study Review Summary:

Ohm's Law	$E = I \times R$	
Power Law	$P = I \times E$	
Power (P)	$P = I^2 \times R$	$P = E^2/R$
Decibels (dB)	3 dB = 2X change	-1 dB = -20.5%
Peak Voltage (E_{PEAK})	$E_{PEAK} = E_{P-P} / 2$	$E_{Peak} = E_{RMS} \times 1.414$
Root Mean Square Voltage (E_{RMS})	$E_{RMS} = E_{PEAK} \times 0.707$	$E_{RMS} = \sqrt{(P \times R)}$
Peak-to-Peak Voltage (E_{P-P})	$E_{P-P} = 2 \times E_{RMS} \times 1.414$	$E_{P-P} = E_{PEAK} \times 2$
Peak Envelope Power (P_{PEP})	$P_{PEP} = (E_{RMS})^2 / 2$	Uses PEV in E_{RMS}

6.2 Components

" We must break problems down into small, digestible bits. We must define the concepts that we use and explain what components they consist of. We must tackle small problems. – Abdolkarim Soroush

When it comes to electronics Dr. Souroush couldn't be more correct. To begin to understand what's really going on inside a transceiver, an amplifier, or any other chunk of radio gear, a lot of insight can be gained from an examination of the individual components from which the equipment is constructed. Let's tackle these small problems, these electronic components, and later we'll put some of them together into bigger working pieces.

You may recall from your Technician studies an introduction to several types of electronic components. Here's a summary of some of those basic components, just to jog your brain into action:

Component	Symbol	Units	Description
Resistor	—/\/\/—	ohm [Ω]	Opposes the flow of current in a circuit; dissipates energy as heat
Capacitor	—||(—	farad	Stores energy in an electric field; passes higher frequency AC, opposes lower frequency AC and DC
Inductor	—ᴜᴜᴜ—	henry	Stores energy in a magnetic field; passes lower frequency AC and DC, opposes higher frequency AC
Diode	—▶|—	N/A	Allows current to flow in only one direction; leads are anode and cathode
Transistor	⊕ ⊕	N/A	May act as an amplifier or as a switch; small controlling current or voltage regulates larger current flow

First we'll consider some common general characteristics of most electronic components, and then we'll tackle each component listed in the table in appropriate General Class detail.

Electronic Component Characteristics: Imagine you're trying to select a car to purchase. Each automobile type is unique, but they all share some common characteristics that you can use for comparison and that will help you judge how well the vehicle will perform for you. For instance, each car will have a gas mileage estimate, an engine size and horsepower, a maximum seating capacity, and so on. In some cases the characteristic will be an approximation, with some variance expected among individual vehicles of the same make and model – gas mileage, for example, will usually vary by individual car and driver, and even by the driving environmental factors, such as altitude.

Electronic components are much the same as cars in this regard. While each type is unique and may perform differently, some common characteristics may be defined for them all. These characteristics will tell you how you may expect the electronic component to perform.

- *Nominal Value* – The intended or designed unit quantity the component should provide. For instance, a resistor may have a nominal value of 1000 Ω resistance; a capacitor may provide 2000 microfarads of capacitance; an inductor may be rated at 0.004 henry of inductance. Consider a component's nominal value to be like an EPA gas mileage rating for the car – it is the target value, but with understanding that variations will occur.

- *Tolerance* – The amount of deviation from the nominal value that is considered to be normal for the quality of the component. Tolerance will typically be a percentage. For instance, the 1000 Ω resistor may have a tolerance of +/- 20%. That means the resistor is within normal operating performance if it provides a measured resistance of anywhere between 800 – 1200 Ω. Similarly, your vehicle's gas mileage may vary from the EPA rating and actually measure somewhat higher or lower than the rating. With electronic components, different tolerances may be specified for a circuit design to ensure the circuit performs within required ranges.

- *Voltage/Current/Power Rating* – The maximum value of voltage, current, or power that the component can handle without being toasted. A component is usually designed for a limited range of input values and if the limits are exceeded the component may not be able to shed the heat generated by the excessive current or power. In such a case the component may break down due to the accumulation of heat or voltage stress. Similarly, your car or truck may be designed with a maximum towing capacity weight. If you try to pull a trailer heavier than the towing capacity, your engine may overheat and fail.

- *Temperature Coefficient* – A description of the component's performance variation with temperature. The nominal value of many components will shift with temperature. For instance, **if the temperature is increased the resistance of a resistor will change depending on its temperature coefficient** – a resistor may be rated at 1000 Ω at 80 degrees Fahrenheit, but its resistance may decrease at temperatures above 80 degrees at a steady rate of 10 Ω per degree. Similarly, your car may accelerate and speed along very well in average temperatures, but on a scorching summer day with the air conditioner running you may find the acceleration to be lacking and the top speed more difficult to achieve due to an overheating engine.

G6A16

Additional characteristics may apply to various component types, but these are the basics that will help you identify the performance parameters of most electronics. Now, let's consider the functioning of each of the component types listed in the preceding table.

Resistors: A resistor offers electrical resistance, opposing the flow of electric current in a circuit. Resistance is measured in units of ohms.

> **Resistor Water Model:** Recalling the water model of electricity from the *HamRadioSchool.com Technician License Course*, an electric circuit can be thought of like plumbing, as in Figure 6.6 on the next page. Water current flows in pipes as electric current flows in wires, and a water pump provides pressure to push the water current through the pipe just as a battery provides electromotive force to push electrical current though wires. If you constrict the pipe, perhaps narrowing its diameter or placing objects inside to interrupt the water flow, you are creating opposition to the flow of the current – resistance! A resistor is like a narrowing or a blockage in the electrical circuit that similarly opposes the flow of current in the circuit. (A load in the circuit, such as an appliance, also imposes resistance.)

Resistors of various types are made from different materials, each with unique characteristics and typical applications. For high power applications, such as power supply circuits, resistors may be wire-wound, using resistive wire wrapped about a non-conductive core such as ceramic. However, such a coil of wire with current flowing will store energy in a magnetic field that is cre-

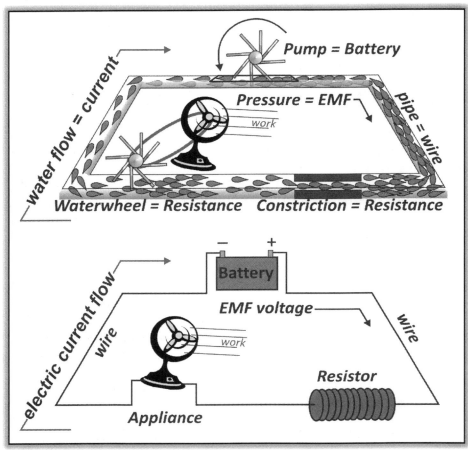

Figure 6.6: Water model of an electric circuit.

ated around the coiled windings. This is called *inductance*, as we will explore further with the *inductor* component. Care must be taken to ensure that a wire-wound resistor's inductance does not interfere with the function of other components in nearby circuits. So, **wire-wound resistors are not typically used in RF circuits because the resistor's inductance could make circuit performance unpredictable.** Rather, non-inductive resistors made from metal oxide or carbon are typically used for RF applications.

A resistor's nominal value will usually be either printed on the resistor or indicated with a series of colored bands around the resistor using a standardized color code. Various tolerances are available from less than 1% precision components to 10% or greater for less demanding applications. Power ratings vary vastly and depend on the construction, material type, and physical size of the resistor. Temperature coefficients also vary substantially, and the coef-

G6A17

ficient may be positive (increased resistance with increased temperature) or negative (decreased resistance with increased temperature).

Thermistor: A device having a specific change in resistance with temperature variation is a *thermistor*. Thermistors may be used to construct temperature sensing and control circuits, such as in a thermostat used to control temperature with a cooling fan, an air conditioner, or a furnace.

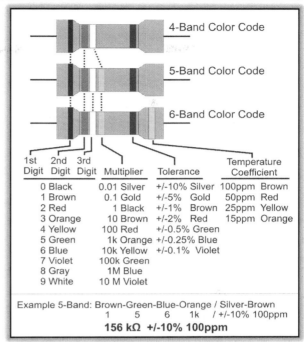

		4-Band Color Code
		5-Band Color Code
		6-Band Color Code

1st Digit	2nd Digit	3rd Digit	Multiplier	Tolerance	Temperature Coefficient
0 Black			0.01 Silver	+/-10% Silver	100ppm Brown
1 Brown			0.1 Gold	+/-5% Gold	50ppm Red
2 Red			1 Black	+/-1% Brown	25ppm Yellow
3 Orange			10 Brown	+/-2% Red	15ppm Orange
4 Yellow			100 Red	+/-0.5% Green	
5 Green			1k Orange	+/-0.25% Blue	
6 Blue			10k Yellow	+/-0.1% Violet	
7 Violet			100k Green		
8 Gray			1M Blue		
9 White			10 M Violet		

Example 5-Band: Brown-Green-Blue-Orange / Silver-Brown
       1   5   6   1k   / +/-10% 100ppm
156 kΩ +/-10% 100ppm

Figure 6.7: Resistor value color codes.

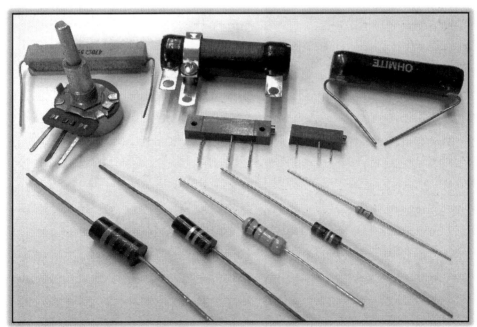

Figure 6.8: Resistors and potentiometers come in a variety of packages for different functions and ranges of power handling capacity.

Potentiometer: A resistor that can be varied in resistance value is called a potentiometer, or a pot. Variable resistors are commonly used to control voltage or current in a circuit by adjusting the potentiometer's resistance, such as in a volume control on a radio. Potentiometers included in some circuits for the purpose of making minor calibrations of the circuit and not regularly controlled by an operator are called *trimmers,* since they are used to tweak or *trim* the final circuit performance.

Capacitors: A capacitor stores electrical energy in an electric field. This component consists of two or more conductive surfaces separated by an insulator, or *dielectric.* Since the surfaces are separated, DC current is prevented from flowing through a capacitor, but AC current is not interrupted – the back-and-forth current flow allows electric charge to build across the capacitor's two surfaces, one surface becoming positively charged and the other negatively charged, until the voltage applied to the capacitor reverses. Upon reversal, the respective surfaces discharge and then recharge with opposite polarity. This repeats with each cycle of AC.

Generally, higher AC frequencies are less impeded by a capacitor since they are less likely to allow the capacitor's plates to reach maximum charge capacity, while lower AC frequencies may accumulate a maximum capacitance charge on the plates that begins to oppose further current flow. Capacitance is measured in units of farads, and greater capacitance (more energy storage capacity) is created with larger surface area and with narrower separation of the surfaces.

Capacitor Water Model: An admittedly over-simplified water model may be used to help comprehend the function of a capacitor. A capacitor may be thought of as a pliable, rubber diaphragm stretching across the interior of the pipe, as in Figure 6.9. The diaphragm will stretch in one direction with the current flow, storing energy elastically. Once the current direction reverses the stored energy is released, accelerating the current flow in the new direction with the force of the elastic contraction. As the current continues to flow, the diaphragm is stretched again, now in the opposite direction, again storing energy until the next cycle of alternating current flow releases it. The stretched diaphragm is loosely analogous to the potential difference that builds across the two plates of the capacitor.

Consistent with the description above about the capacitor's reaction to AC and DC current, you may envision that a high frequency alternating water current would stretch the capacitor diaphragm only mildly before the current direction is reversed, thereby not having a great impeding effect on the current's rapid back and forth flow. However, if the frequency

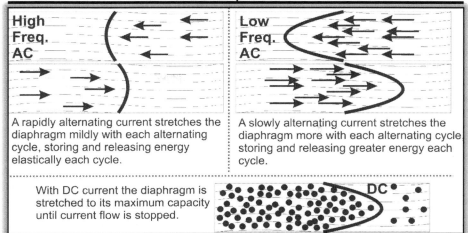

High Freq. AC

Low Freq. AC

A rapidly alternating current stretches the diaphragm mildly with each alternating cycle, storing and releasing energy elastically each cycle.

A slowly alternating current stretches the diaphragm more with each alternating cycle storing and releasing greater energy each cycle.

With DC current the diaphragm is stretched to its maximum capacity until current flow is stopped.

DC

Figure 6.9: In the water model of electricity, a capacitor is like a stretching diaphragm in the water pipe, storing and releasing energy with each alternating cycle of current direction.

of current reversal is low, the diaphragm may be stretched to its maximum capacity before the reversal of flow direction, and the current flow is then significantly impeded. And of course, if the current is DC, never reversing, the capacitor will reach maximum capacity in the one DC direction and then stop further current flow.

Capacitor Packaging: A wide variety of capacitor types and constructions exist. A capacitor may be fabricated from a pair of metal plates separated by air. Sandwich a thin insulating material between two layers of thin metal foil, roll up the sandwich into a cylindrical package, and you have another capacitor form. Stack up multiple alternating layers of insulating and conducting surfaces like a Dagwood sandwich, keeping the layers flat and unrolled, and connect alternating conducting surfaces electrically at their edges, and yet another capacitor packaging is affected.

Plastic Film Capacitors are typically rolled sandwiches of plastic insulating film between metal foil layers. As noted with the wire-wound resistor, a rolled capacitor will impose some undesirable inductance due to its rolled or coiled form. As a result, plastic film capacitors are not typically used in RF circuits requiring higher frequency signal processing where this *parasitic inductance* can affect performance.

Ceramic Capacitors have many narrow plates of ceramic metallically coated on one side and stacked in the Dagwood sandwich configuration. **Compared to other types of capacitors they have the advantage of low cost.** Being a flat stack arrangement, ceramics do not

G6A14

generate parasitic inductance like the rolled capacitors, so they are used in VHF and UHF circuits. However, the wire connection leads do produce small but significant inductance for VHF and above, termed *lead inductance*, which reduces the effective capacitance. As we will see in Section 6.4 inductance and capacitance effects offset one another within a circuit, and even within a component.

Electrolytic Capacitors are typically a rolled form also, but the insulating dielectric is a moist chemical gel (the electrolyte) that coats the conducting layers. **Electrolytic capacitors** are optimized for energy storage, **offering the advantage of high capacitance for a given volume.** Because they are rolled, they produce parasitic inductance, but they are often used in power supply circuits to filter the rectified AC. (See rectifiers in Section 6.5.)

Electrolytic capacitors are usually *polarized* capacitors, meaning that they are used in circuits where the two leads have a consistent applied potential relationship. That is, one lead (+) is always at a higher potential than the other lead (-). **If the applied voltage polarity is reversed the polarized capacitor could overheat and explode, it may short-circuit, or the voltages may destroy the dielectric layer.**

Capacitance Values: Capacitors in RF circuits are often of fractional values of the unit *farad*. The standard mathematical prefixes are attached to the unit to indicate these fractional values of one farad, as follows:

picofarad (pF)	one trillionth	0.000000000001	10^{-12}
nanofarad (nF)	one billionth	0.000000001	10^{-9}
microfarad (µF)	one millionth	0.000001	10^{-6}
millifarad (mF)	one thousandth	0.001	10^{-3}

Converting among these fractional values involves moving the decimal point three places for each of the standard fractional steps. A thorough examination of this is provided in the *HamRadioSchool.com Technician License Course* book, Section 8.3. Let's examine two exam questions regarding conversions.

What is the value in nanofarads (nF) of a 22,000 pF capacitor? Converting from pF to nF is one prefix step, moving the decimal left by three positions. **22,000 pF = 22 nF.**

What is the value in microfarads of a 4700 nanofarad (nF) capacitor? Similarly, this is a one-step conversion moving the decimal left. **4700 nF = 4.7 µF.**

Inductors: Inductors store energy in a magnetic field that is created around the inductor when electric current flows through it. An inductor is usually composed of a coil of wire, in many cases wound about an iron or ferrite core to increase the magnetic energy storage capacity. You may be familiar with the magnetic field generated by an electromagnet, essentially

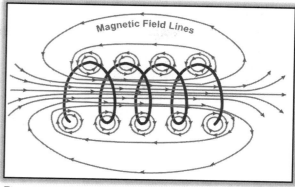

Figure 6.10: A magnetic field "inflates" about an inductor as current flows through the coil.

an inductor comprised of a coil of wire connected to a battery or other DC power source.

An inductor reacts to AC and DC in a manner opposite that of a capacitor. The inductor allows DC current to flow freely once the initial current's magnetic field is established around the inductor, with magnetic field lines stable in one orientation, or *polarization*. However, the constantly reversing AC requires that the magnetic field be created with one polarization, then eliminated and rebuilt with the opposite polarization each AC cycle. This persistent *inflation* and *deflation* of the magnetic field expends electrical energy and thereby opposes AC current. The inductor's opposition to AC increases with frequency. Let's drive home this concept with the water analogy for an inductor.

Inductor Water Model: Imagine the inductor is a very massive waterwheel extending into the water current. As the current begins to flow it will require some time and applied force to get the heavy wheel rotating with the speed of the current. The inertia of the heavy wheel opposes the current flow until it gets up to rotational speed with the flow. Once rotating, the water wheel has kinetic energy stored with its revolving mass, just as the inductor has stored energy in the magnetic field it created.

If the current suddenly stopped flowing the heavy waterwheel would continue to rotate for a while, expending its energy by pushing the water on until the rotation wound down to a stop. As the waterwheel slows to a stop its kinetic energy of rotation is converted back into water current, just as the inductor's magnetic field is converted into continued electrical current until the magnetic field is depleted. Once the wheel's stored energy is depleted and it stops turning, the current flow also stops.

Because energy is expended over time to inflate the magnetic field (to get the waterwheel turning), the inductor offers resistance initially to the current. Once the steady state magnetic field is achieved (waterwheel at current flow speed), the resistance is eliminated. This is the case with a DC current.

If the electrical current reverses direction the magnetic lines of force are induced in the opposite direction also. Thus, the magnetic field must collapse and rebuild with opposite polarity of the lines of force; i.e. the waterwheel would resist the reversed water current, but ultimately it will grind to a halt and gradually pick up rotational speed in the opposite direction with the current. During this process opposition to the flow would be offered until the new steady state is achieved with the waterwheel turning at speed in the opposite direction. This cycle repeats.

As the frequency of current alternation increases, the inductor's opposition also increases. You can imagine the water wheel trying to rapidly start and stop with higher frequencies of AC, never quite getting up to speed and constantly opposing current flow in either direction. You can also imagine the waterwheel just becoming a static blockage in the current if the water flow reversed direction too frequently, with insufficient time to start wheel rotation in either direction before the next reversal.

Inductance: The measure of the ability to store magnetic energy, *inductance*, is determined by the number of wire turns in the inductor, by the area that each turn circumscribes, by the density of turns (longitudinal spacing or length of inductor), and by the *magnetic permeability* of the core material. Permeability is the core's ability to store magnetic energy. Iron or ferrite cores enhance permeability, and permeability may be engineered to fit specific circuit needs.

Variable Inductors: Inductors that provide variable inductance values may be created by shifting the core into or out of the coil, changing the effective permeability. Another technique applied in higher power circuits is to *tap* the inductor with a contact that may be moved among the coil's turns, effectively changing the number of turns used in the circuit by moving the tap position, just as in the tapped coil antenna of Section 5.1.

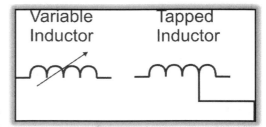

Figure 6.11: Variable and **tapped inductor** symbols.

Mutual Inductance: As noted in the capacitor discussion, an induced magnetic field can extend well beyond a component to affect the performance of other components. In the case of inductors the changing magnetic field of one inductor can induce current flow in another nearby inductor. This is called *mutual inductance*. We will see in Section 6.5 that mutual inductance is the principle by which transformers operate, but it is undesirable in

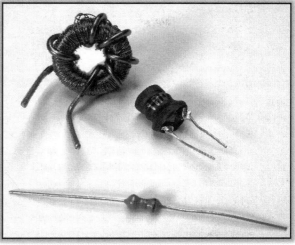

Figure 6.12: Inductors may be toroid coils, solenoid coils, or other forms.

virtually every other type of circuit. It is important to minimize mutual inductance between two inductors to reduce unwanted coupling between circuits. Methods of reducing mutual inductance depend upon inductor form factors.

Inductor Forms: Two common physical forms of inductors are 1) the *solenoid inductor*, having a straight axis or core, and 2) the *toroid inductor*, having a circular or "donut" core on which windings are wrapped. With a solenoid inductor the magnetic field lines loop through the coiled windings and back outside the coil, primarily pointing along the axis of the core. **Placing the winding axes of solenoid inductors at right angles to one another minimizes their mutual inductance,** since the field lines of one inductor are not in an orientation for inducing a current in the other inductor. **The ferrite core toroidal inductor contains most of the magnetic field in the core,** minimizing mutual inductance. **It also has the advantages of relatively large inductance values and optimization for specific frequency ranges by altering the magnetic properties of the core.**

G6A19

G6A18

Inter-turn capacitance in an inductor may cause the inductor to become self resonant at some frequencies. Just as the rolled form of some capacitors creates stray inductance, the gaps between wire coils of an inductor can produce stray capacitance, much like the capacitor's separated plates. This inter-turn capacitance can be significant if an inductor is comprised of many turns. As noted in Chapter 5, a circuit with both capacitance and inductance will resonate at specific frequencies, and these types of circuits are the basis for RF oscillators. However, even an individual component can become undesirably self resonant due to the effects of parasitic capacitance or inductance, altering the component's intended performance by the resonant reinforcement of select frequencies.

Diodes: A diode is a *semiconductor* component that allows current flow in only one direction. It has two connection leads called the *anode* and the *cathode*. Current flows when a positive voltage is applied from the anode to the cathode, and in this condition the diode is said to be *forward biased*. When the diode is reverse biased the voltage is oppositely applied and the diode allows no current flow in the *reverse bias* direction.

> **Diode Water Model:** A diode is analogous to a one-way plumbing valve, such as a check valve or flap valve, that allows water to flow through a pipe in one direction by opening with the flow, but that stops the opposite direction flow by closing the pipe entirely.

A semiconductor is a material with electrical conductivity between that of an insulator such as glass and a conductor such as metal, and its electrical properties may be manipulated by additives or impurities distributed throughout its form. Silicon (Si) is one of the most common semiconductors, and others include germanium, gallium arsenide, and silicon carbide. The addition of impurities is called *doping* the semiconductor. By using two different types of *dopants* in semiconductor, a *junction diode* may be constructed.

Junction Diode: One type of dopant in semiconductor promotes an excess of electrons (negative charge) in the semiconductor. This is called an *N-type* material. Different dopants promote an excess of positively charged ions, usually called "holes." (Think this: A negatively charged electron fits into a positively charged hole as current flows, and holes flow in the opposite direction of electrons in a circuit.) This positive charge inducing material is a *P-type* material.

Place a P-type material and an N-type material together and you form a *junction* of the two types (a "PN junction"). Due to the behavior of the excessive electrons and holes near the junction, current will flow in one direction but not the other, and then it will flow only when a sufficient voltage is applied across the PN junction (forward bias voltage). This is like the minimum water pressure required to open the flap valve and allow water current to flow.

The voltage required to promote forward current flow is called the *junction threshold voltage*. **For a conventional silicon diode the approximate junction threshold voltage is 0.7 volts. For a germanium diode the approximate junction threshold voltage is 0.3 volts.**

Note that the voltage *must* be in the forward bias direction to pull the electrons across the PN junction. Of course, given enough reverse bias voltage, the junction will break down and current will indeed be forced to flow in the reverse direction. This would be like the plumbing backing up with such force the flap valve is collapsed backward and destroyed. Diodes will have a *peak reverse*

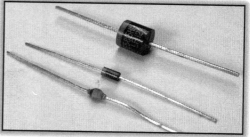

Figure 6.13: Diode packages for various current handling. The stripe indicates the cathode.

voltage rating describing this limit, and a *forward bias current limit* describing the maximum forward current it can handle without being damaged.

There are several different types of diodes that lend themselves to a variety of applications. These include:

- **Schottky Diode** – named for German physicist Walter H. Schottky, it requires a relatively small forward threshold voltage and has the **advantage of lower capacitance compared to a standard silicon diode** as a result. This allows for very fast switching times and **use in RF switching circuits.**

- **Zener Diode** – named for Clarence Zener who discovered the electrical properties of this unique device. When forward biased it acts as a normal diode, but when reverse biased above its reverse break down voltage it will maintain the reverse voltage at or near a stable value even with significant current variations.

- **Light Emitting Diode (LED)** – **When forward biased an LED emits light.** These diodes are commonly used as visual indicators in modern electronics. **Compared to an incandescent indicator, the LED has the advantages of lower power consumption, faster response time, and longer life.**

Additional varieties of diodes are available for specialized applications.

Transistors: A transistor is a semiconductor component capable of using a small current or voltage to control a larger current flow. A transistor may be used as a signal amplifier or as a switch. A transistor has three leads for connections in a circuit. One of the leads is connected to the controlling current or voltage while the larger current flows through the other two leads.

G6A06

G6B08

G6B07

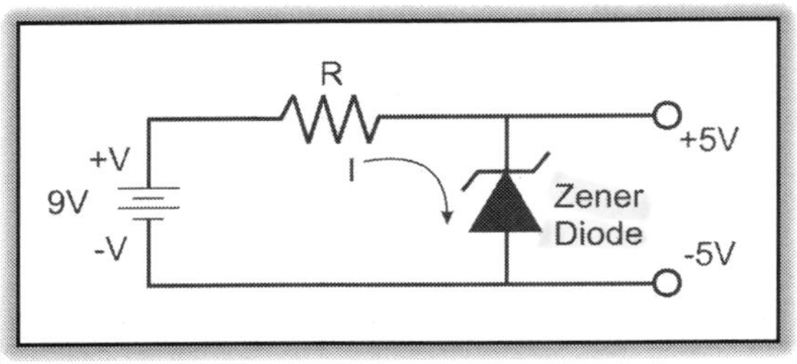

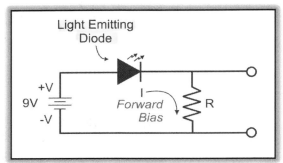

G7A10

Figure 6.14: A Zener diode keeps the reverse bias voltage near a stable value. In this example the 9V reverse bias source is kept at 5V by the Zener diode.

Figure 6.15: The LED will illuminate when forward biased, as shown here. If the voltage is reversed the LED will not emit light.

Transistor Water Analogy: A transistor may be considered like an adjustable valve, as in Figure 6.17. A controlling "signal" is provided by cranking the valve open or closed. Imagine the valve handle is rapidly adjusted so that the water pipe opening is narrow, then widely open, then narrow again in a repeated fashion. With a high current water source available to the pipe, the output "signal" will be a strong fluctuating current that mirrors the small input signal of valve adjustments. While the valve may be adjusted with the light touch of a finger and thumb, the output current flow can be a strong, varying surge of water, depending upon the source current. In this way the transistor valve acts to amplify the input signal, producing a much stronger signal of a pattern identical to the input signal. If the input signal is taken to the end points, closing off the flow entirely or opening it completely wide, it may function as a switch.

Bipolar Junction Transistor (BJT): As the name implies the BJT is a pair of junctions, as described in the previous P-N junction diode discussion. The P-type and N-type materials may be arranged in a PNP sandwich or an NPN sandwich. The center material in the sandwich is connected to the *base* lead that provides the controlling current to the BJT. The outer two materials are connected to the *collector* and *emitter* leads through which the larger controlled current passes.

The BJT has three operating regimes:

1. **Cut-off:** As with the junction diode, a minimum base current (center material connection) is necessary to allow current flow. With no base current greater than the threshold current there is no current flow from

collector to emitter electrode. This stable operating point is called the *cut-off region* for the bipolar transistor.

2. **Amplification:** As base current exceeds the cut-off value, the current flowing from collector to emitter will be proportional to (but usually greater than) the base current. Any base current variations (signals) are amplified as variations in the collector-to-emitter current.

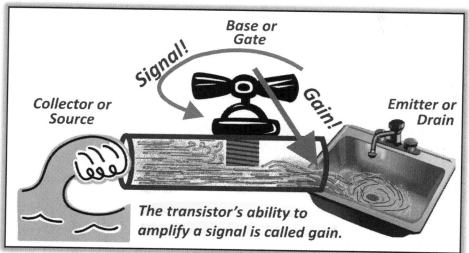

Figure 6.16: Transistors for various power handling.

3. **Saturation:** Some value of high base current will achieve *saturation,* another stable operating point at which increased base current will no longer increase the collector-to-emitter current through the transistor. **The saturation and cut-off regions are the stable operating points for a bipolar transistor used as a switch in a logic circuit.**

G6A07

You may now be wondering what difference is made by the PNP versus NPN material sandwiching? The difference comes in the voltage bias that must be

Base or
Gate

Signal!

Collector or
Source

Gain!

Emitter or
Drain

The transistor's ability to amplify a signal is called gain.

Figure 6.17: A water model for the transistor. A variable valve controls a strong current flow.

applied between the base and emitter to achieve current flow. With the PNP BJT the emitter voltage must exceed the base voltage. For the NPN BJT the base voltage must exceed that of the emitter. The symbol arrows for PNP and NPN BJTs point in opposite directions, with the PNP arrow "pointing in," and the NPN arrow "not pointing in" (NPN).

Field Effect Transistor (FET): The FET utilizes a P-type and N-type combination also, but in a different configuration from the BJT. A *channel* of one material is routed through the other to affect a sort of variably squeezing tunnel for charge passage. The three FET electrodes are referred to as the *gate* (the control signal input, analogous to the BJT base), the *source* (analogous to the BJT collector), and the *drain* (analogous to the BJT emitter).

Like the BJT, the FET amplifies signals input to the gate by controlling current flow from source to drain electrodes. However, instead of a *current signal* to the gate a *voltage signal* is applied. The variable voltage at the gate controls the width of the charge tunnel described above, opening wider or closing smaller to vary current. A variably pinched water hose analogy applies here!

MOSFET: Very similar to the FET is the MOSFET, or *metal-oxide-semiconductor field effect transistor*. A variation on the FET, **the MOSFET inserts a thin insulating layer of oxide to separate the gate from the channel.** This construction can offer some enhanced performance due to improved conductivity.

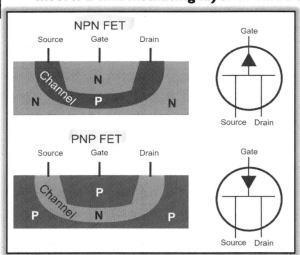

G6A09

Transistor Packaging: Many different packages of transistors are available. Plastic insulated transistors are common for low-power applications. High power transistors will commonly have metal packaging by which heat may be dissipated. In many cases the metal sheath is directly connected to source or collector to improve heat removal.

Figure 6.18: Field Effect Transistors apply a voltage at the gate electrode to vary the width of a charge channel created by the P and N materials. Source-to-drain current varies with channel width, as determined by the gate voltage.

As a result, in order **to avoid contact that would short the collector or drain voltage to ground the cases of some large power transistors must be insulated.**

G6A08

Now you have many of the small, digestible bits of electronics that make radio work! Of course there are other components in most circuits, such as switches, op amps, relays, and more complex combinations of the components we've discussed here. A General Class exam circuit diagram follows below that highlights the component symbols we have covered in this section, and those in the exam question pool are in boldface print. A summary table of electronic components also follows on the next page focusing on the exam question concepts.

Next we'll piece together some of these components to see what they do, and gain greater understanding in the process. But first, review the diagram below and the table on the next page, and then go hit the section 6.2 questions!

HamRadioSchool.com/general_media

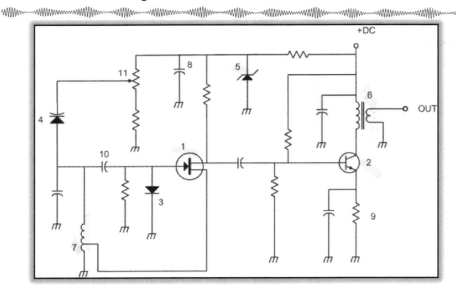

Figure 6.19: Exam Figure G7-1 Review

G7A09 G7A11 G7A10 G7A12 G7A13

1. Field Effect Transistor
2. NPN Junction Transistor
3. Diode
4. Voltage Variable Capacitor
5. Zener Diode
6. Multiple-winding Transformer (See Section 6.5)

7. Tapped Inductor
8. Capacitor
9. Resistor
10. Capacitor
11. Variable resistor

Section 6.2 Components Exam Question Content Review

Component	Symbol	Unit	Exam Question Concept
Resistor		Ohm	Resistance changes depending on temperature coefficient; Wire wound resistors produce inductance that affect circuit performance unpredictably.
Capacitor		farad	Electrolytic type have high capacitance for volume and used in power supplies to filter rectified AC. Ceramic capacitors advantage are low cost. Lead inductance reduces effective capacitance at VHF+ frequencies. Polarized capacitors must not have reversed polarity or explosion, damage dielectric, or short circuit may occur. Convert among pF, nF, µF by moving decimal 3 positions for each prefix step. (Each question item requires moving decimal 3 positions to the left.)
Inductor		henry	Ferrite core toroids increase inductance, keep magnetic field mostly within core, allow optimization for frequencies. Solenoid inductors placed at right angles minimize mutual inductance to reduce unwanted coupling between circuits.
Diode		N/A	Threshold voltages: germanium = 0.3v, silicon = 0.7v.
Schottky Diode		N/A	Schottky diode has lower capacitance advantage. Allows use in RF switching circuits.
Light Emitting Diode (LED)		N/A	Emits light when forward biased. Advantage over incandescent indicators of lower power consumption, faster response time, longer life.
Bipolar Junction Transistor		N/A	Stable operating points for switch function are saturation and cut-off regions. Large power transistor cases must be insulated from ground to avoid shorting collector or drain voltage to ground.
MOSFET		N/A	Construction has gate separated from channel with thin insulating layer.

6.3 / Hamtronics / **Series & Parallel Components**

> ❝ *You can't get more, or less, water out of an upturned bucket than you filled it with.*
> *– Kirchoff's Current Law, restated*

Even though water and electronics do not mix well in everyday applications, using wet analogies for thinking about electronics works remarkably well. Gustav Kirchoff was a German physicist of the mid-nineteenth century who expressed the brilliant concept above about the water in and out of the bucket in much more elegant and mathematical terms. Essentially his current law states that for a closed circuit, the current entering a junction must equal the current exiting the junction. Kirchoff was referring to electricity, of course, but the plumbing analogy to this rule also *holds water. <Ahem.>*

Current Law: Imagine, perhaps, a lawn watering system of pipes. Suppose the pipe from the water spigot (the current source) runs to a junction where three pipes connect, each routed to a different area of the yard where a sprinkler head awaits to scatter the water to parched blades of grass. Kirchoff's insight was that the quantity of current flowing into the junction of the pipes from the spigot must be equivalent to the sum of the current spritzing out of the three sprinklers and onto the grass. Makes perfect sense, right? Duh! Well, keep in mind he was in the early 1800s and working with the relatively new, cutting edge discovery, electricity. I wonder how many times he got shocked.

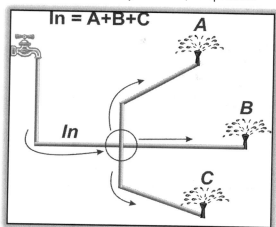

Figure 6.20: Kirchoff's Current Law water model. Current into the junction must equal the sum of sprinkler outputs.

Voltage Law: In spite of any painful jolts he may have received, Kirchoff didn't stop with the consideration of just current. He proved a somewhat more challenging rule about voltage (analogous to water pressure). Imagine that you operate a self-serve car wash that provides high pressure sprayers in each of four washing stalls, but all fed from one central water pump. Folks pull into the stalls, drop a few coins, and blast the crud off their vehicles with the handheld spraying nozzle. If you measure the drop in water pressure that occurs between the high pressure line feeding the spray nozzle to the water released to lower pressure to fly free and splatter against the car, and if you sum up that pressure change across all four wash stalls in operation, it will be equal to the pressure provided by the water pump. Kirchoff discovered that electricity in a closed circuit follows this same concept – the sum of voltage drops across components in a circuit (resistors, appliances, inductors, capacitors, etc.) equals the voltage applied by the battery.

The upshot of Kirchoff's current law and voltage law is that multiple electronic components arranged in series and parallel circuits may be "replaced," mathematically or in reality, by a single *equivalent component*. These neat math tricks are really handy for engineering and circuit design simplification or modification. Thus, from the fine work of Kirchoff we have today a nifty set of simple mathematical relationships for each of the basic component types that define the equivalent single component values of arrangements in either series or parallel. Let's check it out, especially since several question pool items are based upon these equations.

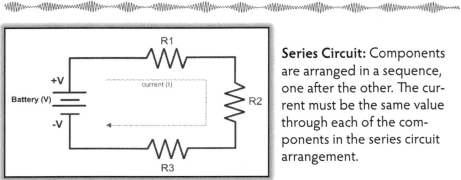

Series Circuit: Components are arranged in a sequence, one after the other. The current must be the same value through each of the components in the series circuit arrangement.

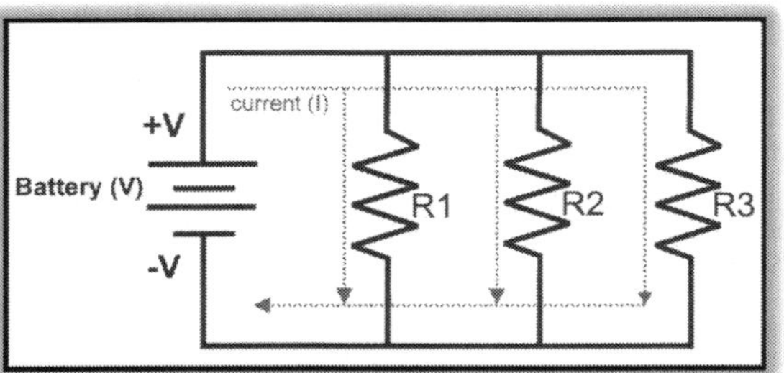

Figure 6.21: Components in series.

Parallel Circuit: Components are arranged in separate, unique paths that branch from a common path. **The total current must equal the sum of the currents through each branch.**

Figure 6.22: Components in parallel.

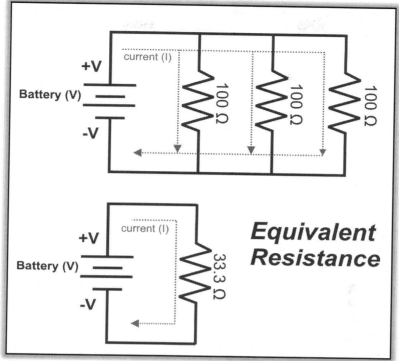

Figure 6.23: The three resistors in parallel may be replaced by a single resistor offering equivalent resistance as calculated from the equation. This concept applies to each type of component.

Two Equations: You need to remember only two simple equations for six circuit scenarios: Each of three components (resistors, inductors, capacitors) may be configured in either of the two arrangements (series or parallel). One of these two general equation forms applies to each of the six cases:

1. *Sum of Components Equation* – If X is the component value, such as resistance in ohms, capacitance in farads, or inductance in henries, the equivalent component value Xeq is simply:

   $X_{eq} = X_1 + X_2 + X_3$ ... and so on for all of the components in the circuit.

2. *The Reciprocal of Reciprocals Equation* – If X is the component value, the equivalent component value Xeq is:

   $$X_{eq} = \cfrac{1}{\cfrac{1}{X_1} + \cfrac{1}{X_2} + \cfrac{1}{X_3}}$$

Resistors and inductors in a series sum as components, using the first equation. **Resistors and inductors in parallel** combine with the reciprocal equation.

Capacitors are the reverse of resistors and inductors. **Capacitors in series** combine as the reciprocal of reciprocals. **Capacitors in parallel** sum as components. See Figure 6.24 for a graphical depiction of these relationships.

Let's consider examples using each of these two equations:

Example 1: What is the inductance (L) of a 20 millihenry inductor in series with a 50 millihenry inductor? Inductors in series add, so we'll use the Sum of Components Equation to simply calculate

$$L_{eq} = 20 \text{ mh} + 50 \text{ mh} = 70 \text{ mh} \quad \text{The correct answer is } \textbf{70 millihenry.}$$

Example 2: What is the total resistance of three 100-ohm resistors in parallel? Resistors in parallel use the Reciprocal of Reciprocals equation, thus

$$R_{eq} = \cfrac{1}{\cfrac{1}{R_1} + \cfrac{1}{R_2} + \cfrac{1}{R_3}}$$

$$= \cfrac{1}{\cfrac{1}{100} + \cfrac{1}{100} + \cfrac{1}{100}}$$

$$= \cfrac{1}{\cfrac{3}{100}} = \textbf{33.3 ohms}$$

Notice that resistors and inductors use the same equation form in the same component arrangements, while capacitors are the *odd component out* in each case, using the opposite form for arrangement. If we perform sample calculations we find the following effects on the equivalent values of components when we add a component:

Component	Adding a Series Component	Adding a Parallel Component
Resistor	**Increases resistance**	Decreases resistance
Inductor	**Increases inductance**	Decreases inductance
Capacitor	Decreases capacitance	**Increases capacitance**

Given the water analogy and what you have learned in the previous section about these components, the table above should make sense. Consider the following observations about each component type that *increases the ef-*

fective value, keeping in mind the opposite arrangement will have the decreasing value impact:

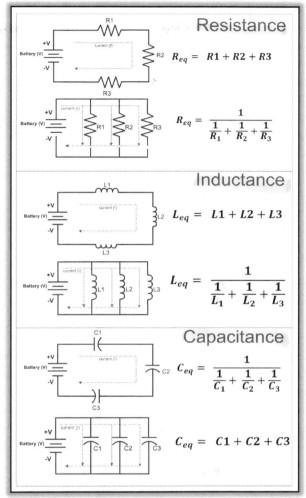

- Stringing resistors along in a series line is like making one longer resistor, so resistance increases.

- Stringing inductors along in a series line is like lengthening a single inductor, increasing its number of windings, and thereby increasing its inductance.

- Arranging capacitors in parallel is like creating a single capacitor of much larger surface area, thereby increasing its capacitance.

Let's work through a few more examples. Sharpen your pencil and grab your calculator, and let's get comfortable with series and parallel computation.

Figure 6.24: Series and parallel components with equations.

Example: What is the total resistance of a 10 ohm, a 20 ohm, and a 50 ohm resistor in parallel? Resistors in parallel use the Reciprocal of Reciprocals equation form, thus

$$R_{eq} = \frac{1}{\frac{1}{R_1} + \frac{1}{R_2} + \frac{1}{R_3}} = \frac{1}{\frac{1}{10} + \frac{1}{20} + \frac{1}{50}}$$

$$= \frac{1}{\frac{17}{100}} = 5.9 \text{ ohms}$$

Think back to middle school math on this one… when adding those three fractions together in the denominator, the denominator of each fraction must be common. Convert each fraction so that it has a denominator of 100, and the numerator values convert to 10, 5, and 2, respectively, summing to 17/100. Following this conversion and summation, use the "1/x" or "reciprocal" key on your calculator to easily compute the final solution.

Example: What is the capacitance of three 100 microfarad capacitors connected in series? Capacitors in series use the Reciprocal of Reciprocals equation form.

$$C_{eq} = \cfrac{1}{\cfrac{1}{C_1} + \cfrac{1}{C_2} + \cfrac{1}{C_3}}$$

$$= \cfrac{1}{\cfrac{1}{100} + \cfrac{1}{100} + \cfrac{1}{100}}$$

$$= \cfrac{1}{\cfrac{3}{100}} = 33.3 \text{ microfarads}$$

In contrast with the resistance example above, this problem already has common denominators since the capacitors are of equivalent value. Again, the "1/x" calculator key comes in handy for computing the final reciprocal.

Example: What is the inductance of three 10 millihenry inductors connected in parallel? Inductors in parallel also use the Reciprocal of Reciprocals equation form.

$$L_{eq} = \cfrac{1}{\cfrac{1}{L_1} + \cfrac{1}{L_2} + \cfrac{1}{L_3}} = \cfrac{1}{\cfrac{1}{10} + \cfrac{1}{10} + \cfrac{1}{10}} = \cfrac{1}{\cfrac{3}{10}} = 3.3 \text{ millihenry}$$

Example: What is the capacitance of a 20 microfarad capacitor in series with a 50 microfarad capacitor? Again, the Reciprocal of Reciprocals equation form, but only two capacitors:

$$C_{eq} = \cfrac{1}{\cfrac{1}{C_1} + \cfrac{1}{C_2}} = \cfrac{1}{\cfrac{1}{20} + \cfrac{1}{50}} = \cfrac{1}{\cfrac{7}{100}} = 14.3 \text{ microfarads}$$

Once again, obtaining a common denominator for the two fractions is necessary before adding them.

Example: What is the equivalent capacitance of two 5.0 nanofarad capacitors and one 750 picofarad capacitors connected in parallel? First, convert picofarads to nanofarads by moving the decimal left three places, making the units common as nF. Then, capacitors in parallel use the Sum of Components equation form.

$$750 \text{ pF} = 0.750 \text{ nF}$$

$$C_{eq} = 5.0 \text{ nf} + 5.0 \text{ nf} + 0.750 \text{ nf} = \textbf{10.750 nanofarads}$$

Example: If three equal value resistors in series produce 450 ohms, what is the value of each resistor? Resistors in series add together, so the value of three equal value resistors summing to 450 ohms must each be **150 ohms.**

$$150 + 150 + 150 = \textbf{450 ohms}$$

Diodes in Parallel: Beyond the resistors, capacitors, and inductors, diodes are sometimes used in a parallel arrangement to increase current handling capacity. Although either diode alone may not have sufficient current rating to handle the circuit's peak current, the pair of them in combination can handle it with one-half

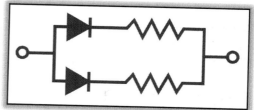

Figure 6.25: Diodes in parallel for increased current handling, with low-value resistors in series.

of the current flowing through each of the two diodes. The pair of diodes are equivalent to a single larger or higher rated diode.

However, it is necessary to ensure that the current is indeed shared equally between the two parallel diodes, or one of them could carry most of the current unintentionally. A resistor placed in series with each diode ensures that one diode doesn't carry most of the current, but that it is equally shared. Low value resistors are typically used as shown in Figure 6.25 to balance the current throughput between the diodes.

Hopefully your bucket is now filled sufficiently with series and parallel circuit concepts that you may pour forth equivalent knowledge on your VE exam and ace any of these questions you see. Make sure you have the pattern of equation use in your bucket for the combinations of arrangement and component type, make sure the equation forms don't leak out, and be familiar with the use of your calculator! Good luck!

Go snag the questions for this section online and practice again, and then come back to learn more about the reaction we get from these components – less math, more science.

HamRadioSchool.com/general_media

❝ *The impeded stream is the one that sings.*
— *Wendell Berry*

Indeed, currents in the absence of impedance would be boring. In many ways it is impedance that allows our radios to modulate and to radiate – in essence, to *sing*. In this section we will examine impedance more closely, including the component reactions to alternating current that contribute to impedances. We will also consider how the manipulation of impedance with electronics is important to our control and transfer of power, from the wall socket to the antenna feedpoint.

Impedance (Z): The opposition to the flow of current in an AC circuit. The unit of measure for impedance is the ohm (Ω). Much like simple resistance to DC, impedance opposes the back-and-forth current flow of AC. However, impedance is resistance combined with another oppositional force called *reactance*.

G5A01 G5A10

Reactance (X): Opposition to the flow of alternating current caused by capacitance or inductance. The unit of measure for reactance is also the ohm. Capacitors and inductors *react* to AC in different, quite opposite, ways. The reactance imposed by capacitors and inductors depends upon the component value of capacitance or inductance and upon the frequency of AC.

G5A02 G5A09

Capacitive Reactance (X_C): Opposition to the flow of alternating current in a capacitor. The designation for capacitive reactance is X_C, and it is calculated as

G5A04

$$X_C = \frac{1}{2\pi f C}$$

The frequency in hertz of the AC is designated by f and the capacitance in farads of the component by C. ($\pi \approx 3.14$.) Although there are no question pool items requiring this computation, it is useful to illustrate the reactance to capacitance and frequency. **As frequency of the applied**

G5A06

205

AC increases, the reactance decreases. And as capacitance increases, reactance decreases.

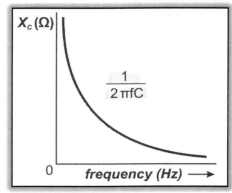

Figure 6.26: Capacitive reactance decreases as frequency increases. A capacitor passes high frequency signals and impedes low frequency signals.

Recalling our water model of capacitors, this makes sense. The capacitor was imagined to be a stretchy diaphragm across the interior of the water pipe, stretching back and forth with the alternating current flow, storing energy in the elastic stretch, but having a maximum capacity that when reached stops further stretching and storage. For a given AC voltage, if the frequency of alternation is rapid enough (high frequency) the maximum charge capacity may never be reached in either direction of current, so little opposition to the AC flow results (low reactance). But with the same voltage and a low AC frequency, the diaphragm may stretch to maximum capacity (maximum charge) and reduce or stop further current flow (increased reactance) until the AC cycle reverses. The greater the capacitance the less opposition to current flow results from cycle to cycle (lower reactance).

Strictly in electrical terms, the capacitor is storing electric charge until the maximum feasible charge is accumulated on its plates, and opposition to current flow builds up gradually over that time of accumulation each AC cycle. At higher frequencies or with higher capacitance, the plates do not approach the maximum charge and reactance remains low. At lower frequencies or lower capacitance the plates approach or achieve maximum charge capacity and offer great opposition each AC cycle, or higher reactance. So, the capacitor readily passes high frequency AC and opposes low frequency AC and DC.

Inductive Reactance (X_L): Opposition to the flow of alternating current in an inductor. The designation for inductive reactance is X_L, and it is calculated as

$$X_L = 2\pi f L$$

Again, the frequency in hertz is designated f, and the inductance of the component is L. Note that **if either frequency** or inductance **increas-**

es, the inductive reactance will increase. Notice that these effects are opposite that of the capacitive reactance.

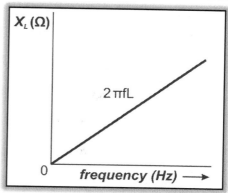

Figure 6.27: Inductive reactance increases as frequency increases. Inductors pass low frequency signals and impede high frequency signals.

In the water model an inductor was likened to a massive water wheel extending into the current flow. It stores energy in the rotational inertia of the heavy wheel turning, analogous to the inductor *inflating* a magnetic field to store energy. Inflating the magnetic field requires time and work, as accelerating the wheel rotation up to current speed. During this initial inflation period (wheel acceleration) great opposition to the current flow is offered, but it diminishes gradually with time and once fully inflated (spinning at speed) the opposition is eliminated. This effect is opposite that of the capacitor where initially little opposition is offered in the cycle but great opposition builds over time as the plates charge, or the diaphragm stretches toward its limit.

The inductor readily passes DC or low frequency AC that allows the magnetic field time to inflate and stabilize during the AC cycle. A rapid reversal of current with high frequency AC requires constant work inflating the magnetic field in opposite polarizations each cycle, never achieving stability, and thus providing constant opposition to current flow.

Resonance: In the language of physics (*no, don't run!*), resonance occurs in a system when it is easily able to store and transfer energy between two (or more) storage modes. Think about a playground swing, for instance. At the bottom of a swing's cycle the energy is *kinetic*, stored as the high velocity of your body's mass moving along the swing's arc. As the swing rises and slows the energy is transferred into *gravitational potential*, your body suspended high above the ground, and the maximum transfer to potential energy has occurred at the moment of weightlessness when you get that little thrill in the pit of your stomach! That energy transfer was pretty easy, huh? Fun, too! (*See, physics can be fun!*)

Following that high suspended state of abdominal delight you will fall. Gravity will pull you down. Your potential energy is being transferred back to the

Figure 6.28: Resonance, like that of a swing, occurs in circuits having both capacitance and inductance.

kinetic energy of speed once again. Fortunately, the swing directs that speed onto the arc defined by the length of its chains or ropes, and the kinetic-potential-kinetic cycle is repeated again and again, much to your intestine's joy.

This is easy transfer of energy between two storage modes. But there is some opposition to this swinging cycle presented by air resistance as you zip along and by the rubbing friction at the chain attachment points. However, if only a tiny amount of energy is added each cycle, perhaps by someone giving just the slightest push regularly timed with your downward motion, the small amount of resistance to your swinging cycle is overcome and perhaps exceeded, sending you higher and higher! The natural frequency of the swing's oscillation, and the frequency with which reinforcing pushes are added to be most effective, is the *resonant frequency.*

The same condition can arise in AC circuits containing inductors and capacitors. This type of circuit is an *LC oscillator,* also known as a *tank circuit* because of its similarity to a sloshing tank of water transferring energy between kinetic and potential modes. *When the inductive reactance and capacitive reactance are equivalent the circuit will achieve a state of resonance.*

The two energy storage modes in an LC oscillator are magnetic field storage (inductance L) and electric field storage (capacitance C). When a circuit's inductive reactance and

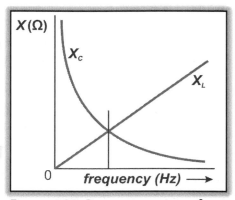

Figure 6.29: Resonance occurs for the frequency at which inductive and capacitive reactances are equivalent.

capacitive reactance
are equal the two
components can
easily transfer
energy back and
forth, just like the
swing. In a series
circuit arrangement
the opposite effects
of the inductive
and capacitive
reactances cancel
one another out,
leaving only the
internal resistance
of the inductor
and capacitor
to contribute to
overall impedance,

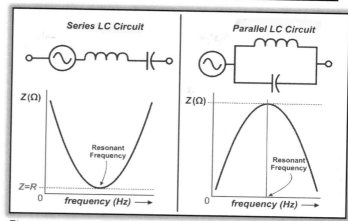

Figure 6.30: Impedance of a series LC circuit minimizes to simple resistance at the resonant frequency. Impedance of a parallel LC circuit maximizes at the resonant frequency and includes simple resistance and reactances.

as shown in the left of Figure 6.30. In a parallel circuit these reactances reinforce one another, causing circuit impedance to peak to a maximum, as in the right of Figure 6.30. You may recognize this case from the antenna trap discussed in Section 5.1 (and Figure 5.9) where the resonant frequency causes high impedance and electrically terminates the inner antenna segments.

Further like the swing, the transfer of energy back and forth between capacitor and inductor will have a characteristic frequency of oscillation, or resonant frequency. The swing's resonant frequency is determined by the length of the swing and by the strength of gravity's pull. (A longer swing has a lower resonant frequency, and a swing on the moon would have a lower resonant frequency than the same swing on earth.) Similarly, **the frequency of an LC oscillator is determined by the inductance and capacitance in the tank circuit.** By selecting appropriate values of inductance and capacitance, an LC oscillator can be created to resonate at a specific frequency for the purposes of filtering (as in the antenna trap) or in tuning circuits to selected frequencies. As noted in Section 6.2 *Components*, some inductors create inter-turn capacitance that causes them to be self-resonant at some frequencies where the parasitic capacitive reactance equals the inductive reactance. One final analog to our swing: In an LC oscillator circuit the applied AC frequency is the reinforcing push provided each cycle of energy transfer to overcome the remaining simple resistance.

G7B09

Impedance Matching: Thanks to another 19th Century German physicist with the impressive name *Moritz Hermann von Jacobi*, we are able to take advantage of the *Maximum Power Transfer Theorem* in our radio circuits. With this theorem von Jacobi proved that **a power source can deliver maximum power to an electrical load when the impedance of the load is equal to the internal impedance of the power source.** Let's untangle that mouthful just a bit.

In a radio station an electrical load may be an antenna, a dummy load, a resistor, coaxial cable, or other circuit type – it is the thing to which we wish to transfer power with the source, or transmitter. A load will have characteristic impedance resulting from the combination of resistance, capacitive reactance, and inductive reactance. In some cases, such as antennas, coaxial cable, and engineered circuits, we can adjust the impedance of the load to a desired value by manipulating components or materials. Similarly, with signal sources like an RF transmitter, the output impedance (at the connector) may be engineered to a desired value. As an example noted in Chapter 5, *Antennas*, most amateur radio transmitters and commonly used coaxial cables are designed to have 50 ohm impedance.

The Maximum Power Transfer Theorem reveals that **impedance matching is important so the source can deliver maximum power to the load.** To deliver maximum power to our station antenna the impedance of the transmitter, feed line, and antenna feed point should be well matched. As discussed in Section 5.3, an impedance mismatch will result in power reflections, reducing power delivered to the antenna.

Impedance Matching Devices: Depending upon the application or situation, various practical circuits may be used to match the impedance of a load to that of the source. **At radio frequencies impedance matching may be achieved with a transformer, an LC circuit (Pi-network or T-circuit), or even a simple length of transmission line.** Impedance matching transformers will be described in the next section, but let's examine two popular LC circuit matches.

LC Circuit: Inserting an LC network between two circuits is one method of impedance matching between AC circuits. The *Pi-network* and *T-circuit* are two common LC circuits used for this purpose. (Network is just a more formal term for a circuit, particularly when a general design concept is to be related.)

By selecting appropriate inductor and capacitor values these circuits will present the desired matching impedance on each side of the circuit

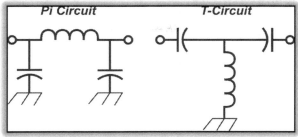

Figure 6.31: The Pi Circuit and T-Circuit used for impedance matching.

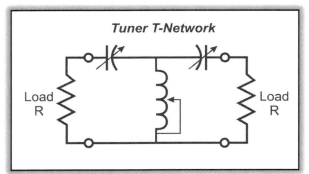

Figure 6.32: A T-Network using variable components for tuning the impedance match between two loads.

to the source or load to which it is connected. Variable inductor and capacitor components may be used to create adjustable matching networks when load impedance is expected to vary, such as in an antenna tuner used to match impedance between a transmitter and an antenna across a broad band of RF frequencies. The T-circuit is commonly used in antenna tuning devices, and the Pi-network is often incorporated in higher power applications such as amplifiers.

Practical Application: The most common application of impedance matching for most amateurs is in the realm of antenna tuning. The maximum power will be transferred to your antenna when the antenna system's impedance matches that of the transmitter. In the simplest and most common scenario this will mean a 50 Ω transmitter output with 50 Ω coaxial cable connected as a feedline. The feedline will attach to the antenna feed point. The impedance presented at the antenna feedpoint will be a function of the antenna design, antenna installation height, and the environment near the antenna.

Rarely will an antenna present a feed point impedance of precisely 50 Ω, especially across a wide range of frequencies in a typical amateur band. Thus, it is at the antenna feed point connection where an impedance mismatch will most commonly occur and thereby generate power reflections and elevate SWR.

Using an antenna tuner or an impedance matching network between the transmitter and feedline is a partial solution. Most modern transmitters will begin reducing power as SWR exceeds values of about 2:1. The matching network presents 50 Ω to the transmitter so it will not reduce power, but the impedance mismatch is still present at the feed point and causing a higher SWR on the antenna system. The matching network or tuner does not improve power transfer to the antenna, but it helps avoid power reduction by the transmitter. The reflections are still bouncing back and forth along your feedline. *Your antenna system is not at resonance,* but that's OK.

Your antenna SWR will rarely, if ever, be 1:1 on the nose. This *might* happen at one frequency on one band when the humidity is just right, the moon is full, and you wear two different colored socks, one of wool and the other of cotton, while your spouse pulls the aluminum gutter away from the house at the precise angle required. But even without all that you can get it *good enough* for superb operation. The perfect antenna system impedance match is a very rare thing.

So you see, the impeded stream really is the one that sings. The impeded transceiver sings its RF melody, particularly when the impeded antenna system is singing in harmony. Next we'll examine power sources and learn about their inner workings. First, the questions on impedance and reactance!

HamRadioSchool.com/general_media

Note: If you would like to learn more about complex impedance and the relationship among resistance, capacitive reactance, and inductive reactance, see the *HamRadioSchool.com* three-part article on Complex Impedance in the *Ham Radio 101* category of online articles.

❝❝ *With great power often comes great confusion.*
– Dan Allen, Seam in Action

When it comes to supplying power to your station, great confusion should be avoided. In this section we will examine the workings of power sources. We'll cover several types of power sources, but we will focus on what's going on inside those DC power supplies that you plug into the 120 VAC wall socket and that provide about +13.8 VDC to power your ham radio. This should help to clear up, or at least reduce, any great confusion you may have about supplying power.

Power Supply Overview: You have probably used a DC power supply of one type or another a million times. Plug in a battery charger for an HT ham radio, a cell phone, a tablet computing device, an electric razor, an electronic toy, or nearly any other battery operated electronic device on the market today and you're using a power supply. Many small appliances will have them integrated internally, such as clocks, commercial radios, and computers. An amateur radio base station will often be operated with a supply capable of delivering the power necessary for transmitter RF output of 50 to 100 watts. A power supply will integrate three basic circuits to convert higher voltage AC into lower voltage DC:

1. *Transformer:* Shifts AC voltage from one value to another. For example, 120 VAC may be transformed into an AC voltage nearer the desired 13.8 volts output level.
2. *Rectifier:* Converts the AC waveform into a varying voltage DC. Even though the voltage is providing EMF in only one direction after being rectified, it still contains the sine wave-like variability in voltage value over time.
3. *Filter Circuit:* Smooths the varying DC voltage into a steady DC voltage that is usable by the radio electronics.

Let's consider each of these types of circuits and the tasks they accomplish for the power supply.

Transformer: Contrary to popular belief a transformer is not a giant alien robot that can camouflage itself as a tractor trailer rig or spiffy hotrod car. In electronics a transformer is two (or more) inductors whose wire windings are wrapped around the same core. The symbol for a transformer looks like a pair of parallel inductors with a bar between them, mimicking the physical reality. While not nearly as sensational as a giant alien robot destroying high rise buildings, real transformers are a lot more practically useful and a lot less trouble.

Recall from the 6.2 *Components* section that an inductor creates a magnetic field about itself to store energy when a current passes through its coiled form. Recall also that inductors near one another may have *mutual inductance* – that is, the changing magnetic field of one inductor can induce an electric current in the other inductor as its magnetic field inflates and deflates with AC cycles. While mutual inductance is to be avoided in most circuits, a transformer is designed specifically to take advantage of mutual inductance. This is why the windings share a common core.

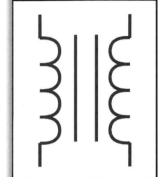

Figure 6.33: Symbol for a transformer.

If AC is applied to one of the windings it will produce a magnetic field that inflates and deflates with the AC cycle with alternating polarity of the magnetic flux. This part of a transformer that is normally connected to the incoming source of energy is called the primary, or *primary winding*, and it is the primary that is energized by household 120 VAC. The other winding on the core, called the secondary winding, is also within the alternating magnetic field of the primary. As the primary's magnetic field inflates and deflates an alternating current is induced in the secondary winding. **A voltage across the secondary winding of a transformer when an AC voltage source is connected across its primary winding is caused by mutual inductance.**

Transforming Voltage: The AC voltage and current induced in the secondary winding depends upon the ratio of the number of turns between the two windings. Specifically, the ratio of the voltages of the two windings will equal the ratio of the number of windings. Letting E_p and E_s be the primary and secondary voltages (EMF), and letting N_p and N_s be the number of turns in the primary and secondary, the relationship is

$$\frac{E_S}{E_P} = \frac{N_S}{N_P}$$ or, solving for the secondary voltage $$E_S = E_P \times \frac{N_S}{N_P}$$

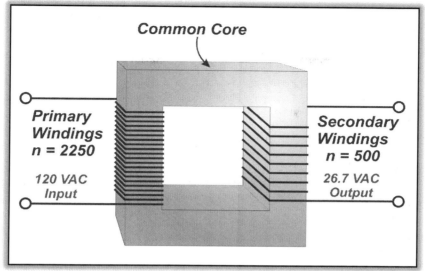

Common Core

Primary Windings n = 2250

120 VAC Input

Secondary Windings n = 500

26.7 VAC Output

Figure 6.34: A "step down" transformer has more windings on the primary than on the secondary, and it reduces voltage by the ratio of windings.

The second form of the equation lets us compute the voltage induced in the secondary from the primary voltage and the windings ratio, as in the following example. We will work with RMS voltages as described in the 6.1 *Power and Principles* section.

Example: **What is the RMS voltage across a 500-turn secondary winding in a transformer if the 2250-turn primary is connected to 120 VAC?** (Figure 6.34)

$$E_S = E_P \times \frac{N_S}{N_P} = 120v \times \frac{500}{2250} = 120v \times 0.222 = \textbf{26.7} \textbf{\textit{v}}$$

This is an example of a *step down* transformer, since the voltage is decreased from the primary to the secondary windings. The current of the secondary will be proportionally greater than the current of the primary, as the power (P=EI) transfer of the two sets of windings must be equivalent (in an ideal case). **In a step up transformer** in which the primary conducts greater current so that the secondary may have a higher voltage, **the primary winding conductor (wire) may be larger in diameter than the conductor of the secondary to accommodate the higher current of the primary.**

A reversal of the number of windings between primary and secondary will reverse the step up or step down nature of the transformer. For example, **if**

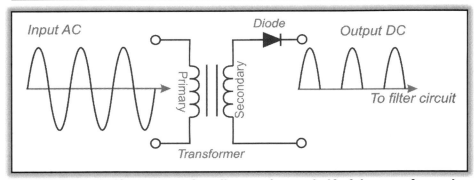

Figure 6.35: A half-wave rectifier allows only one-half of the transformed AC waveform to pass, resulting in a pulsing and varying DC output.

G5C02 **you reverse the primary and secondary windings of a 4:1 voltage step down transformer the secondary voltage becomes 4 times the primary voltage** in a step up windings arrangement.

Rectifier: After the AC voltage has been adjusted to a desired value by the transformer the rectifier will convert the AC to DC. That is, the back-and-forth alternating direction cycle of current will be changed to flow in just one direction. Let's consider two basic types of rectifiers, the *half-wave* and the *full-wave* rectifier.

G7A05 Half-Wave Rectifier: **A half-wave rectifier converts** to DC only one-half of the AC wave, or **180 degrees of the full AC waveform**, as depicted in Figure 6.35. The complete 360 degree AC waveform is applied to the primary winding of the transformer, but the diode circuit on the secondary winding output allows only one-half of the transformed AC waveform to pass – the positive voltage portion in this figure. The sine wave-like variation of voltage remains, but all voltage is in a single direction. The voltage "pulses" and varies however, since the negative voltage half of the waveform is deleted, leaving the positive voltage sine wave signal and a gap of zero volts during the negative voltage times of the AC source.

The diode selected for the half-wave rectifier must be rated to withstand the negative peak voltage of the transformer for which current will attempt to flow in the inverse (non-conducting) direction through the diode. This is referred to as the peak-inverse-voltage (PIV) rating of a rectifier, the maximum voltage it will handle in the non-conducting direction. **G7A04** **For the half-wave power supply the PIV is typically two times the normal peak output voltage of the power supply** for reasons we will explore under the filter circuit topic later in this section.

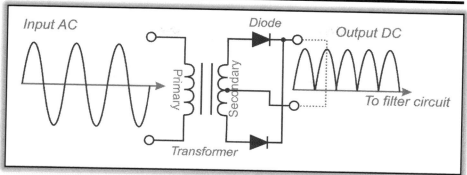

Figure 6.36: A center-tapped full-wave rectifier passes the entire transformed AC waveform, resulting in a varying DC output.

Full-Wave Rectifier: **A full-wave rectifier converts to DC the entire
360 degree portion of the AC cycle,** as depicted in Figure 6.36. Each
of the two diodes in the full-wave rectifier circuit passes one-half of the AC
voltage waveform, either the positive or the negative half. And due to the
circuit arrangement, each diode passes its current to a common directional
path beyond the diodes and toward the filter circuit of the power supply. This
is like having two one-half wave rectifiers working together, each converting
to DC one-half of the AC waveform. As a result, **the output waveform of
an unfiltered full-wave rectifier is a series of DC pulses at twice the
frequency of the AC input.**

Notice, however, that the full-wave rectifier requires the current return connection to be tapped at the center of the secondary winding of the transformer. The return cannot go to the opposite side of the winding as in the half-
wave rectifier or the negative side (lower) diode would impede the return
current flow. Thus, each half of the transformer winding must produce the
full output voltage required of the power supply. Stated differently, the total
transformer output capability must be twice the required output voltage. So,
when either diode is reversed bias during its non-conducting portion of the
waveform, it must be peak-inverse-rated for the *full voltage of the transformer,*
not just its half-winding voltage. [*See G7A04 on previous page.*]

Full-Wave Bridge Rectifier: Another full-wave rectifier design sidesteps the
disadvantages of the center tapped full-wave design – the bridge rectifier. As
shown in Figure 6.37 on the next page, this rectifier uses an arrangement of
four diodes instead of two, but it does not require the double-voltage transformer like the center tapped design.

Instead, the four diodes of the full-wave bridge rectifier allow two different
current paths to the load (or to the filter circuit of the power supply), with

G7A06

G7A07

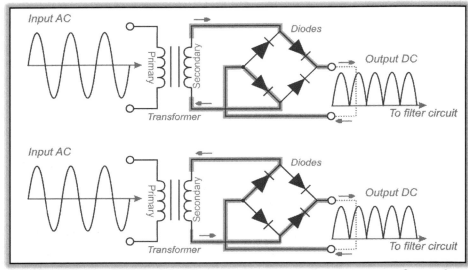

Figure 6.37: The full-wave bridge rectifier passes the entire transformed AC waveform using a diode bridge to ensure output current flows in only one direction. The current paths of each half of the AC cycle are highlighted in grey.

each path arranged for identical output current direction as illustrated in Figure 6.37. Unlike the center tapped full-wave rectifier, **the peak-inverse-voltage across the rectifier in a full-wave bridge power supply is equal to the normal peak output voltage of the power supply,** not double it.

G7A03

Filter Circuits: The output of a rectifier is DC, but a pulsed DC. Most electronics are designed to use a constant, stable DC voltage. It is the job of the power supply's filter circuit to smooth the variable DC pulses of a rectifier into a steady voltage for output. One of the simplest forms of a filter circuit is a *filter capacitor* following the rectifier circuit, as depicted for a half-wave rectifier power supply in Figure 6.38.

The filter capacitor connected across the output of the rectifier will reduce the variability in the voltage. The capacitor will be charged by the rectifier output when the rectifier voltage exceeds the capacitor's voltage, and the capacitor will discharge when the rectifier voltage is lower than its own. With the water analogy you may imagine the filter capacitor swelling and stretching during the higher voltage portion of the rectifier output, storing energy in its elasticity, and then supplementing the power supply output current by releasing its energy during the lower voltage portions of the rectifier cycle. The capacitor

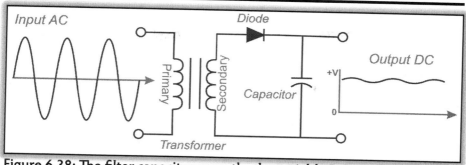

Figure 6.38: The filter capacitor smooths the variable DC output from the rectifier circuit, charging during high voltage periods and discharging during low voltage periods. Some ripple remains in the output voltage.

will constantly charge and discharge commensurately with the voltage of the rectifier, providing a steady output voltage. [Note, this is an idealized description, and some *ripple* will remain in the DC voltage, depending upon filter capacitor ratings and performance.]

Bleeder Resistor: Notice the bleeder resistor included in the bridge rectifier power supply diagram of Figure 6.39. **The bleeder resistor is a power supply safety feature that discharges the filter capacitor when the power is removed.** Any charge remaining on the capacitor will *bleed off* through the resistor over a short time, eliminating its stored energy as heat,

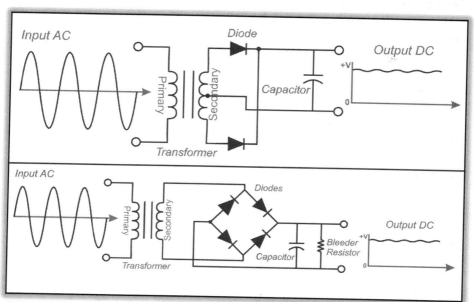

Figure 6.39: Full-wave rectifier power supply circuits including simple filters.

and eliminating a potential shock hazard. Large power supply capacitors can hold substantial and potentially deadly electric charge.

Choke Input: More elaborate filter networks are commonly used that may provide greater smoothing than a lone filter capacitor. An *inductor input filter*, also called a *choke input filter*, **combines inductor components with capacitor components in a power supply filter network.** Since an inductor opposes changes to current the choke input filter helps to smooth current variations as well as voltage variations. The inductor as a choke was introduced in Section 6.2, *Components*.

[margin: G7A02]

Switch-Mode Power Supply: Also known as a *switching supply*, this unique and popular type of power supply **offers the advantage of high frequency operation that allows the use of smaller components.** The switch-mode supply uses a power *switching transistor* to provide high frequency output that is rectified and smoothed by a filter network. The high frequency DC pulses allow the switching supply to rapidly respond to changes in current demands, such as when a transmitter is keyed on and off. And since the pulses are brief the transformer (and other components) may be of reduced performance capacity, smaller and lighter, relative to other types of power supplies.

[margin: G7A08]

Batteries: Many amateur operators prefer to use battery systems to power a station. Batteries are used with HTs regularly, and mobile stations are usually wired to the automobile battery. But batteries may also be used to power base stations in the shack, to serve as a backup supply in the event of power outage, or to operate a portable rig in the field. Batteries store energy chemically, and a variety of chemical types are available, each with unique characteristics and performance.

Storage Cells (Lead-Acid): Perhaps the most commonly used batteries for higher power rigs such as base stations are so-called *storage cells*. Storage cells include deep-cycle marine or recreational vehicle batteries that use lead-acid chemistry and are rechargeable. Lead-acid storage cells offer low internal resistance that provides excellent surge current capability for transmissions at higher power levels. Lead-acid batteries tend to hold charge well over time and require only occasional *maintenance charging*, or *topping off*. The lead-acid electrolyte may be a liquid (as in car batteries) or the very popular *gel cell* type in which the electrolyte remains in a semi-solid gel form greatly reducing the potential for spills or leaks. Most storage cells should be maintained at 13.8 V, even as they may be rated, and called, "12 V batteries." **The minimum allowable discharge voltage for maximum life of a stan-**

[margin: G6A01]

dard 12 volt lead-acid battery is 10.5 volts. Below this output voltage the battery's voltage will fall off sharply with time. Discharging below this level can reduce the effective life of the battery, so recharge at or before reaching the 10.5 volt level. However, deep-cycle batteries are just that – they are designed to be discharged to a very low percentage of their capacity, and a commensurately low voltage, with little long-term negative effects.

The table below summarizes the features of several additional battery types that are popular for amateur radio use. The energy storage rating in *milliamp-hours* is an indication of the capacity of the battery to provide current with a stable voltage for a period of time, and it may be used as an index to compare relative capacities of cells.

Internal Resistance: A battery will have *internal resistance* resulting from its own construction and materials, and this internal resistance will govern the rate of electric current that may flow from the source. For example, **an advantage of the low internal resistance of nickel-cadmium batteries is high discharge current,** and the same has been noted already for lead-acid cells. This comes in handy when a strong surge of current is required to power an HT radio transmission, for instance. Other batteries may impose high internal resistance to insure current is limited to a low value for stable, long term operations such as powering a wrist watch.

Battery Type Summary

Chemistry	Typical Packaging	Voltage (V)	Energy (mAh)	Notes
Alkaline	AAA to D 9v 6v	1.5v 9v 6v	1100 to 12000 580 11000	Disposable; Recharge only if designated "rechargeable." Good for emergency backup of HT or other portable devices.
Nickel-Metal Hydride	AA 9v	1.2v 9v	1500 to 2200 200	Rechargeable; Often multiple AA cells in molded package for HT snap-on.
Nickel-Cadmium	AA 9v	1.2v 9v	700 120	Rechargeable; Older technology. AA cells combined in snap-on package.
Lithiom-Ion	AA Coin Cell	1.7v ~3v	2100 to 2400 25 to 600	Rechargeable; New technology. AA cells combined in snap-on package. Now used in many HT products.
Carbon-Zinc	AA	1.5	600	Disposable. **Never recharge.** Older technology moving out of use.

G6A02

G6A04

Alternative Power Sources: Even with batteries it is sometimes desired to have longer term power available. Solar and wind power are becoming more prominent as personal power sources for the home or the field. Having a solar panel to recharge batteries when camping or backpacking can come in handy, and modest modern solar power systems can keep your home station storage cell batteries charged up and even power your rig directly while the sun shines.

Light weight, compact, foldable or roll-up panels are available on the market complete with the simple electronics needed to affect recharging of a battery or voltage conversion for powering a small device. Generally, the power available from a panel or panel array will be a function of the total area of the panels, the conversion efficiency, and the illumination available. Different types of solar cells are made from different materials and each type has an efficiency rating that may be used to estimate the output of the system. Higher quality silicon cells have efficiency ratings greater than 20% and advances in efficiency are being made rapidly. More than 100 watts of power may be generated by a large, modern solar panel in bright sunlight.

G4E08 **The name of the process by which sunlight is changed directly into electricity is photovoltaic conversion.** Typical solar cells from which panels are constructed are special PN-junctions that generate small currents when sunlight is absorbed by the material. **G4E09** **If you measure the open-circuit voltage of a modern, well illuminated photovoltaic cell it will usually be 0.5 VDC.** By connecting cells in various series and parallel arrangements, panels of a variety of output voltages may be created. For instance, a 12 volt system for powering a radio station could be fabricated from a set of 24 cells of 0.5 volts all connected in series. Multiple 12 volt strings like this can be connected in parallel to provide increased current and available power. **G4E10** **Usually a diode will be connected in series between a solar panel and a storage battery that is being charged by the panel to prevent self discharge of the battery through the panel during times of low or no illumination.** (Blocking diode.)

Check out solar power for your station or for your portable field operations. It's remarkably easy and much more convenient than lugging batteries around!

Wind generators may be effective in some locations, depending upon the typical atmospherics. Wind power generation requires heavier mechanical systems than solar – a generator and gearbox typically, and more complex electronics to ensure voltage regulation with variable speed generators. This

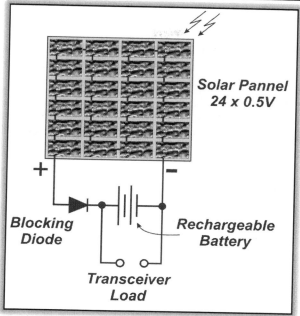

Figure 6.40: A simple solar panel circuit for powering a transceiver and charging a battery.

increases costs associated with wind power. Further, **the disadvantage of using wind as a primary source of power, such as for an emergency station, is that a large energy storage system is needed to supply power when the wind is not blowing.** Nature can be unreliable in this way, and if your luck is like mine the wind will die exactly when I need it most.

The bottom line is that wind generation may work well for some locations and with a solid battery storage system, but solar is usually more reliable and becoming less expensive. The combination of solar panels and modest storage capacity is usually a winning one.

Transforming Impedance: Let's return briefly to the topic of transformers to consider one other task they can accomplish. In addition to transforming voltage a transformer may be used to match impedances! Transformers are sometimes used at antenna feed points to achieve a match. Here's how it works.

The power (P) into the transformer must equal the power out of the transformer by the power law P = EI. Thus, if the voltage (E) of the secondary winding differs from the voltage of the primary, the current (I) of the secondary must also change in order that input and output power equate. And for AC, impedance (Z) is the ratio of voltage to current, as noted in Section 5.1 *Antennas - Theory and Principles:* Z = E/I. Putting this together, since the voltage and current of the secondary differs from the voltage and current of the primary, the impedance (Z_s) of the secondary must also differ from the primary impedance (Z_p). A relationship of the turns ratio and impedances is

$$\frac{N_P}{N_S} = \sqrt{\frac{Z_P}{Z_S}}$$

Notice that since a transformer adjusts impedance it can be used as a method of impedance matching. **An impedance matching transformer may be used to maximize the transfer of power.** Antennas may use a matching transformer, as will other components of a station besides power supplies, such as an audio amplifier driving a speaker.

Example: **What is the turns ratio of a transformer used to match an audio amplifier having a 600 ohm output impedance to a speaker having a 4 ohm impedance?**

$$\frac{N_P}{N_S} = \sqrt{\frac{Z_P}{Z_S}} = \sqrt{\frac{600\Omega}{4\Omega}} = \sqrt{150} = 12.2$$

The turns ratio is 12.2 to 1. Note that in this example the amplifier is serving as the primary winding source voltage, and the turn ratio is stated with the larger number (12.2) first, as 12.2 : 1.

How's the confusion? Some of it wiped away? If not, review this section and online materials, and particularly practice the questions on *Power Sources!* And if you've really got it all, no more confusion at all…. More power to you!

HamRadioSchool.com/general_media

❝ *Nigel Tufnel: The numbers all go to eleven. Look, right across the board, eleven, eleven, eleven and...*

Marty DiBergi: Oh, I see. And most amps go up to ten?

Nigel Tufnel: Exactly.

Marty DiBergi: Does that mean it's louder? Is it any louder?

Nigel Tufnel: Well, it's one louder, isn't it? It's not ten. These go to eleven.

- This is Spinal Tap,
Rob Reiner, Director

Let's be clear: Nigel was *not* a licensed amateur radio operator. Thankfully. However, many stations do use RF amplifiers to boost signal strength. Most of them probably go only to ten, but they can still be very effective when atmospheric propagation conditions are poor or when it is important to provide a solid, clear signal over a large area – perhaps to serve as net control for an HF band net, for instance. Let's consider two basic categories of amps: *Solid State and Vacuum Tube* amplifiers.

Solid State Amplifiers: Recall from Section 6.2 *Components* that transistors will behave as amplifiers in the region between high and low stable states. The controlling signal input to the base (BJT) or gate (FET) is represented in the stronger current flowing from collector to emitter (BJT) or source to drain (FET). Amplifiers for amateur radio may be *solid state*, meaning the construction is entirely of solid materials such as semiconductor electronics including amplifying transistors. That is, no glass vacuum tubes. With most solid state amps you may essentially plug them in and operate with little concern for meticulous adjustment or tuning. Most of that is handled automatically by cleverly designed circuits, although **permanent damage to a solid-state amplifier can be caused by a condition of excessive drive power** (the control input signal power from the transmitter). But, particularly for higher power HF, solid state amps tend to come at a premium price point.

G4A07

Vacuum Tube Amplifiers: Vacuum tubes are like *glass FETs* – they behave in a very similar manner to field effect transistors, amplifying a control input signal across other electrodes. In fact, you might say that vacuum tubes were transistors before there were transistors! Some of us recall a day when televisions emitted a warm glow through the ventilation holes in the TV's cabinet housing due to the vacuum tubes helping to amplify signals for display on a giant vacuum tube called a cathode ray tube (CRT).

Generally, the price point for RF power with vacuum tubes is a bit lower than with solid state RF amps. Vacuum tube RF amplifiers remain very popular in amateur radio for not only the price advantages but for the quality of performance and high power output provided. Tube type amplifiers require more careful adjustment during use, usually with manual impedance tuning and power control.

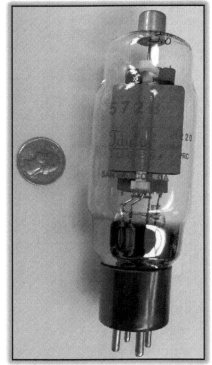

Figure 6.41: An RF amplifier vacuum tube.

So, crank it up to eleven and let's rock out to some tubular amplification of RF. Dude.

Amplifier Classes: Amplifiers are categorized by *class*, as determined by the characteristics of signal amplification and resulting performance. Different classes of amplifier are appropriate for different types of radio operations. Along with each description that follows is a figure depicting the portion of each AC cycle that the class of amplifier operates upon. That is, only the high-lighted portion of each waveform will have its amplitude boosted to a greater value by the affiliated amplifier, and this has an impact on the accuracy with which the amplifier can recreate the input signal without distortion as well as the efficiency with which the amplifier class operates.

Amplifier efficiency is computed as the RF output power divided by the DC input power – the ratio of output to input power.

Class A: A *linear amplifier* **offering low distortion** of the amplified signal. It amplifies the entire waveform of the input signal (full 360 degrees of each cycle), but it is the least efficient type of amplifier.

A linear amplifier is one in which the output preserves the input waveform.
With amplitude modulated signals such as SSB phone this is critical to preserving the modulation envelope by which audio signals are encoded in the RF. (*See SSB and AM section.*) Unlike the other types of amps, the Class A amplifies the entire RF waveform cycle equivalently, boosting the signal amplitude while maintaining the amplitude-derived envelope shape.

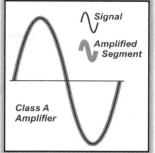

Figure 6.42: Class A amplifier signal.

Class B: Given high quality of design the Class B amplifier can also be highly linear. This amplifier uses two complementary signal amplifying components, one to boost only the negative half of the input waveform (180 degrees) and one to boost only the positive half (opposite 180

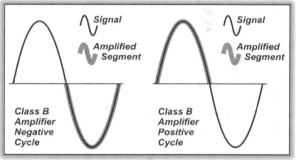

Figure 6.43: Two Class B amplifier signal halves

degrees). For this reason the Class B amp is also known as a *push-pull amplifier*. If both amplifiers perform identically with well-matched, duplicate input signals, good linearity of the output amplified signal can result. Power efficiency of a push-pull is significantly improved over the Class A.

Class AB: A combination of Class A and Class B types. A push-pull configuration is used as in Type B, but each complementary amplifying device boosts slightly more than one-half of the input signal cycle, either positive or negative plus a bit of the other. Both devices operate around the crossover time from positive to negative, helping to eliminate distortion problems of the Class B push-pull design. The AB amplifier is sufficiently linear for SSB mode, but less power efficient than the Type B due to the longer cycle active periods.

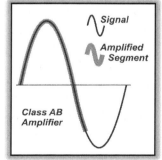

Figure 6.44: The positive cycle of a Class AB amplifier signal.

Class C: Less than one-half of the input signal is amplified, typically between 100 – 150 degrees. **Class C is the highest efficiency class of amplifier,** but its linearity is very poor. This can be inferred by examining the amplified segment of the waveform – any modulating amplitude envelope would be severely distorted by this amplifier's small active period. So, Class C amplifiers should not be used with SSB or AM. However, since FM depends only upon frequency deviations, this amp is quite suitable for FM amplification. Further, since **CW mode** requires only a narrow bandwidth tone and does not contain a modulating envelope, **the very efficient Class C amplifier is quite appropriate for CW operations.**

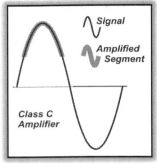

Figure 6.45: Class C amplifier signal.

Some RF amplifiers for amateur use may be operated as Class AB and also as Class C. A longer amplification period Class AB functioning supports SSB mode with low distortion while a brief period Class C functioning provides excellent efficiency in CW mode.

We will examine the operating adjustments and cautions required of RF tube amplifiers, but to better understand those adjustments we'll next consider the workings of the vacuum tubes used as amplifying components in many RF amplifiers. Let's go tubing.

Vacuum Tubes: The solid state Field Effect Transistor (see *Components* section) **is most like a vacuum tube in its general operating characteristics,** as a tube uses a controlling input signal to regulate a larger current flow much like the FET. Recall from Section 6.2 that the FET base electrode receives a controlling voltage that regulates the current passing between the source and gate electrodes. The vacuum tube has similarly functioning elements.

With some variation depending upon specific design, a tube will have the following basic elements:

- *Cathode* – a source of electrons, analogous to the FET *source* electrode.

- *Heater* – a resistive heating filament that heats the cathode to cause electron emission.

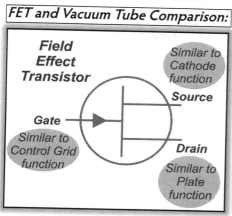

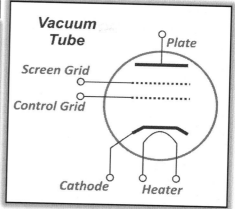

Figure 6.46: The FET is similar to the vacuum tube in its functions for amplification.

Figure 6.47 Tetrode (4-element) Vacuum Tube controls current with an input voltage, similar to a FET.

- *Control Grid* – the **control grid** located between the cathode and plate **is used to regulate the flow of electrons between the cathode and plate;** analogous to the FET *gate* electrode; the controlling signal (*drive power*) is applied here.

- *Screen Grid* – located between the control grid and plate, **the primary purpose of the screen grid is reducing the grid-to-plate capacitance** that degrades high frequency amplification performance.

- *Plate* – an electrode that collects electrons as the *plate current*, analogous to the FET *drain.*

The heater heats the cathode which begins to emit electrons into the vacuum within the tube. Relative to the cathode's voltage, the plate is placed at a positive voltage to attract the electrons. The electrons must pass through the open gaps of the control grid to reach the plate. The grid is mainly open gaps between fine interlaced wire or other conductive material, so few electrons are actually collected by the grid. The voltage of the control grid controls the passage of electrons. If the control grid voltage is negative with respect to the cathode the electrons will be repelled, reducing the plate current or even terminating it completely (*cutoff state*). If the control grid voltage is positive relative to the cathode the electrons will be accelerated to the plate, increasing plate current. An input voltage signal to the control grid varies the plate current, and since the plate current may be quite large the input signal is amplified via the plate electrode.

A vacuum tube with three elements (excluding the screen grid) is a *triode*, and a four-element tube such as that depicted in Figure 6.47 is a *tetrode*. Additional grids may be included in design variations and other physical configurations are common.

Amplifier Adjustments: Radio frequency power amplifiers will receive a signal from the transmitter, amplify it, and output a signal to the antenna system. Since the amplifier is coupled to the antenna load, all of the previous discussions of impedance matching and power transfer apply. The amplifier must be tuned for the band and frequency of operation, and the input and output power must be adjusted for the desired safe operating levels. Typically three types of operator controls will be used to get the amp set up for operating:

- *Band Switch* – used to select the frequency band of operation. Impedance matching networks and filters for both input and output signals are configured. This is typically a set of discrete selections of amateur bands requiring no fine adjustment. The band may be automatically detected and selected on some amplifiers without user intervention.

- *Tune Control* – used to tune the amplifier output circuit for the selected operating frequency. Component values of an impedance matching circuit, such as a Pi-network (see *Impedance and Reactance* Section 6.4) are adjusted until a match is achieved as indicated by the plate current. This adjustment interacts with the *load adjustment*.

- *Load Control* – used to adjust the coupling of the amplifier to the antenna load. Component values of an impedance matching network are adjusted to achieve an output impedance match with the antenna as indicated by the output power reading. This adjustment interacts with the *tune adjustment*.

Read and heed your vacuum tube amplifier manufacturer's instructions for tuning and operating your amplifier, as specific tuning requirements may vary.

A tube amplifier tuning activity will generally proceed something like this:

1. Select the operating band with the band switch.

2. Apply a small amount of drive power from the transmitter.

3. **Adjust the tune control to obtain a pronounced dip** (minimum value) **on the plate current meter, indicating correct adjustment** and that the matching network is resonant for the operating frequency.

G4A04

4. **Adjust the load control (coupling control) to achieve maximum power output without exceeding maximum allowable plate current, indicating correct adjustment.**

G4A08

5. Repeat adjustment to the tune control to achieve plate current dip and load control adjustment to obtain peak power iteratively until the desired operating output power or plate current is achieved. Drive power may also be adjusted during these iterations to achieve the manufacturer's recommended value or recommended control grid current.

Drive Power: Refer to your transmitter manufacturer's instructions on adjusting the drive power provided to an RF amplifier. If too much current is applied to a vacuum tube control grid the grid may be damaged or destroyed, and excessive plate current can also result, causing overheating failure. Many manufacturers will provide special protection circuits in amplifiers to ensure that excessive grid drive cannot damage the tube. These protection circuits are a great feature to look for when amp shopping.

Excessive drive may also cause distortion of your signal, particularly at modulating signal peaks, such as loud audio. As noted in Section 4.1 *SSB and AM*, the Automatic Level Control (ALC) can be used to reduce the transmitter drive when power becomes too great for proper modulation. **The purpose of using Automatic Level Control with RF power amplifiers is to reduce distortion due to excessive drive.** Refer to your transmitter user's manual for proper implementation of ALC with RF power amplifiers.

G4A05

Neutralization: Due to the capacitance that arises between electrodes, some amplifiers (particularly triode tube amps) can become self-oscillating circuits at some frequencies. Such component resonance was discussed in the Section 6.2. This can cause erratic behavior or poor operation of the amplifier. To combat this problem that is very rare in most modern amplifiers, **the final amplifier stage of a transmitter may need to be neutralized to eliminate self-oscillations.** This process imposes negative feedback in the circuit at the frequency of oscillation, eliminating the oscillatory positive feedback. Usually this is accomplished by inserting a variable capacitor of manufacturer-recommended range between the output and input filtering circuits and adjusting the capacitor to neutralize the oscillation. Most modern amplifiers will not require this modification be implemented by the user.

G7B13

So, dude… Now you can safely operate your RF amplifier, cutting through the difficult conditions with the power of eleven!

Or maybe just ten. Or perhaps with the maximum rated plate current for your amp, properly tuned up for frequency and with correct grid drive. As always with the more complex operations of amateur radio it is a good idea to seek the initial sage advice of an experienced elmer. That policy certainly applies to RF amplifier ops. Besides, that old head-banging elmer may just be able to show you how to wheedle an eleven out of your system!

Rock on over to the web site and quiz yourself on the question pool items.

HamRadioSchool.com/general_media

6.7   Hamtronics

ICs and Computers

" *The number of transistors on a chip will double approximately every two years.*
— *Moore's Law, Gordon Moore*

M r. Moore, cofounder of Intel Corporation, posited his law in 1965 and claimed that it should apply for at least ten years into the future. Fully 50 years later the trend he identified remains generally valid. The forming of multiple miniature transistors, resistors, capacitors, diodes, inductors, switches and more on a tiny slab of silicon all wired together into functional complex circuits has had an incalculable impact on our world and on amateur radio technology.

As a General Class operator you should have a basic comprehension of integrated circuits (ICs) and digital logic, the combination of ICs as microprocessors and computers, the common language and names in this domain, and familiarity with IC interfaces and connectors that may be used with radios. Let's integrate and connect these topics.

Analog versus Digital ICs: The broadest categories of ICs are analog or digital logic. Analog ICs are also called linear circuits, operating over a range of voltage and current values and outputting continuous signals. Digital circuits use discrete voltage and current values rather than a range, usually activated in either of two stable states – "on" or "off," representing binary digits of 1 and 0, respectively.

Analog ICs:
Operational Amplifiers (op amp) and linear voltage regulators are two common analog integrated circuits.
The op amp schematic symbols and packaging

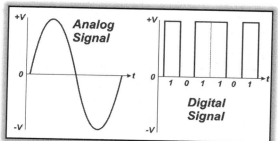

G6B06   G6B01

Figure 6.48: Analog vs. Digital Signal representations.

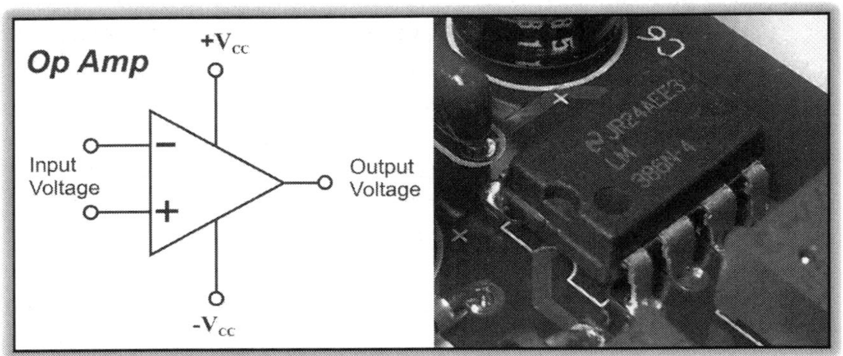

Figure 6.49: Operational Amplifier symbol and typical packaging on a circuit board.

are represented in Figure 6.49. The op amp is used in audio and other circuit types to provide signal gain. Typically a voltage difference is applied between the + and – input terminals (differential input) and the output voltage (relative to the input voltage) is hundreds or thousands of times greater than the input differential value. The VCC inputs are the supply voltage source supporting amplification. **Most sine wave oscillator circuits will use an amplifier and a filter operating in a feedback loop** to produce a sine wave voltage signal by varying the op amp input voltage in a regular repeating cycle.

Linear voltage regulators supply a constant voltage output across a range of current for stable power supply to circuits. A voltage regulator will have *input, output,* and *ground* terminals.

Digital ICs: **When processing digital signals ICs take advantage of the ease of representing binary "ones" and "zeros" with an "on" state or an "off" state,** analogous to the two stable states of transistors described in *Components* Section 6.2 (saturation and cut-off regions). Combinations of digital ICs can be constructed to perform complex computational tasks using binary logic.

TTL and CMOS Logic Families: Although several different families of digital ICs have been created, two commonly used families are the *transistor-transistor logic* (TTL) family and the *complementary metal-oxide semiconductor* (CMOS) family. These names refer to the types of materials and component construction used in the logic circuits. **As compared to TTL, CMOS integrated circuits have the advantage of low power consumption.**

G7B07

G7B02

G6B03

Logic Gates: Digital circuits of great complexity are built from basic logic building blocks called logic gates. Logic gates are created with combinations of transistors and other electronic components to provide specific binary outputs (on or off, 1 or 0) for given binary inputs. In the language of binary gate circuit logic, inputs and outputs are said to be "high" (high voltage) if the saturation voltage is applied (on, or 1), and "low" (low voltage, off or 0) if in the cut-off state. Gates are given names that reflect their input-output logical function. Consider a few salient examples:

Two Input AND Gate: Output is high only when both inputs are high. In other words, if the two inputs are called A and B, this gate outputs a binary 1 (high) only in the case that Input A *AND* input B are provided binary 1s, or high voltage. If either or both of the two inputs are a binary 0 ("low") the output will be 0. The logic of the two input AND gate is summarized in Figure 6.50 along with other gate examples and associated schematic symbols.

Two Input NAND Gate: Meaning "Not AND" the NAND gate is the logical inverse of the AND gate. The output is low only when both inputs are high.

Two Input OR Gate: As the name implies, the output is high when either or both inputs are high. The output is low only when both inputs are low.

Two Input NOR Gate: This is the logical inverse of the OR gate. **Output is low when either or both inputs are high.**

Two Input XOR Gate: Meaning "Exclusive OR," the output is high when either, but not both, inputs are high. That is, for an output 1 to occur just one, and only one, input must be high.

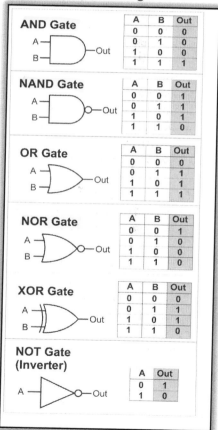

AND Gate

A	B	Out
0	0	0
0	1	0
1	0	0
1	1	1

NAND Gate

A	B	Out
0	0	1
0	1	1
1	0	1
1	1	0

OR Gate

A	B	Out
0	0	0
0	1	1
1	0	1
1	1	1

NOR Gate

A	B	Out
0	0	1
0	1	0
1	0	0
1	1	0

XOR Gate

A	B	Out
0	0	0
0	1	1
1	0	1
1	1	0

NOT Gate (Inverter)

A	Out
0	1
1	0

Figure 6.50: Common logic gates with symbol and input-output truth table.

NOT (Inverter): The NOT Gate has but a single input. The output state is always the opposite of the input state.

Sequential Logic Circuits: Another type of digital IC is the sequential logic circuit. The output state of these ICs depends upon time or upon sequential input states. The foundational building block of sequential logic is a storage element called the *flip-flop*. A flip-flop circuit has two stable states and it can be made to change state by applying the appropriate high or low states to its inputs. The flip flop will maintain its state (storing a value) until the inputs are properly cycled or changed. If several flip flops are sequenced together such that the output of one is fed to the input of the next, a *counter* or a *shift register* may be constructed.

Counters: A counter represents a binary number in the latched states of the linked flip flops. A clocked signal (input state change) affects state changes through the flip flops such that the collective 1 and 0 states increment sequentially with each clock signal or input state change. The binary representation counts up (or counts down) the input signal occurrences. One flip flop stores one bit of data with its latched state. For a set of flip flops in a counter circuit, the number of different binary states that can be represented is 2^n, where n is the quantity of flip flops. This determines the largest number that the counter can represent. For example,

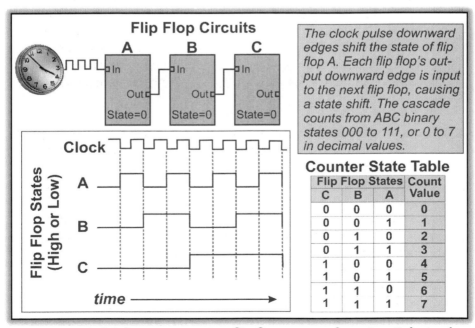

Figure 6.51: A 3-bit counter using flip flops counts from 0 to 7 decimal.

Figure 6.51 depicts three linked flip flops as **a 3-bit binary counter having 8 states: $2^3 = 8$.**

Shift Registers: Essentially a memory element, **a shift register is a clocked array of circuits that passes data in steps along the array.** A 3-bit shift register would operate similarly to the 3-bit counter except that the arrangement between flip flops (or other memory elements) is altered. In the simplest case the sequence of flip flops are linked such that a new input state fed into the first flip flop results in the former state of the first flip flop being *shifted* into the second flip flop in the sequence. Similarly, the former state of the second flip flop is shifted to the third. When the register runs out of flip flops the last data state is lost, as there is no flip flop element for it to be shifted into. You might imagine the states of each shift register flip flop getting shoved from one flip flop to the next in a left-to-right sequence through the flip flops, with the last one falling out of the far right flip flop to be lost! Other arrangements of shift registers are feasible to affect various input and output functions and memory storage or recall.

Microprocessor ICs: With millions or billions of tiny gates and logic arrays integrated onto a single chip, **the microprocessor is essentially a computer on a single integrated circuit.** (Actually, that last statement is not perfectly accurate, but that's what the question pool says!) It can perform millions or billions of logic operations each second by implementing a program of sequenced steps using binary computations in a *machine language* of programming. The ability to execute a stored *program* from *software* or *firmware* is what distinguishes a microprocessor from mere digital logic circuits. Microprocessors are used in personal computers and other general purpose devices.

Microcontroller: An integrated circuit often replacing complex digital circuitry. A microcontroller may have a core microprocessor, memory, and input/output peripheral devices to serve an imbedded function in a device. Your transceiver may have one or more microcontrollers, as do most modern automobile engines, TV remote controls, electronic toys, military missiles, and lots of other commercial products. The microcontroller is programmable, and thus more flexible than the simpler, custom-engineered digital logic circuits.

MMIC: *Monolithic Microwave Integrated Circuit.* The MMIC is a specially designed RF integrated circuit to affect functions up to microwave frequencies of operation such as modulation, demodulation, frequency mixing, and amplification. An MMIC may contain several

G7B05

G7B06

G6B11

G7B01

G6B02

transceiver block functions in a single chip, and they are used extensively in cellular telephone devices.

G6B04

G6B05

Digital Memory: Microprocessors and microcontrollers require digital memory capacity in order to store and recall input and output data or programming options. ***Read Only Memory, or ROM,*** means exactly that – the memory data cannot be changed or altered or replaced, but only accessed to read out. ROM will be **non-volatile memory, meaning that the stored information is maintained even if power is removed** from the circuit. A ROM memory bank may contain the start-up or core programming for a processing IC. *Random Access Memory* (RAM) is flexible and may be read, written, rewritten, or deleted altogether. RAM is used to hold temporary data for computation, display, or data output operations. The *flash memory* used in small solid state plug-in memory devices ("thumb" or "flash" drives) is a type of *non-volatile RAM*, providing random access to data but also retaining it following the termination of power.

Visual Displays for ICs: Several types of visual displays may be driven by ICs and used in amateur radio. The following summarizes two of the most common display types in modern use that are easily driven with ICs.

LED: The LED discussed in the *Components* section is commonly used to create visual displays that may be a simple on-off illuminated indicator or a multi-character digital readout. LEDs are self-illuminated requiring no separate light source. Segmented LEDs used to create numbers, letters, or other characters are turned on or off by the digital logic of ICs.

Figure 6.52: Self-illuminated segmented LED display (upper) and a backlit LCD display (lower).

Liquid Crystal Display (LCD): Very common on newer amateur radio transceivers and related components, the LCD uses a crystal material between two layers of glass. The crystal blocks, filters, or reflects light with crystal patterns driven by electronic circuits. **A characteristic of the liquid crystal display is that it requires ambient or back lighting** to be clearly visible.

G6B09

Connectors: It takes a lot of cables and connections to make ham radio stuff happen. Hooking up computers to radios, audio devices and speakers, power supplies and meters... It's just a lot of stuff passing all those signals back and forth for amateur radio bliss! The zoo of various connectors can get a little confusing, even frustrating, so let's review a few common connector types.

Keyed Connectors: Many connectors will have multiple individual connectors, or *pins,* that must be aligned and connected with specific commensurate sockets to properly route signals. In order to assure that the proper connection alignment, or *mating*, is achieved by a user the connector body housings, inserts, and pin configurations will often be designed so that only a single connection orientation is possible with complementary connectors. **The main reason to use such keyed connectors instead of non-keyed types is to reduce the chance of incorrect mating.** Incorrect mating in the ham shack is just trouble.

G6B15

Numerous types of data and audio signal connectors are available, but the following are a few of the more common connectors you will encounter when linking together IC-based modules.

USB Interface: The *Universal Serial Bus* interface has become almost... well... *universal* as a connector for modern electronic devices. (USB – has absolutely nothing to do with the upper sideband!) It can transfer data and power

Figure 6.53: Common USB connector formats, left-to-right:
Type B, Type A, Mini B, and Micro B.

between devices, and it has at least six different keyed physical forms, four of which are depicted in Figure 6.53. Nearly every smart phone, tablet device, computer, digital camera, printer, and video game will have one or more USB ports. **A USB interface might be used in an amateur radio station to connect a computer and transceiver.** For example, a sound card interface used between computer and transceiver for some digital modes may use a USB interface. Some channel programming utilities will use a USB connection between computer and transceiver.

G6B10

Figure 6.54: DE-9 Connector

G6B12 DE-9: **A good choice for a serial data port would be the DE-9 connector,** very commonly misrepresented as "DB-9." The D refers to the shape of the keyed shell which resembles the letter D. The E refers to the size of the shell, and the 9 refers to the number of pins within the shell. Many other D type connectors exist, but the DE-9 is very common for many data interfaces, including amateur radio connections to computers or other devices.

G6B17 **DIN Connector: A family of multiple circuit connectors suitable for audio and control signals.** The DIN family is a round, slotted key form with multiple pins. DIN connectors are popular on many amateur radios for connecting external control devices. Some computers still use DIN connectors for keyboard and mouse connections, although the USB is rapidly replacing the DIN for those functions.

RCA Phono Connector: An older connector still **commonly used for audio signals in amateur radio stations and other audio devices.** This non-keyed connector has a single pin/socket and can be used for

G6B14

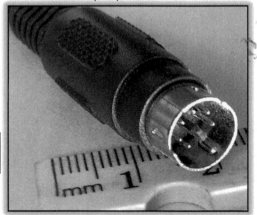

Figure 6.55: DIN connector

numerous applications including video signals, control signals, and some RF signals.

Many other connector types may be used in amateur radio for power connections, RF feedline connections, network connections, even audio and data connections. *It is good to be connected,* so familiarize yourself with the range of options in your station and integrated circuit-based devices.

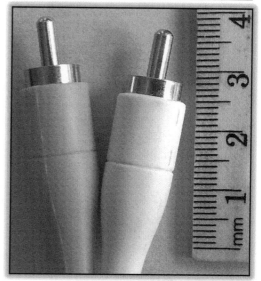

Figure 6.56: RCA phono connectors

Much like Moore's Law, perhaps your knowledge of integrated circuits has doubled in just the last few minutes! It's quite likely that you have encountered hundreds, even thousands of integrated circuits, microprocessors, electronic displays, connectors, and myriad other things that create, manipulate, and pass electronic signals. Now you have a little taste of what's going on inside all that electronic wizardry so you can intelligently integrate and connect your General Class station!

See the chart on the next page summarizing IC characteristics, and don't forget to review the question pool items for this section!

HamRadioSchool.com/general_media

A Summary Organization of Integrated Circuits

Integrated Circuits			
Analog	Digital [TTL & CMOS]		
Op Amp Linear Voltage Regulator MMIC Other devices	Logic Gates	Sequential Logic	Microprocessors Microcontrollers
	AND Gate NAND Gate OR Gate NOR Gate XOR Gate Not (inverter)	Flip Flops Counters Shift Registers	Memory Modules

Hamtronics

6.8

Measurement

ff *Every line is the perfect length if you don't measure it.*

— Marty Rubin

And every circuit has the perfect voltage if you don't measure it.

And every transmitter creates the perfect signal if you don't measure it.
And every antenna radiates the perfect pattern if you don't measure it.

You get the point. In order to ensure that your radio station is operating properly you must, on occasion, measure things. Let's take a look at some basic test and measurement equipment and techniques for amateur radio so that the "perfect station" may be avoided.

Meters: Perhaps the most fundamental piece of test equipment for the ham is a meter for electrical measurements. While individually functioning voltmeters, ammeters, and ohmmeters are available, the *multimeter* is now the most common type of handheld meter. The multimeter combines several measurement functions into one device and provides user-selectable controls for measurement type and display scales. You can pick up one at the hardware store, but be careful of quality – generally you get what you pay for, and some low-end meters may not have the resolution or accuracy for RF electronics applications.

Analog versus Digital: Analog meters typically use a needle indicator that moves against one or more static calibrated scales. Digital meters will usually present numerical digits by LCD or LED display. **An advantage of a digital meter (such as a voltmeter) as compared to an analog meter is better precision for most uses** – the digital readout can provide better resolution of values than the analog needle display. However, in a measurement task in which a null value or peak value is sought among a continuous range, such as **when adjusting tuned circuits, an analog readout may be preferred over an instrument with a numerical digital readout** – the analog meter movement and

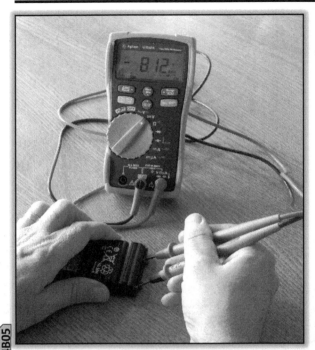

Figure 6.57: Measuring cell voltage with a multimeter.   *Photo: Sara Ray, KCØAMO*

maximum or minimum position is usually easier to interpret than dancing digits! However, many digital meters now include analog-like bar graphs to aid visual perception.

Regardless of the type of meter, digital or analog, it is important that the measurement device itself not affect the circuit being measured. At least, the impact upon the circuit should be minimized to avoid grossly inaccurate measurements. For example, **high input impedance is desirable for a voltmeter to decrease the loading on circuits being measured.** If the meter's input impedance were relatively low, significant current would flow from the circuit being measured through the meter circuits, altering the normal voltage drop across the measured circuit positions. High impedance avoids significant current flow through the meter, keeping the voltage drops very near the non-measurement activity value.

Oscilloscopes: The most versatile electronic measurement instrument, the *oscilloscope,* displays a real-time image of voltage over time. The voltage is displayed for a window of time that may be adjusted by the user. Typically the window of time is depicted across the horizontal extent of the oscilloscope display with a time scale superimposed on the

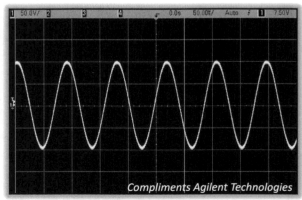

Compliments Agilent Technologies

Figure 6.58: A sine wave signal voltage displayed on an oscilloscope. The vertical scale is voltage units, and the horizontal is time.

image, left to right. The voltage signal is depicted in the vertical dimension, usually as a continuous function – an unbroken curve or line. A vertical scale is also provided to indicate specific voltage values. As an example, a well-formed AC voltage sine wave would be depicted as in Figure 6.58. The time window from left edge to right edge can be varied to "zoom in" or "zoom out," viewing less or more of the signal waveform.

Most modern oscilloscopes will provide horizontal as well as vertical signal inputs so that another signal can drive the horizontal dimension of the signal, in lieu of simply time. In this way very complex signals may be depicted on the scope. Further, **an oscilloscope will contain horizontal and vertical channel amplifiers** to boost weak signals for improved display.

G4B01

The clear advantage of an oscilloscope versus a digital voltmeter is that complex waveforms can be measured. For example, the RF output of a transmitter may be displayed to examine the modulated waveforms generated. **To check the RF envelope pattern of a transmitted signal the attenuated RF output of the transmitter is connected as the signal source to the vertical input of the oscilloscope.** For a single modulated tone the display would look similar to Figure 6.59. In a similar manner **the keying waveform of a CW transmitter may be checked with an oscilloscope** to identify any undesired noise or anomalies in the keyed signals.

G4B02

G4B04

G4B03

An oscilloscope can also be useful in analyzing your station audio processing, microphone gain, digital signal output from a circuit, a computer, or a sound card interface, and more! It takes a little practice to become adept at adjusting and interpreting an *O-scope*, but it is a measurement skill that will come in handy for ensuring your station is functioning properly. One typical use of a scope in an amateur station is for the *two-tone test*.

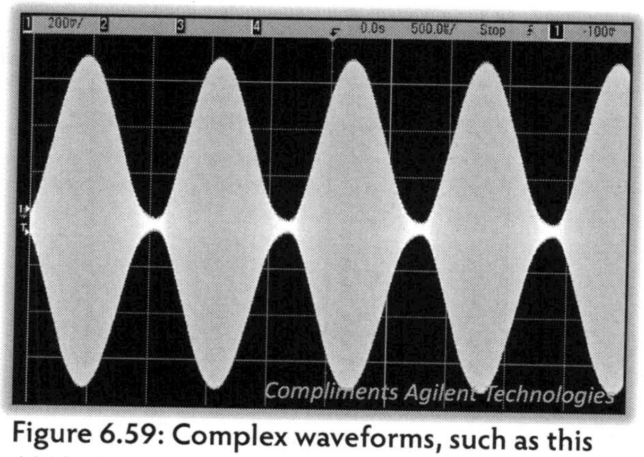

Figure 6.59: Complex waveforms, such as this 100% AM modulated RF signal, can be measured with an oscilloscope.

Two-Tone Test: **The two-tone test analyzes transmitter linearity.** If two different audio frequency signals have equivalent amplitude, a transmitter should modulate those two different signals with equivalent amplitude, or RF power. If the transmitter does

G4B15

modulate with equivalent RF power it is exhibiting good linearity. If the two audio signals are modulated with different RF power output the transmitter is not linear. Of course, each of the pair of audio frequency signals is perceived as a different audio tone by our ears, hence the *two-tone test.* **To conduct a two-tone test two non-harmonically related audio signals are used** (700 Hz and 1900 Hz are a common pair selection). The oscilloscope representation of each modulated tone is examined for any RF power output differences, or distortion. Transmitter adjustments may be made to alleviate the *distortion* while monitoring the signals in real-time via the oscilloscope.

G4B07

Field Strength Meter: A field strength meter is used to measure the strength of a transmitted RF field. For instance, **a field strength meter may be used to monitor relative RF output when making antenna and transmitter adjustments.**

G4B08

Figure 6.60: A simple field strength meter for relative measures. A collapsible dipole antenna extends left and right from this meter.

Signals are received with a conventional antenna (such as a dipole or ¼ wave monopole) and routed to circuits that detect the relative strength of the RF voltages. Unless the meter is carefully calibrated all measurements are relative – no specific signal strength measurements are made, only "stronger or weaker" measurements on a unitless scale. However, with such relative signal strength readings **the radiation pattern of an antenna may be determined with a field strength meter.**

G4B09

Go forth and measure! Using the tools and techniques of this section you can now absolutely, positively, unquestionably ascertain that your station is imperfect. And just exactly how imperfect. And you can be proud of the imperfections and your ability to quantify them! But first, please perfectly answer the online quiz for the questions of this section. Good luck!

HamRadioSchool.com/general_media

ﬀ *No matter which way they pointed the antenna, no matter how clean and precise the receiving apparatus, a persistent background hiss inter-fered with the measurements.*
— *Regarding Penzius and Wilson's discovery of Cosmic Background Radiation*

What Penzius and Wilson accidentally discovered in 1965 is that radio frequency interference has been around since the beginning of the universe. Really. The annoying hiss detected by the giant horn-shaped micro-wave antenna they were using at Bell Telephone Laboratories in New Jersey in relation to a set of experiments on communication satellites was actually part of the radio echo left over from the cosmic Big Bang from which the universe originated. In spite of numerous tweaks and adjustments, including the scrub-bing of all pigeon droppings accumulated in the horn and the purging of all pigeons seeking to roost within it, the interference persisted and they were awarded a Nobel Prize in physics for it.

So, while it has been around for about 14 billion years, give or take a few hun-dred millennia, radio frequency interference is a relatively recent bother to human kind. And while the Cosmic Background Radiation is unlikely to annoy most hams, the several billion new radio emitters that have sprung up on our planet in the last 100 years are sure to get in one another's way on occasion. Let's take a look at some of the things you can do to reduce the chances of RF interference between your station and other radiating or receiving devices, and even between your station and your body!

RF Interference: The undesired reception of RF signals produced properly or improperly by an electronic device is *interference*. Interference may be received by your radio station from other emitters, either intended emitters like other radio stations or unintended emitters such as poor or faulty electronic devices. Additionally, some devices may be unintentional

Figure 6.61: Other electronic devices may become inadvertent receivers of amateur signals.

or incorrectly operating RF receivers that will pick up signals from your station's transmitter by mistake. These may include telephones or audio equipment. Let's characterize some common types of RF interference and common solutions to avoid it.

Fundamental Overload: If your transceiver or another device is unable to reject very strong signals from a nearby transmitter the electronics may be overloaded, and distorted or unintelligible audio may result. For example, your HT radio may experience fundamental overload when another nearby amateur station transmits strongly on the same band to which you are tuned, even if the two are not on the same frequency. This will usually override any weaker signals you may be intending to receive.

Solution: To alleviate fundamental overload you must reduce the signal level hitting the receiver. This may be accomplished in one or more ways: 1) By separating the offending transmitter and receiver by a greater distance, 2) By reducing the offending transmitter's power, 3) By using a directional antenna on one or both transmitting and receiving stations, or 4) By putting a filter on the receiver. The filtering option usually applies to non-amateur radio receiving devices that are inadvertent receivers, such as telephones, televisions, or other electronic devices.

Direct Detection or Unintentional Receivers: Strong RF signals can be picked up by nearly any kind of electronic device, particularly those with lengths of speaker leads, power cords, or cables. These wires can act as unintentional antennas directing signals into the electronic circuits to cause erratic behavior or noise. For instance, **Interference from a nearby single-sideband phone transmitter unintentionally received by a telephone or audio device will sound like distorted speech, while**

a CW transmitter will produce on-and-off humming or clicking effects. Transmitted RF picked up by an audio cable carrying AFSK data signals between a computer and a transceiver may cause VOX circuit un-key failure, distorted transmissions, and frequent connection timeouts.

G4C04 G4A15

Solution: **RF Interference of this kind caused by *common-mode currents* on an audio cable (or other types) can be reduced by placing a ferrite bead around the cable.** Also referred to as ferrite *chokes*, snap-on filters of various sizes are readily available at radio and electronics retail outlets. **Alternatively, RF signal interference to audio-frequency devices may be reduced with a bypass capacitor.** Also called a *decoupling capacitor*, a small capacitor from an audio connection to ground voltage (such as a chassis connection) will "bypass" the higher RF frequency signals, allowing them to go directly to ground without effecting the much lower frequency audio signals.

G4C08

G4C01

Figure 6.62: Ferrite chokes for common-mode filtering come in many packages including snap-on beads and rings.

Harmonics: Spurious emissions that are frequency multiples of the intended (fundamental) frequency of a transmitter are called *harmonics*. For instance, the 2nd harmonic will be twice the fundamental frequency, the 3rd harmonic three times the fundamental, and so on. Virtually all transmitters produce some harmonics of much lower power levels than the fundamental frequency. Harmonics generated by your station may lie outside of the amateur bands and cause interference in non-amateur receivers or devices.

Solution: Harmonics can be reduced or eliminated by proper implementation of RF filters in a feedline. A low-pass filter selected to allow the fundamental to pass while impeding the higher frequency harmonics can be inserted into the feedline, but take care that the filter is matched to the feedline impedance. (See Section 5.3 *Antennas, SWR*

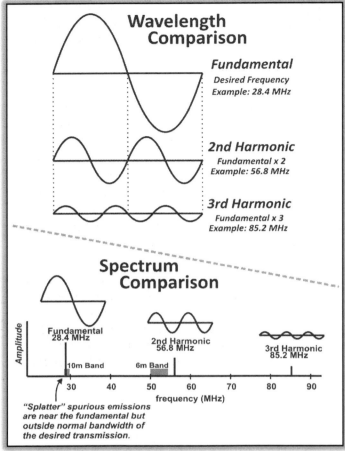

Figure 6.63: Example comparison of fundamental frequency with 2nd and 3rd harmonic frequencies.

and Impedance Matching.) Harmonic filters are a common integrated feature in most modern transceivers.

Splatter: A spurious emission beyond the necessary and proper bandwidth for the mode and frequency band in use is referred to as splatter. Poor or faulty transmitters may generate excessively broad signals that interfere with communications on adjacent frequencies. For example, a SSB transmitter emitting a 20 kHz signal instead of the necessary and proper 3 kHz maximum bandwidth is splattering 17 kHz of spurious emissions. Correct your transmitter operation if you are splattering. A transmitter repair or simply an adjustment of microphone gain or ALC may be needed.

Arcing: Arcing at a poor electrical connection could be the cause of interference covering a wide range of frequencies. Electrical arcing may be generated by almost any electric device, sometimes intentionally such as an electric igniter on a furnace. High voltage utility power lines or transformers can have faults that produce regular arcing and generate a broad band crackle or buzzing on receiver audio. To eliminate local suspect arcing equipment, simply turn off equipment and see if the interference goes away.

Solution: For malfunctioning equipment or appliances, electrical repair or replacement may be warranted. Power line noise will usually need to be isolated to an offending location or device, perhaps with the use of simple direction finding equipment. A request should be made to the power utility company to check and correct the offending source.

Mobile Station Interference Sources: Automobiles can produce arcing and sparking and all sorts of RF noise from electrical and electronic devices. Alternator whine is a common source of high-pitched whine that varies with engine speed. Popping or crackling that varies with speed is likely spark plug noise. Connect your transceiver's power leads directly to the battery with in-line fuses and avoid using any of the automobile wiring to reduce the effects of alternator whine – don't use the cigarette lighter or power connections provided in the cabin of your vehicle. Using the transceiver noise blanker can also help to filter this kind of regular pulsing interference.

Many automobile microcontrollers operate at frequencies in the HF range of 3 – 30 MHz. **An HF radio receiver installed in a recent model vehicle may obtain interference from the battery charging system, the fuel delivery system, or the vehicle control computer.** Alleviating computer interference can be a challenge in some cases. Check with your automotive dealer for available upgrades or replacement controllers, or consider options for shielding the controller enclosure.

G4E07

Grounding: Proper grounding of your station is necessary to alleviate *ground loops* and to reduce "*RF in the shack*" These problems can promote noise, erratic equipment behavior, and even offer a nasty RF burn or shock to the operator.

Ground Loops: If the various components of your station have differing ground level voltages, a ground loop may result – currents flowing among the components due to the ground level potential differences. **One symptom of a ground loop somewhere in your station is received reports of "hum" on your station's transmitted signal.** A ground loop may also cause erratic behavior of some equipment. **Avoid ground loops by connecting all ground conductors to a single point,** as depicted in Figure 6.64 on the next page. Typically this will involve using a broad conductive flat strap to connect individual station equipment chassis to a common single ground panel or ground bus. This common connection among station component grounds will maintain a common ground voltage level and alleviate ground loops.

G4C10

G4C09

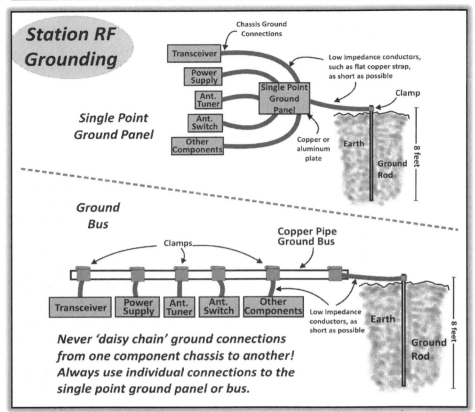

Figure 6.64: Station single point ground configurations.

RF in the Shack: The conductors in your station – ground connections, equipment chassis, cables and wires – all act as antennas. Some antennas are better than others, but radio frequencies can induce currents in your shack on any conductor, and particularly on longer ones. A low impedance connection to earth ground can help reduce this problem.

The single point ground panel or bus should be connected by a short, low impedance conductor to a ground rod imbedded in the earth. Any stray currents on your station equipment will have a direct path to earth ground level. **Connecting all equipment grounds together is a good way to avoid unwanted effects of stray RF energy in an amateur station,** and a solid earth ground will route them away from your equipment. (Be sure that you are following the National Electric Code [NEC] recommendations for grounding systems in your home or shack. If unsure, check with an electrician.)

G4C07

Ground Conductors: Broad, flat conductive strap with only gentle bends or turns is best for station grounding. A broad conductor such as copper strap provides very low impedance at RF frequencies due to the large surface area of the conductor, helping to ensure that RF currents easily flow to ground. **If you receive an RF burn when touching your equipment while transmitting on an HF band** (*RF hot spot*), **the ground wire likely has high impedance on that frequency even if connected to a ground rod,** or your grounding system may be poorly implemented (or not at all implemented).

RF Hot Spots: The ground conductors should be made as short as physically possible for your station arrangement. Any conductor that approaches 1/8 wavelength or longer will serve as a nice antenna for receiving RF and inducing currents on the conductor. A ground conductor can become resonant with the RF resulting in "hot spots" of RF currents on its length. **A resonant ground connection can affect high RF voltages on the enclosures of station equipment,** representing a significant hazard for burn or shock. Note that on the 10 meter band a ¼ wavelength conductor is only about 2.5 meters long, or under 8 feet. Achieving this short of grounding conductor from the single

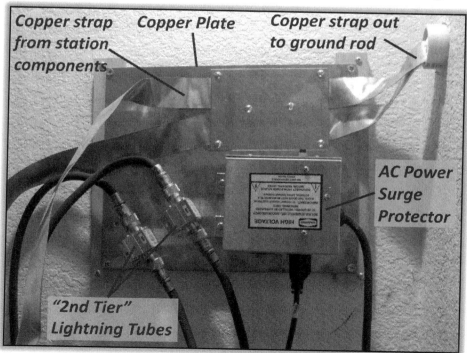

Figure 6.65: An example wall-mounted single-point ground panel. AC surge protector and second-tier coaxial lightning protection tubes are grounded to panel along with flat strap from station component chassis.

point panel or bus to an external ground rod may be infeasible for many stations. In a difficult situation, careful planning with the use of multiple lengths of grounding conductor, avoiding the resonant multiples, may help to avoid potential resonance hot spots for your favorite HF operating bands.

Interference happens. It will happen to you eventually. It has been around a lot longer than any of us mere humans, and it'll exist long after we've departed. It's something we just live with as hams.

Don't panic, you can handle most interference that you will encounter. Sometimes you may need the patience and dogged determination of Penzius and Wilson to chase down the source of an annoying interference source, but hopefully you won't have to scrub up pigeon poop or trap the flying rats. Plan and implement your HF station RF grounding arrangement as best you can, and snag a nice set of ferrite snap-on chokes and telephone filters to distribute to your neighbors, should the occasion arise. Good luck, and be sure to cover the online questions from this section.

HamRadioSchool.com/general_media

7.0 Safety

" Better dead sure than sure dead.
– Anonymous

Hams take safety seriously. It's good to do so when you're handling equipment that can produce many deadly amps of electrical current, or when you're climbing a tower many dozens of feet high, or when you're erecting an antenna and power lines are near, or even if you're just soldering together a connector and coaxial cable. There are a million ways to get hurt or killed, but only one dead sure way to avoid it. Practice safety.

In Section 7.1 we will review basic precautions for handling electricity and for erecting towers and antennas. Section 7.2 is all about RF exposure safety and how to ensure your station is not overexposing you, your family or your neighbors to RF radiation. Read on to help ensure you're dead sure.

7.1 Safety Electrical & Antenna Precautions

" Electricity can be dangerous. My nephew tried to stick a penny into a plug. Whoever said a penny doesn't go far didn't see him shoot across that floor. I told him he was grounded. – Tim Allen

The chances of getting seriously injured with amateur radio are probably a lot less than playing with Tim's nephew. Still, it is prudent to be very familiar with common hazards affiliated with ham radio and, most importantly, to understand how to take precautions and avoid those hazards. Let's consider a few hazards and precautions regarding electrical safety in the shack and some related safety factors with antennas and towers.

Electric Shock: The commonly accepted value for the lowest voltage that can cause a dangerous amount of current to flow through the human body is 30 volts. However, it is the current flow and not the voltage that is dangerous. Currents flowing through the body cause health hazards by heating tissue (burning), by disrupting the electrical functions of cells (nervous system dysfunction or loss of consciousness), and by causing involuntary muscle contraction (inability to control movement and interruption of heart rhythm).

How much current is dangerous? Just 10 mA or so can cause involuntary muscle contractions, 30 mA begins to feel painful, and at 50 mA you may not be able to "let go" of the conductor before losing consciousness! Your heart rhythm can be disrupted by 100 mA, possibly leading to death if the current continues for some time. Of course, greater amperage can lead to more rapid serious injury, and very high currents can burn tissues.

Typical household AC of 120 volts RMS is more than enough to be deadly. Take great precaution to avoid injury by powering down equipment before working on it unless it is absolutely necessary to work with a powered circuit. Disconnect power sources or transmitters altogether before working. Remember that large capacitors can hold a dangerous charge for long periods, so carefully discharge them with a bleeder resistor before working.

Codes and Wiring Conventions: The National Electric Code (NEC) covers electrical safety inside your home and ham shack. It describes the requirements for safe electrical wiring and handling conventions. Local codes may also apply and be more restrictive than the NEC, so check with your local authorities if you are modifying your shack electrical wiring. If you are not comfortable doing your own work in this regard be sure to consult a licensed electrician. The following are some commonly applied conventions and guidelines from the NEC.

120 V and 240 V Household Circuits: Most US households receive AC power in a 240 volt circuit with two wires each at 120 volts relative to a third "neutral" wire. The neutral wire is insulated white while the two "hot" wires will usually be insulated red or black. (Variations do occur, so use your meter to check!) Most household circuits are 120 volts provided by one of the hot wires and the neutral wire. Some household circuits for large appliances (or for high power amplifiers) will utilize both hot wires and the neutral wire to provide 240 volts. A separate *safety ground* wire, either green insulated or bare, is also included for the typical modern 120 V "three-prong outlet" circuits and for the four-conductor 240 volt source receptacle. Note: Standards in other countries may vary.

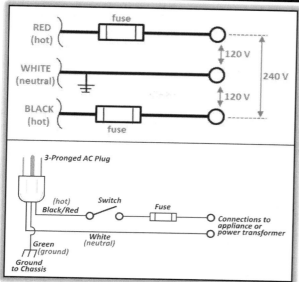

Figure 7.1: Typical 240 VAC and 120 VAC household circuit configurations.

Fuses and Circuit Breakers: Any 120 V hot wire should use a fuse or circuit breaker in the hot wire connection. **In a device operated from a 240 VAC single phase source, only the two wires carrying voltage in the four-conductor connection should be attached to fuses or circuit breakers.** A fuse has a wire that will melt from heat when too much current is drawn through it, thereby opening the circuit and avoiding a dangerous over-current condition. A circuit breaker will "trip" to open the circuit in overload conditions, but it may be reset after the cause of the overload has been resolved.

Wire Current Ratings: *Ampacity* is the maximum safe current carrying capacity of a wire. Generally, larger diameter wire can handle greater current. *American Wire Gauge* (AWG) defines wire diameter, with smaller AWG values being larger diameters. Exceeding the current rating of a wire may cause the wire to overheat, possibly causing a fire.

Two of the most commonly used AWG wire sizes are number 12 and number 14, depicted in the ampacity table on the following page. **For a circuit drawing up to 20 amperes of continuous current, the AWG number 12 is the minimum wire size that may safely be used** – the NEC requires that no more than a 20 amp fuse or circuit breaker be used in combination with AWG

Figure 7.2: One form of common 240 VAC electrical outlet.

GOB03 #12. Similarly, by NEC restrictions, **a 15 ampere fuse or circuit breaker would be appropriate to use with a circuit that uses AWG number 14 wiring.** (This NEC-extracted table is for insulated copper wire, and separate values for aluminum conductors are specified by NEC.)

Copper Wire AWG	Allowable Safe Ampacity (A)	Maximum Fuse or Circuit Breaker Allowed (A)
8	40	40
10	30	30
12	25	20
14	20	15

Preventing Electric Shock: Special types of devices and circuits can be used to help prevent electric shock. These include Ground Fault Circuit Interrupter (GFCI) circuits, equipment cabinet safety interlocks, and equipment chassis grounding.

Ground Fault Circuit Interrupter (GFCI): This special circuit and associated electrical outlet contains a circuit breaker that will trip when an imbalance is detected in the hot wire to neutral wire current. The current drawn through the GFCI circuit should equal the current returning to the GFCI, else a problem exists. A short circuit or current flow on an unintended path will cause the trip. Thus, if current flows into a person an imbalance will cause the trip, quickly terminating the shock. **GOB05 Current flowing from one or more hot wires directly to ground will cause a GFCI to disconnect the 120 volt or 240 volt AC line power to the device.**

Safety Interlock: Many pieces of equipment using high power, such as **GOB12 a transmitter power supply,** will incorporate a cabinet safety interlock. **The purpose of a safety interlock is to ensure that dangerous voltages are removed if the**

Figure 7.3: A GFCI 120 VAC electrical outlet.

cabinet is opened. The interlock is a switch, often integrated with the chassis housing, that will disconnect the powering circuit if the enclosing cabinet chassis is unlocked or opened. With the interlock switch in the open position dangerous or unprotected electrical contacts inside the enclosure cannot offer electrical shock if they are touched.

Chassis Grounding: Equipment with a metal chassis should always have the chassis connected to the green safety ground wire of the powering circuit. **Grounding the metal enclosure of every item of the station equipment ensures that hazardous voltages cannot appear on the chassis.** Most modern amateur radio equipment will use a power cord that includes a safety ground wire that is already connected to the chassis of the device, and the ground connection is made automatically when you "plug in." In the case that an improper short or contact occurs with the enclosure, the safety ground wire provides a path to ground for the currents, reducing the chance of someone receiving an electric shock from touching the metal chassis.

G0B06

Mobile Station Electrical Precautions: Although most often operated from the 12 volt battery of an automobile, electrical precautions must also be taken even with this lower voltage level. Caution must be exercised as significant current can be drawn from the car battery. **If you are operating a 100-watt HF transceiver in an automobile, it is best NOT to draw the DC power from an automobile's auxiliary power socket** (lighter socket) **because the socket's wiring may be inadequate for the current being drawn.** The wires feeding the socket could overheat quickly and start a fire. Rather, **a fused power connection direct to the battery with heavy gauge wire would be best for the 100-watt HF**

G4E04

G4E03

Figure 7.4: For mobile station power connections use dedicated heavy gauge wire with in-line fuses routed directly to the battery.

mobile installation, and this is a good precaution to use with any portable or mobile station. The heavy gauge wire ensures the current can be safely handled, the direct connection avoids any possibility of using lighter gauge automobile wiring, and the in-line fuse is the safety switch in the case of a short or other fault that draws an excessive amount of current through the power wire.

Backup Power Safety: In an emergency or portable operating scenario such as a power outage or a field operation, hams may use power from liquid-fueled portable generators or from storage cells such as lead-acid based batteries. Each of these backup power sources introduces safety concerns.

Electrical Generators: Portable electric generators using gasoline or diesel fuel are popular emergency preparedness and portable power supply equipment items. Because they burn petroleum-based fuels, care must be taken to properly ventilate the area in which they are used. Carbon monoxide in exhaust fumes can accumulate quickly in a poorly ventilated enclosure, and CO is a deadly gas. **The danger of carbon monoxide poisoning is a primary reason for not placing gasoline-fueled generators inside an occupied area.** Don't take chances. Follow these guidelines:

- **For emergency generator installation the generator should be located in a well-ventilated area.**
- Ensure that the generator is positioned so that fumes cannot be drawn into windows, air intakes, or any other breach into occupied areas.
- Install a carbon monoxide detector in any enclosed occupied area near the generator installation.

Additionally, take proper precautions in the handling of liquid fuels for a generator. Keep a fire extinguisher nearby and avoid spark, flame, or exhaust system heat when refueling the generator. Use the generator's ground terminal and connect it to an earth ground to avoid potential arcing, and store fuels well away from the generator.

If you are using an emergency generator to power your home or other structure that receives commercial utility power **you must disconnect the incoming utility power feed.** Typically the disconnection is accomplished by tripping the large "Main" circuit breakers (usually two). If the utility service power is not completely disconnected the generator may *back-feed* onto the utility power lines creating a potential hazard of unusually high voltage on the lines.

G0B04

G0B15

G0B13

Restored utility power may also damage the generator if it is still connected. Once utility service power is completely disconnected it is safe to power the structure with an emergency generator. You may wish to have a *transfer switch* installed by a licensed electrician that safely disconnects utility power and connects your generator, disallowing both to be connected simultaneously. **CAUTION!** If you are not completely confident of the procedures necessary to safely connect and disconnect an emergency generator to your home or shack, consult a licensed electrician.

Storage Cells: As described in the Chapter 6 Power Sources section, storage cells can be a good emergency or portable power source for amateur radio operations. They require proper care in recharging to avoid hazardous conditions. Many newer lead-acid-based storage cells require a smart charger to ensure a proper voltage profile is maintained over the duration of the charging process. Check the battery manufacturer's recommendation for charging and stick to it to avoid overheating that can occur from recharging too rapidly. Lead-acid storage batteries can give off explosive hydrogen gas when being charged, so they should be maintained in a well-ventilated area outside the shack to avoid hydrogen build-up in an enclosed area and potential resultant explosion or fire.

Soldering Safety: Plenty of hams enjoy *home brewing* electronics, building up coaxial cables, and making their own equipment repairs. Soldering is a very common activity for those involved in amateur radio. And of course soldering has a couple of safety precautions that should be attended.

Solder is a blend of metals that melt at temperatures of about 190° F and higher, with specific melting temperatures depending upon the metal blend. Solder is melted around electrical

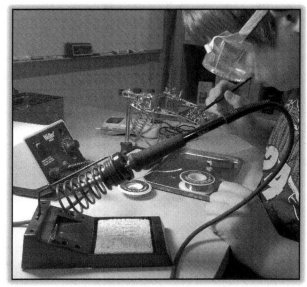

Figure 7.5: A stable iron holder, safety glasses, and good ventilation keep soldering safe.

contacts using a hot iron and allowed to cool and solidify to provide a jointing or connection with excellent electrical conductivity. Of course, with a hot iron up to several hundred degrees Fahrenheit you should take great care to avoid burns. Use a stable soldering iron holder and place the iron within it any time you are not heating the solder connection.

A common blend of solder combines tin with lead, and often a small amount of silver to enhance electrical conductivity. Lead is a toxic metal and you should avoid ingesting it. **A danger from lead-tin solder is that lead can contaminate food if hands are not washed carefully after handling it.** When lead-tin solder is melted it will release fumes with visible smoke. While solder smoke can contain isocyanates, aldehydes, and other unhealthy particulates that should be avoided, the lead metal is not typically heated sufficiently to vaporize it and cause lead particles to be included in the smoke. A solder fume absorber or other ventilation method is recommended, especially if you frequently engage in soldering work. And finally, safety glasses can help to avoid getting a hot splatter of solder or an ill-aimed soldering iron in the eye! Ouch!

GOB10

Antenna Safety: Whether your antenna work requires scaling a high tower or simply raising or lowering wire from a tree, always take proper precautions before starting your work. Especially if you are erecting a new antenna in a new or unfamiliar location, go slowly, attend to the local environment, think through every step, and double check all precautions.

As you learned in your Technician Class studies, keep all antennas well clear of utility lines and service feed lines to your home or shack! If the antenna should fall it should have absolutely no possibility of contacting electrical lines, and vice versa – a fallen utility line should not be able to contact your antenna. Keep the two well separated, with plenty of extra clearance. The following additional precautions are prudent for safe antenna work.

> **Electrical Clearance:** It pays to reiterate this point – make sure your antenna absolutely cannot contact electrical lines. This may be the #1 greatest hazard for most ham operators!
>
> **Power Down: Any time you make adjustments or repairs to an antenna, turn off the transmitter and disconnect the feed line.** This removes any possibility of the antenna being energized while you are handling it, potentially avoiding painful RF burns or excessive RF exposure. Similarly, **if any person is preparing to climb a tower that**

GOA12

GOB08

supports electrically powered devices, make sure all circuits that supply power to the tower are locked out and tagged, whenever possible. This means physically securing the circuits with locks so they cannot accidentally be powered until all personnel are safely clear of the tower.

Photo: Perry Jager NØWMZ
Pictured: Dave Novotny WA6IFI

Figure 7.6: Tower climbing safety gear includes goggles, hardhat, and properly configured harness.

Climbing Gear: All members of a tower work team should wear safety goggles and hard hats to protect the head and eyes from falling tools or other objects. Members climbing a tower should use a proper climbing harness to protect against that sudden stop at the end of a long fall. **When using a safety belt or harness on a tower climb, confirm the belt is rated for the weight of the climber and that it is within its allowable service life.**

G0B07

Safe Clearance: **Any antenna, and particularly ground-mounted antennas, should be installed so that it is protected against unauthorized access.** (See Section 7.2, *RF Safety.*) A ground mounted antenna, such as the ¼-wave vertical, may need to be located where it cannot be readily accessed by people, perhaps within a fenced enclosure. Avoid areas easily entered by the public or near property lines. If possible, raise the antenna out of reach.

G0A06

Lightning Safety: It is good practice to protect against lightning strikes and the potential of lightning energy being routed into your radio shack. Grounding towers and antennas properly is one primary precaution to take against lightning. Grounding requirements for amateur radio towers or antennas are established by local electrical codes, so ensure that you comply with them.

Grounding arrangements for towers should use a minimum of a separate eight-foot long ground rod for each tower leg, bonded to the tower and also to each other, as depicted in Figure 7.7. Tower ground connections should be short and direct. A broad conductor such as copper strap is best for grounding connections since it provides large surface area and low impedance for

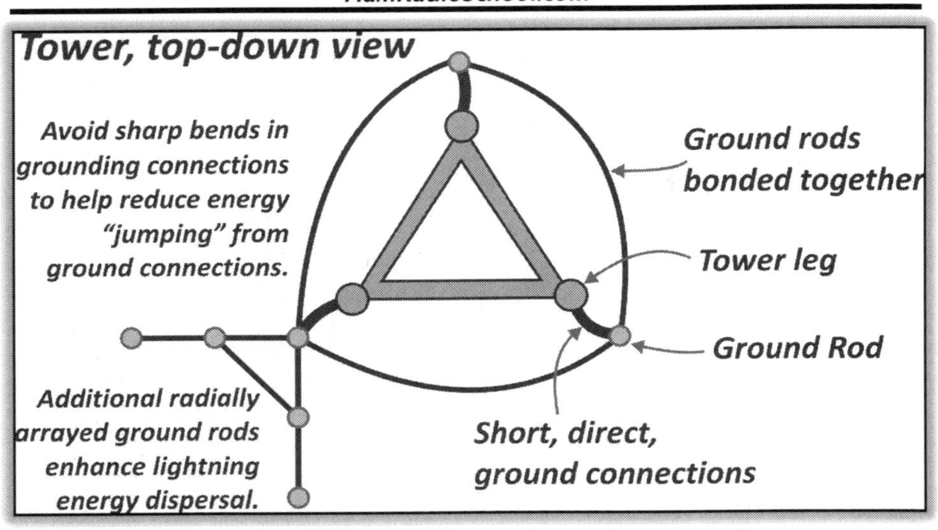

Tower, top-down view

Avoid sharp bends in grounding connections to help reduce energy "jumping" from ground connections.

Ground rods bonded together

Tower leg

Ground Rod

Additional radially arrayed ground rods enhance lightning energy dispersal.

Short, direct, ground connections

Figure 7.7: Top-down view of a tower grounding configuration.

current flow to ground. Sharp bends or creases in the grounding strap should be avoided as these increase impedance and encourage lightning energy to depart from the conductor and jump to nearby structures or objects.

For enhanced lightning mitigation more ground rods are better! They help to dissipate the lightning energy into the earth when a strike occurs. To avoid saturating the local earth with charge, rods should be separated 16 to 20 feet. If saturation occurs the energy will seek other paths to ground level voltage, such as through your shack or equipment! Again, **good engineering practice for lightning protection grounds calls for them to be bonded together with all other grounds,** thereby distributing the energy most effectively for dissipation. **However, soldered joints should not be used with the wires** (or strap) **that connect the base of a tower to a system of ground rods because a soldered joint will likely be destroyed by the heat of a lightning strike.**

GOB11

GOB09

Feed Line Lightning Protectors: Lightning protectors or "tubes" use common coaxial connector interfaces such as the N-connector or the SO-239/PL-259 so they may be easily inserted into a coaxial feed line. If a strong electrical surge from lightning strike energy flows down the coaxial cable the lightning tube will break like a fuse very rapidly to minimize the surge currents that continue down the feed line toward the shack, and instead route the lightning energy directly to earth ground. Lightning protectors should be mounted to a grounded conductor plate on an external wall of your radio shack or home structure. This entry panel should be well grounded to earth rods in a manner similar to that described for a tower so that lightning energy has a direct, low impedance path to earth ground.

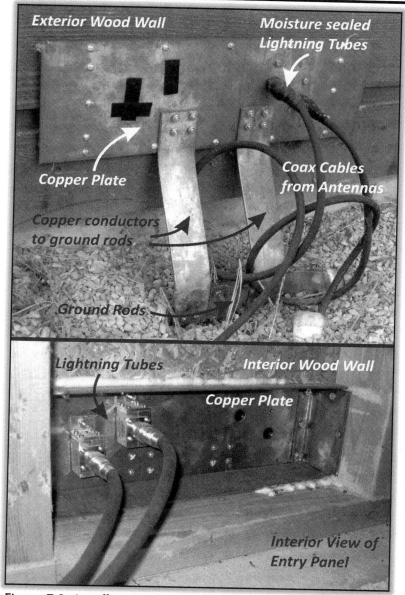

Figure 7.8: A well-grounded copper entry panel with lightning protection tubes.

Many hams prefer to insert a secondary set of lightning protectors in the feed line inside the shack grounded to the single-point ground panel or bus, as described in Section 6.9. These secondary tubes will help to stop any residual surge current on the feed line that was not stopped by the primary protectors and shunt it to ground.

Indeed, electricity can be dangerous, especially when it comes to lightning! And fumes from generators, batteries, or solder can also be hazardous, especially when combined with ignorance. And antennas and towers can be dangerous, especially when combined with live transmitters or utility power lines. So, what are the lessons learned?

- Protect against electric shock by ensuring your antenna cannot contact electrical lines even if it falls.

- Protect against lightning with a robust grounding system and protection tubes.

- Protect against electrical shock by powering down gear for any work, by sticking to codes, and by using proper fuses, proper wiring, good grounding procedures, and safety devices.

- Protect against fumes with good ventilation and careful positioning of sources.

- Protect against antenna and tower mishaps by avoiding power lines, powering down equipment before work, using all the proper climbing gear, and positioning to avoid human contact.

In spite of our humorous start to this section, compliments of Mr. Allen, safety is no joke. Most ham radio operations will present little if any hazards, but some circumstances can be quite dangerous. Here we have presented only a surface scratch of the most common safety considerations for the ham. Be careful and be smart, and become more educated about safety, perhaps with the help of a wise and experienced elmer. Good luck, stay safe!

But it is always safe to examine the question pool items for the section!

HamRadioSchool.com/general_media

Safety

7.2	RF Exposure

❝ *I have this complex. I don't like too much exposure. I don't know why it is.*
— *Mark Viduka*

When it comes to radio frequencies too much exposure can indeed be a bad thing, but it's really not very *complex*. We know why it is that we don't like it. Let's wrap up our General Class studies with a simple explanation of RF exposure hazards and mitigation practices. Here we *glow…*

RF Exposure Safety involves understanding the FCC RF exposure limits and how to apply them with your station, ensuring that your station does not expose any person to levels of RF energy that exceed recommended levels. In most amateur stations RF exposure is not a great concern, but as a General Class amateur operator you should be very familiar with limits and requirements to evaluate exposure to assure safe operations for yourself, your family, and your neighbors. You should also understand how to mitigate excessive exposure when the potential for it arises. First, a little clarity about RF radiation.

Non-Ionizing Radiation: UHF, VHF, and HF emissions are non-ionizing radiation. This means that the RF emissions do not strip electrons from atoms in the way that ionizing radiation does. (Examples of ionizing radiation are ultraviolet rays and X-rays, the EM waves of much higher frequency than RF.) Non-ionizing radiation does not directly cause biological molecular changes or adverse effects on DNA genetic material.

RF Heating of Tissues: RF energy is absorbed by tissues in our body causing heating of those tissues. With excessive RF exposure tissue damage can occur due to the body's inability to dissipate the heat delivered. Think of the way a microwave oven works – a great amount of microwave RF energy is delivered inside the oven, rapidly cooking the items placed there that have no way of shedding the absorbed energy and resultant heat. This type of damage is referred to as *radiation burn*, and radiation exposure is the primary topic of this section. The term *RF burn* has a somewhat different connotation referring to damage due to RF electric shock, as follows.

G0A01

RF Burns: Electric currents at RF frequencies flowing through your body's tissues can cause an RF burn. RF burns are painful and may happen if a person accidentally touches your antenna while you are transmitting. Unlike conventional heat burns, RF burns may extend deep below the skin surface and may require long healing times. RF burns are not a significant hazard with HT radios emitting 5W or less, but take care to ensure that no person touches your mobile or fixed station transmitting at higher power levels.

Maximum Permissible Exposure (MPE): The FCC recommends radiation exposure limits for each amateur frequency range that are referred to as the *Maximum Permissible Exposure* (MPE). You may need to evaluate your station to determine whether anyone is exposed to RF radiation beyond the MPE. Several different factors of your station operations affect RF exposure.

Factors Affecting RF Radiation Exposure: **Each of the following properties is important in estimating whether an RF signal exceeds the Maximum Permissible Exposure (MPE):**

- **Frequency** of the signal
- **Power density** of the signal
- **Duty Cycle** of transmissions

Frequency: Radiation exposure limits vary with frequency because the human body absorbs more RF energy at some frequencies than at others. The greatest absorption, and thus the lowest Maximum Permissible Exposure limit, is found for the VHF band of 30 to 300 MHz. Note that this includes the popular 2m band (near 144 MHz) and 6m band (near 50 MHz). The HF frequencies are less readily absorbed by the human body than VHF or UHF.

	Wavelength Band	Evaluation Required if Power* (watts) Exceeds
MF	160 meters	500
HF	80 meters	500
	75 meters	500
	40 meters	500
	30 meters	425
	20 meters	225
	17 meters	125
	15 meters	100
	12 meters	75
	10 meters	50
VHF	All bands	50
UHF	70 cm	70
	33 cm	150
	23 cm	200
	13 cm	250
SHF	All bands	250
EHF	All bands	250

* Power = PEP input to antenna

Figure 7.9: You must evaluate your station for RF exposure compliance if the transmitter power exceeds established power limits.

Power Density: *Power Density* is the measure of RF power over area. Typically this is expressed as milliwatts per square centimeter (mW/cm²). The MPE values are expressed in these units for each frequency band, as summarized in Figure 7.13, an FCC bulletin extract at the end of this section. Power density is determined primarily by the *output power* and *antenna distance* from the exposure location, and antenna gain must also be factored into the evaluation.

Power Output: Greater power output from your antenna increases the power density of the RF field. **A routine RF exposure evaluation must be performed to ensure compliance with RF safety regulations when transmitter power exceeds levels specified in FCC Part 97.13.** These transmitter power levels, expressed in watts, are summarized by frequency band in Figure 7.9. Regardless of power transmitted, **make sure MPE limits are not exceeded in occupied areas if you install an indoor transmitting antenna.**

G0A08

G0A11

Distance from Antenna: Radio frequency energy spreads out as distance from the antenna increases, reducing the power density. Specifically, power levels fall off as the square of the distance, so doubling the distance from the antenna reduces your exposure by a factor of four (1/4). Thus, relocating or elevating antennas is one of the most common actions an amateur might take to prevent exposure to RF radiation in excess of FCC-supplied limits.

Antenna Radiation Pattern & Gain: Directional antennas will concentrate power in one direction, increasing the power density in that direction as compared to isotropic or dipole antennas. Assessments of RF exposure should take into account the power gain of all antennas used by the station. The output power must be determined with the antenna gain as a multiplying factor.

Duty Cycle: The ratio of on-air transmission time to total operating time of a transmitted signal is duty cycle. Duty cycle affects the **time-averaged RF radiation exposure (the total RF radiation exposure averaged over a certain time).** So, duty cycle is a factor used to determine safe RF radiation exposure levels. **A lower transmitter duty cycle permits greater short-term exposure levels,** while a greater duty cycle allows less exposure over time.

G0A04

G0A07

Duty cycle varies with the mode of transmission used. FM signals transmit at 100% power for the entire transmission time. SSB signals vary in power with your audio, dropping to near zero between words and sentences, and causing the duty cycle to be reduced. The ratio of transmission time to receive time also impacts the exposure calculation.

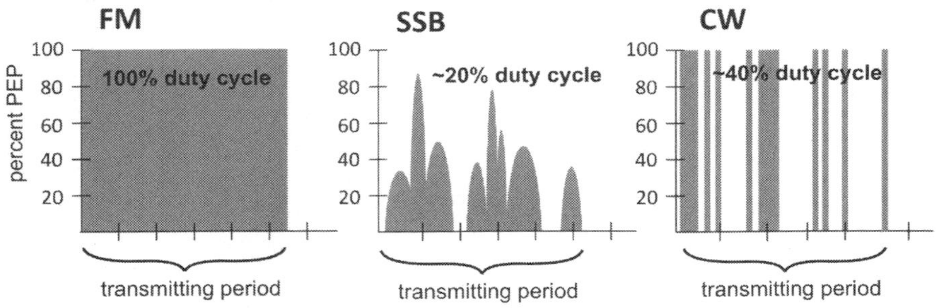

The duty cycle of transmission modes is determined by transmitter "on air" time and percent PEP within any single transmission. For 100% PEP modes (FM, CW) duty cycle is simply the ratio of "on air" time to total operating time. Multiple transmitter operating periods and receiver "listening periods" may comprise a standard averaging period of 6 or 30 minutes for estimating RF exposure levels.

Figure 7.10: Duty cycle of a transmitter varies with mode.

Complying with Limits: If your station requires an exposure evaluation, **you can determine that your station complies with FCC RF exposure regulations by any of the following methods of determining compliance:**

G0A03

- **By calculation based on FCC OET Bulletin 65** (see upcoming Practical Advice topic)
- **By calculation based on computer modeling** (see upcoming Practical Advice topic)
- **By measurement of field strength using calibrated equipment (Accurate measurement of an RF field requires a calibrated field-strength meter instrument with a calibrated antenna.)**

G0A09

If an evaluation of your station shows RF energy radiated from your station exceeds permissible limits you must take action to prevent human exposure to the excessive RF fields. Figure 7.11 characterizes common actions to prevent excessive exposure. For example, **if evaluation shows that a neighbor might receive more than the allowable limit of RF exposure from the main lobe of a directional antenna, you can take precautions to ensure that the antenna cannot be pointed in their direction.** A mechanical stop or limiters on an antenna rotator system may help to accomplish this mitigating action. Elevating the antenna or narrowing its elevation pattern with stacked elements may also alleviate this type of exposure problem.

G0A05

G0A10

Practical Advice on RF Exposure Compliance:

Most ham stations are not going to require an evaluation if antenna placement has been well planned, if space constraints are not too imposing, and if high output power levels are not used. But if you plan to use higher power levels, if you plan to use a directional antenna with substantial gain figures, or if your antenna must be in close proximity to people, it is your responsibility to ensure your station is not exposing humans to RF levels in excess of the Maximum Permissible Exposure limits defined in FCC OET Bulletin 65.

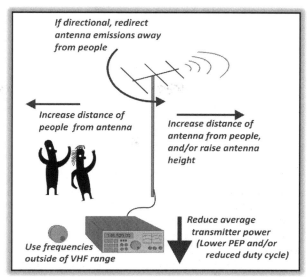

If directional, redirect antenna emissions away from people

Increase distance of people from antenna

Increase distance of antenna from people, and/or raise antenna height

Use frequencies outside of VHF range

Reduce average transmitter power (Lower PEP and/or reduced duty cycle)

Figure 7.11: RF exposure can be mitigated by several methods or combinations of methods.

The FCC Office of Engineering and Technology (OET) Bulletin 65 from August 1997 contains more information than most new hams are likely to absorb in a short time. However, the tables and graph of MPE from the bulletin's appendix A is quite useful. Armed with a computed estimate of exposure in mW/cm^2 (milliwatts per square centimeter), you can use these tables to make a good estimate of whether or not your station is complying with MPE limits.

How can you easily make such a computation, you ask? The internet comes to the rescue! In addition to commercial and freeware computer software programs, several good internet sites are now available to estimate exposure levels using basic information that is easily known to you about your station and the exposure environment. Most of these sites utilize the formulas given in FCC OET Bulletin 65, but research sufficiently to be sure these equations are indeed used. An internet search of "RF Exposure Calculator" will turn up multiple options. You will also find links to online exposure calculators in the learning media at HamRadioSchool.com.

In most software or online MPE calculators using the FCC formulas, you will need to enter the following types of information:

- **Average PEP** power at the antenna. This should be very close to your

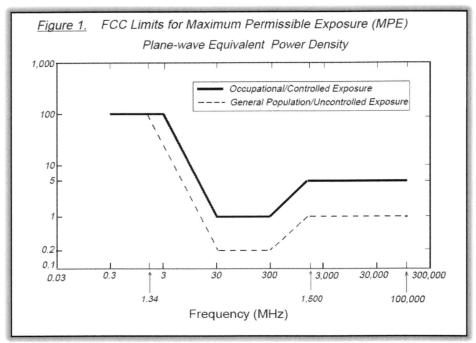

Figure 1. FCC Limits for Maximum Permissible Exposure (MPE) Plane-wave Equivalent Power Density

Figure 7.12 OET Bulletin 65 Chart of MPE (mW/cm2) by Frequency.

transmitter power, and you may measure close to your antenna with a power meter on the feedline. You may also need to adjust the power value for the duty cycle that is typical of your operational mode.

- **Gain** of your antenna in the direction of interest, or the isotropic gain.

- **Distance** to the area of interest for your measurement. That is, how far from your antenna to the living room or to your neighbor's house.

- **Frequency** of transmission, usually in MHz.

To use the FCC tables:

1. Make your estimates of exposure power density in mW/cm^2, perhaps using an online calculator as described earlier in this section.

2. Reference the frequency range in megahertz in the left column of the OET Bulletin 65 table (included at the end of this section)

Note that MPE is specified for controlled exposure (you, the operator) and for uncontrolled exposure (other people), and note that some frequency ranges require a simple MPE calculation based upon the specific frequency of exposure.

3. Compare your computed exposure level for your station with the MPE values in the table to determine if your station is exceeding the MPE.

4. If you find your station is exceeding the MPE, take steps to reduce the exposure.

Congratulations! You have completed all of the testable material for your FCC General Class VE exam! Review the last set of question pool items for this section, take plenty of practice exams, and go upgrade your license!

HamRadioSchool.com/general_media

Good luck, and we'll catch you on the HF bands soon! 73. WØSTU, clear.

Table 1. LIMITS FOR MAXIMUM PERMISSIBLE EXPOSURE (MPE)

(A) Limits for Occupational/Controlled Exposure

Frequency Range (MHz)	Electric Field Strength (E) (V/m)	Magnetic Field Strength (H) (A/m)	Power Density (S) (mW/cm²)	Averaging Time $|E|^2$, $|H|^2$ or S (minutes)
0.3-3.0	614	1.63	(100)*	6
3.0-30	1842/f	4.89/f	(900/f²)*	6
30-300	61.4	0.163	1.0	6
300-1500	--	--	f/300	6
1500-100,000	--	--	5	6

(B) Limits for General Population/Uncontrolled Exposure

Frequency Range (MHz)	Electric Field Strength (E) (V/m)	Magnetic Field Strength (H) (A/m)	Power Density (S) (mW/cm²)	Averaging Time $|E|^2$, $|H|^2$ or S (minutes)
0.3-1.34	614	1.63	(100)*	30
1.34-30	824/f	2.19/f	(180/f²)*	30
30-300	27.5	0.073	0.2	30
300-1500	--	--	f/1500	30
1500-100,000	--	--	1.0	30

f = frequency in MHz   *Plane-wave equivalent power density

NOTE 1: *Occupational/controlled* limits apply in situations in which persons are exposed as a consequence of their employment provided those persons are fully aware of the potential for exposure and can exercise control over their exposure. Limits for occupational/controlled exposure also apply in situations when an individual is transient through a location where occupational/controlled limits apply provided he or she is made aware of the potential for exposure.

NOTE 2: *General population/uncontrolled* exposures apply in situations in which the general public may be exposed, or in which persons that are exposed as a consequence of their employment may not be fully aware of the potential for exposure or can not exercise control over their exposure.

Figure 7.13: FCC OET Bulletin 65 Table of MPE Limits.

Index of Terms

Element 3 General Class Exam Pool Question Page Index

Element 3 General Class Exam Pool Question Page Index

Element 3 General Class Exam Pool Question Page Index